Student Learning Outcomes and Law School Assessment

Student Learning Outcomes and Law School Assessment

A Practical Guide to Measuring Institutional Effectiveness

Lori E. Shaw
Victoria L. VanZandt

CAROLINA ACADEMIC PRESS
Durham, North Carolina

Library of Congress Cataloging in Publication Data

Shaw, Lori E., author.
 Student learning outcomes and law school assessment : a practical
guide to measuring institutional effectiveness / Lori E. Shaw and Victoria L. VanZandt.
  pages cm
 Includes bibliographical references and index.
 ISBN 978-1-61163-266-8 (alk. paper)
 1. Law--Study and teaching--United States--Evaluation. 2. Law
schools--United States--Evaluation. I. VanZandt, Victoria L., author.
II. Title.

 KF272.S52 2015
 340.071'173--dc23

     2014047211

Carolina Academic Press
700 Kent Street
Durham, NC 27701
Telephone (919) 489-7486
Fax (919) 493-5668
www.cap-press.com

From Victoria L. VanZandt

To my honorable, ornery, and wise father, Joe T. Fergus, memories of you make me smile every day. I love you and will always miss you.

From Lori E. Shaw

To my loving parents, William and Wilma Shaw, for their unfailing love and support.

From both authors

To Dean Lisa Kloppenberg for starting us on the assessment journey and providing support and guidance along the way.

To the University of Dayton Assessment Committee and the University of Dayton School of Law Assessment Committee for sharing the assessment journey with us and providing their wisdom and perspectives.

To Denise Platfoot-Lacey and Elise Bernal for reviewing this Guide and providing their invaluable input and insight.

Contents

Preface

Excellence is the gradual result of always striving to do better.

Pat Riley

As you begin your exploration of this Guide, you may be wondering what prompted us to write about the use of student learning outcomes to measure institutional effectiveness. The answer is simple. We believe that legal education is good, but with some effort on all our parts, it can be so much better.

Surprisingly, our lawyer-dominated academic discipline has rarely relied on evidence in making critical decisions about curriculum, pedagogy, etc. Institutional outcomes assessment allows us (*i.e.*, law schools and law faculty) to use the collective performance of our students as evidence of our own performance as educators. The empirical data it provides allows us to advance from mere guesswork to prudent decision making.

We owe it to our students to analyze our own efforts with the same critical eye we apply to theirs. We owe it to our students to identify exactly what we want them to learn and to weigh the evidence of what works and what doesn't work in achieving those desired learning outcomes. And we owe it to them (and to their future clients) to take thoughtful action to address any failure to achieve those outcomes.

The American Bar Association and other accrediting bodies agree that we owe our students more. As a result, they now mandate that every law school engage in institutional student learning outcomes assessment. This Guide is intended to help you understand and satisfy the new accreditation requirements. It will walk you through the process step by step.

Because this is a "how-to" guide, we have adopted an informal tone. We want to keep it simple and focus more on the practical than the theoretical aspects of assessment. We realize that our approach is basic. We are only skimming the surface here. There are many excellent texts that delve into the theory and provide in-depth treatment of our various topics. We encourage you to explore those texts, many of which have been cited throughout the Guide.

We embarked on this project knowing that we were on an uncharted course in legal education. We have attempted to set out the best practices for what should be done. No system is perfect. And, we admit that we are learning from our own mistakes. On more than one occasion as we worked on the Guide, one of us looked at the other and exclaimed, "Wow. I wish we'd done it that way!" Because we are all still learning, we encourage you to share your experiences, good and bad, with the academy, as we have shared ours.

Most of all, we encourage you to always keep sight of why you are undertaking this new and sometimes overwhelming task—it's all about helping your students learn. And isn't that what we're all here to do?

Measurement is the first step that leads to control and eventually to improvement. If you can't measure something, you can't understand it. If you can't understand it, you can't control it. If you can't control it, you can't improve it.

H. James Harrington

Student Learning Outcomes and Law School Assessment

Chapter 1

What?
Outcomes Assessment:
The Big Picture

Learning Outcome: Readers will accurately explain assessment basics.

Readers will demonstrate achievement of this learning outcome by

- ✓ Defining basic assessment terms.
- ✓ Explaining the various types and levels of assessment and the interplay between and among them.
- ✓ Articulating the basic tasks needed to create and to implement an institutional assessment plan.

You just received the following email from the dean:

Dear Chris,

Hope you're having a great summer. Service assignments are coming out next week, and I just wanted to let you know that I'd like for you to help lead our efforts to create an institutional assessment plan. (I'm not quite sure yet what the planning team and process will look like. I want your input and that of a few others before anything is etched in stone.)

You're never afraid to take on something new. The University has been on me to do something about assessment planning for years and with the changes to the ABA Standards, I thought now would be a good time. Don't worry. We'll talk about it soon.

Regards,

The Dean

The Language Challenge

Assessment has its own terminology or jargon, which can be off-putting to those new to assessment. To add to the confusion, there is no standardized assessment terminology. Various institutions, accreditors, assessment experts, and individuals use different assessment terms. To keep things simple and avoid confusion, we have adopted a uniform set of defined terms, which are presented in bold text throughout the Guide. The definitions for the terms are presented in italic text. Wherever necessary, we also provide the synonyms for the terms. A comprehensive glossary of these key terms can be found in Appendix A.

As a first step, we urge you to adopt a standard assessment vocabulary within your institution so that assessment of student learning on the institution level, program level, or course level will have a shared vocabulary. A shared vocabulary will assist in alignment of outcomes across the curriculum and provide for a cohesive assessment process within your institution.

Your initial thoughts: "Another service assignment. And a leader, no less. Great. Just what I need when I'm trying to get this article finished. *Institutional* assessment? I'm not sure I even know what that is. And the University and the ABA are both involved? That can't be good. I'd better schedule an appointment with the dean to find out what this is all about."

That was us a few years ago. Our school, the University of Dayton School of Law, assigned us to lead its institutional outcomes assessment efforts and, among other things, tasked us to create something called "student learning outcomes" by the end of the summer. When we started, we knew almost nothing about this thing called "institutional outcomes assessment." Since then, we have become among its biggest fans and strongest boosters.

If you are reading this Guide, it is likely because you and your school are about to undertake the same journey we did. Our goal is to walk you through the process step by step, answering questions, giving tips on best practices, and, perhaps most important, providing you with action lists for each stage of your school's institutional outcomes assessment efforts. Our desired learning outcome is for you to finish this Guide with a completed institutional outcomes assessment plan in hand fully prepared to implement the plan, evaluate the data you collect, and "close the loop" by making any needed changes to your educational program.

Getting Started: A Brief Overview of Institutional Outcomes Assessment

Let's start with the most basic question of all. When we talk about "institutional outcomes assessment planning" what do we mean? We will provide much more detailed definitions and explanations later in this Chapter, but here is a quick-and-dirty explanation that you can use to explain institutional outcomes assessment planning to colleagues and others.

First, what do we mean when we say "institutional"? Assessment at the institutional level typically refers to assessment of the performance of the highest level of an organization. We know that most of you teach at law schools affiliated with a university, but to avoid any possible confusion, **for purposes of this Guide, when we use the word "institutional," think "law school."**

Second, what do we mean when we say "outcomes"? An outcome is a desired result. Desired institutional outcomes can include results that are not necessarily related to student learning (*e.g.,* desired levels of advising effectiveness, student satisfaction, etc.). But to avoid any possible confusion, **for purposes of this Guide, when we use the word "outcome," think "student learning outcome."**

Like every law school, your law school markets itself to potential students as being a great place to learn (*i.e.,* acquire necessary knowledge, skills, and values). In other words, it promises certain student learning outcomes (*e.g.,* "If you come to Dayton Law, you will learn to be a skilled advocate."). But what real proof does your school have to support that assertion? (Any statement that begins with "It's my sense that ..." is not real proof!)

The only way to know if your students are truly learning is to identify the knowledge, skills, and values that you seek to teach them (*i.e.,* the learning outcomes your school desires) and develop and implement ways of measuring to what extent the student body as a group is achieving those outcomes. If your students collectively are achieving an outcome, it is a cause for celebration and a sign that your educational program is in good shape. If your students collectively are coming up short on an outcome, it is a sign that your school should take steps to improve their performance, and then measure again to see if those steps worked. Continuous improvement, not perfection, is the goal.

> When choosing terminology, we suggest that you start with the accreditor's language and make sure faculty understand and agree to use the terminology. For example, we have adopted the term "learning outcome" as that term is used by the ABA in its standards.

A good institutional outcomes assessment plan ensures that your students' collective achievement of each learning outcome is measured periodically and that your law school responds to any problems identified. Institutional outcomes assessment is about helping students learn. It's as simple as that.

But if all of this is so simple, why haven't we been doing it for years? Perhaps more to the point, why the abrupt push by your law school to develop an outcomes assessment plan now? We will explain all of that in Chapter 2. For now, let's focus on getting you up to speed on what outcomes assessment is and how it works.

Before you dive into the process (or even meet with your dean), you need to understand the larger picture on assessment and begin to develop a working vocabulary of key assessment terms.

At this point, you are probably feeling at somewhat of a loss as to where to even begin what sounds like a big task. Chapter 1 is intended to provide you with a starting point.

Any discussion of assessment is made more complex by the existence of different types and levels of assessment and by the often-confusing terminology. As a result, before you begin developing your school's institutional outcomes assessment plan, you should make certain that all of those involved in your school's assessment efforts have adopted a common language and are on the same page with regard to some basic concepts.

This Chapter provides a bird's eye view of assessment planning, explaining the various types of assessment and the various levels of assessment planning. It concludes with a strategy for getting started on your school's assessment plan. Along the way, it will introduce you to many of the key terms of art.

Assessment and Non-Academic Goals

This Guide focuses on the achievement of student learning outcomes as a measure of institutional effectiveness, but you should be aware that many different strategic goals can come into play in assessing institutional effectiveness.

For example, your school may have the goal of being seen as a provider of legal services to the poor and marginalized in the community or achieving student satisfaction with advising, financial aid, and other services. And the ABA Standards contain some requirements unrelated to the academic program, such as the requirement that schools take "reasonable steps to minimize student loan defaults."

You may or may not be charged with assessing whether these non-academic goals are being achieved, but someone at your law school is (or should be) gathering and reviewing evidence about the achievement of these goals and using that information to improve the institution.

Institutional Assessment in Context

When developing any assessment plan, the first logical step is to consider what individual, group, or entity is being assessed. Sometimes the goal is to assess our students' performance as scholars, and sometimes the goal is to assess our own performance as educators. As educators, we are accustomed to focusing on assessing the performance of individual students. Institutional assessment requires us *to instead use the collective performance of our students to assess **our own performance** as educators.*

Individual Student Assessment

Although this Guide will focus on institutional outcomes assessment, those engaging in institutional assessment must also be familiar with the fundamentals of and terms of art relating to individual student assessment (also sometimes referred to as "classroom assessment"). **Individual student assessment** *provides your students with feedback for improvement and/or a measure of their achievement.* Every grade and every critique you provide a student is a form of individual student assessment.

Within assessment of individual student learning, there are two different sub-types of assessment: formative assessment and summative assessment. As discussed in Chapter 2, the ABA Standards for accreditation now require both formative and summative assessment of individual students.

Formative Assessment

Formative assessment is traditionally defined as *assessment conducted throughout the course of study through which students are provided feedback to improve their learning.* Ideally, students are given multiple formative assessments. A mid-term exam would be an example of formative assessment. Formative assessments may or may not count toward the final grade.

The best formative assessments involve individual feedback not only as to the product produced, but the process employed. So, for example, if a student fails to discuss an important issue in a paper, it is important that her professor specifically identify what was wrong with her product. In other words, instead of simply providing a numeric score or letter grade (or grading by gestalt), ideally the professor should point out the error (*i.e.*, the missing issue). A grading rubric is a great tool for pinpointing the issues to be covered and for breaking down an assignment or exam into the learning outcomes that the assignment is meant to assess. Additional information on rubrics can be found in Chapters 5 and 6.

Ideally, her professor will also help the student explore the reasons for this failure, which could range from not reading a case with sufficient care to deleting the discussion in a last-minute editing frenzy. A professor will not have time for this level of assessment on every assignment, but even sitting down with a student for 10 minutes to discuss one assignment can create some "light bulb" moments.

Formative assessment helps a student see where in the learning process he made a wrong (or a correct) turn and make any needed changes on his next assignment.

Summative Assessment

On the other hand, **summative assessment** is traditionally defined as *"assessment after the fact," assessment that occurs after a course of study. It provides no opportunity for individual students to improve their learning and typically provides little or no feedback to the students.*

Summative assessment informs a student where his level of achievement falls on a standardized scale and/or in comparison to his peers. Final course grades and the bar exam are examples of summative assessment.

Institutional Assessment

As will be discussed in Chapter 2, under the new ABA accreditation standards, along with assessing the performance of individual students, your school must assess its own effectiveness as an educational institution. We need to "grade" ourselves. *In undertaking the outcomes assessment process, always keep in mind that your ultimate goal is not only to measure outcomes, but to use the data you have collected to continuously improve the effectiveness of your law school's (i.e., your institution's) educational programs.*

The assessment process will require your school to determine what it means to be "effective" as a law school; how effectiveness might be measured; and where effectiveness should be measured. Each of these questions will be addressed in far greater depth in the chapters that follow, but here is a brief overview of the basic concepts.

What Does "Effectiveness" Mean?

While it is easy to say that you want your institution to be effective, it is sometimes all too difficult to articulate what "effective" means. The effectiveness of any institution ultimately is measured by whether it is achieving its stated **mission**.

Desired Student Learning Outcomes

Throughout the Guide, when we use the term "learning outcome," we are actually using a short-hand version of the term, "**desired student learning outcome.**" Note that the more precise (or long-hand) version emphasizes that outcomes assessment focuses on **collective student learning**. (As previously noted, your school may have desired outcomes that relate to something other than student learning. This Guide does not address the assessment of such non-academic outcomes.)

The long-hand version also reflects that the learning outcomes to which we refer in this Guide are the knowledge, skills, and values that you desire your graduates to have upon graduation. It does not assume that every graduate will achieve the desired outcome.

ABA Standard 204 requires every law school to submit a mission statement as part of the accreditation process. **Mission statements** *are broad statements of purpose. Essentially, they explain why the law school exists.*

For example, the University of Dayton School of Law's mission statement states in part, "Our mission is to enroll a diverse group of intellectually curious, self-disciplined and well-motivated men and women and to educate them in the substantive and procedural principles of public and private law. The School of Law seeks to graduate highly qualified attorneys…."

As you can see, a mission statement standing alone does not provide sufficient guidance to allow an institution to measure its effectiveness. We cannot say whether our school is graduating "highly qualified attorneys" without more clearly defining what that means to us as an institution.

Developing a list of desired **learning outcomes** helps provide that definition. *Learning outcomes describe what we want the result of obtaining an education at our institution to be: what our graduates will know, what they will be able to do, and what they will value.*

For example, one of our learning outcomes is that "Graduates will demonstrate competency in analytical and problem-solving skills." We have determined that this skill set is required for someone to be considered "a highly qualified attorney." Granted, outcomes at the institutional level are written in broad terms, but they still provide a much clearer vision of the institution's intent than does its mission statement.

To take an example from the world of industry, a multitude of manufacturers may have the mission "to produce and sell high quality automobiles." But "high quality" could be defined in very different ways. Some outcomes, such as satisfying federal safety regulations, will be common to all manufacturers, but some will be unique. One manufacturer could have an outcome of putting cars on the road that handle like racecars, while another could have the outcome of putting cars on the road that are environmentally friendly.

The list of outcomes you develop will not be etched in stone. A law school's overall mission may stay the same forever, but its learning outcomes can change as the profession changes. For instance, we could envision a time when our school might adopt outcomes related to the use of technology, familiarity with international law, or something of which we have yet to even dream.

Many schools have adopted **goals** and/or **objectives** to further define their mission statements as part of the strategic planning process. *Goals and objectives describe the more specific aims of the school. They are somewhere in between mission statements and learning outcomes in terms of their level of specificity.*

For example, Loyola University Chicago School of Law has adopted the goal of "assur[ing] a Curriculum that Prepares Loyola Students to be Accomplished and Ethical Leaders in the Legal Profession and the Larger Community" and the objective of "ensur[ing] a Core Curriculum of Essential Knowledge, Skills, and Values."

Note that, like mission statements, statements of goals and/or objectives, typically focus on what the *institution* will do. In contrast, learning outcomes focus on what the *student* knows, does, or thinks. As the following graphic demonstrates, if your school has adopted specific goals and/or objectives, they, too, can help direct you in drafting your learning outcomes.

We will discuss how to develop a list of your school's learning outcomes in Chapter 4.

Figure 1.A

How Can "Effectiveness" Be Measured?

Having identified what your learning outcomes are (*i.e.*, what student achievements it would take for your faculty to deem its educational process effective), the question becomes how to measure the achievement of those outcomes. In considering this question, it is helpful to think about education as a process.

Our students are our raw materials. Some students/materials are of higher quality in terms of academics than others. They walk in the door with knowledge, skills, work ethic, etc. greater than that of their peers. But by admitting a student, we are saying that this student meets certain minimum requirements (*i.e.*, that we can produce a qualified attorney from this raw material).

We are making promises as to the quality of our product (*i.e.*, our graduates) not only to the graduates themselves, but to our customers, the bench, the bar, and the public. Most states require three things for attorney licensure: the applicant must 1) satisfy a character and fitness requirement; 2) pass the bar; *and* 3) graduate from an accredited law school. We are holding out our graduates as being qualified to practice law.

In producing/manufacturing an attorney, we combine various **inputs**, *educational experiences*, with our raw materials. **Inputs** *are the resources that we devote to producing our final product.* We require our students to attend classes, to do readings, and to complete assignments of various kinds. We provide libraries filled with books, learned faculty members, academic support personnel, and assistance of all types. The goal of all of these efforts is to produce the learning outcomes.

Finally, we ask our students to produce certain **outputs**, *work products*, to document what they have learned. Students are required to take final exams, write papers, make oral arguments, etc.

Figure 1.B

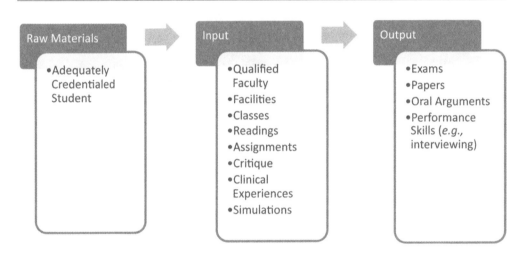

Historically, law schools have attempted to measure their effectiveness by looking to the quality of their *inputs*. While analysis of inputs has not been entirely eliminated, accreditors are now asking law schools to shift their attention to the quality of their students' *outputs*. Institutional outcomes assessment uses the quality of student outputs as a measure of institutional effectiveness.

Inputs Assessment

Accreditors in all fields have long relied on inputs as an assessment tool. Deans and promotion, retention, and tenure committees have often done the same thing. Our favorite assessment joke illustrates the difference between input and output/outcomes assessment.

*Law Professor 1, Lori, comes across Law Professor 2, Vicki, walking
her dog, Peyton.*
Lori: *Vicki, I will bet you $100 that I can teach your dog to sing
"You Ain't Nothin' But a Hound Dog."*
Vicki: *I'll take that bet. Peyton is gifted, but a singing dog? I
don't think so.*
Lori *sits Peyton on top of the sheet music for "You Ain't Nothin'
But a Hound Dog" and proceeds to lecture on the topic of how
to read music. She then shows Peyton a video of Elvis singing
the tune. When the video ends, she asks Peyton to sing the song.
Peyton politely woofs and wags her tail, but does not sing.*
Vicki: *Pay up, Lori, you failed. Peyton didn't learn to sing, "You
Ain't Nothin' But a Hound Dog." You owe me $100.*
Lori: *No, Vicki. You owe me $100. I never said she would learn
to sing. I said I would teach her, and that is exactly what I did.
Pay up.*

For decades, legal education's focus has been on what law schools
are trying to teach, not on what students are actually learning. An accreditor might ask a school to provide sample syllabi or might sit in
on all or part of a class. Inputs are certainly relevant to learning—
garbage in, garbage out—but looking solely at inputs does not provide
any real insights as to the success of our teaching efforts.

As the old proverb goes, "The proof of the pudding is in the eating."

Outcomes Assessment

Outcomes assessment shifts the focus from what we put in to the
educational process to what results from the educational process.
Simply defined, **outcomes assessment** is *an ongoing, formalized or systematic process to improve something, in which outcomes are created;
data is gathered to measure the achievement of the outcomes; the data
is analyzed; and then, the data is used to improve the achievement of the
outcomes.*

The process requires your law school to undertake the following steps:

1. identify student learning outcomes (*See* Chapter 4);
2. measure student achievement of the learning outcomes, using
   data collected from student outputs (*See* Chapter 5);
3. analyze the data obtained from such measurements (*See* Chapter
   6); and
4. use the data gathered to improve student learning (*i.e.,* "close the
   loop") (*See* Chapter 6).

These steps are often represented as a circular process:

Figure 1.C

From this point forward, you will be asked to use your students' outputs not only to measure their individual achievement, but your school's effectiveness. You will periodically evaluate/measure a sampling of student outputs to take a snapshot of whether your students are achieving the desired outcomes in acceptable numbers.

While you will be using the same student outputs (*e.g.,* papers, exams, etc.) used in providing students with individual assessments (*i.e.,* grades), you will be using these outputs in a very different way. Assessment and grading are not synonymous.

An example may help illustrate the differences. Let's say that the outcome you wish to measure is that students will demonstrate the ability to identify legal issues. To measure the achievement of this outcome, you pull a sampling of essay exam answers to question three of the Property final exam. Using a rubric that identifies the issues that should have been addressed, you assign each answer a score of 1 to 3 with 2 being "competent."

How is this different than the typical grading process? One, you are focusing in on a single outcome. Grading is typically a gestalt process that requires a professor to weigh multiple factors. A poor grade could be the result of a failure to spot issues, a failure to accurately describe the law, or a failure to make adequate use of the facts. Other factors, like class participation, attendance, and penalties for late papers, that may not be directly related to the outcome at issue may also influence the final grade.

In contrast, the type of evaluation undertaken as part of the assessment process allows you to pinpoint areas of strength and weakness. You are able to focus like a laser on one skill, value, etc.

Two, there is no curve. All of us have had some classes (groups of students) that are stronger than others. But if your school is like ours and has a mandatory curve, the overall course grades are essentially the same from year to year, regardless of student performance. Outcome measures allow us to track ups and downs in student performance.

Three, when assessing institutional achievement of outcomes, data is typically culled across courses, professors, and dates using a variety of tools. You are not relying on a single measure. As discussed in Chapter 5, using multiple tools to measure each outcome is a best practice. The use of multiple tools provides you with a more nuanced view of student achievement of the learning outcome.

For all of the reasons noted above, grades are not acceptable outcome measures. When you think about a grade, it is essentially an artificial construct designed to compare the performance of one student to another and rank them accordingly. As discussed in Chapter 5, you may well be able to use raw scores on outputs like multiple-choice exams to measure achievement of outcomes, but you will be evaluating these scores using a different standard than is used in assigning a grade.

Some supporters of input measures will argue that it is impossible to obtain the perfect measure of any outcome, and they are absolutely right. There is a subjective aspect to every measure of a student's performance. But that has never stopped us from assigning grades to students, and it should not stop us from seeking to grade ourselves.

Further, as discussed in Chapters 5 and 6, there are ways in which you can improve the reliability of your measures. For example, you can assign multiple evaluators to each project, and you can and should use multiple projects in measuring the achievement of each outcome.

The measures used in outcomes assessment are not perfect, but they do provide valuable insight into our strengths and weaknesses. They allow us to evaluate if and how changes to our inputs affect our outcomes. For example, did adding an additional writing requirement improve students' writing skills or do we need to look for another way to achieve that goal, such as requiring writing across the curriculum?

Outcomes assessment allows important decisions regarding curriculum and other academic issues to be guided by hard data, rather than intuition and guesswork.

Assessment and the Bar Exam

We are often asked why law schools cannot simply rely on the bar exam as the ultimate output/outcomes measure. Although an assessment measure, the bar exam cannot be the only method of assessing our students' learning. First, as we will discuss in Chapter 5 and Chapter 6, multiple measures are required for valid and reliable assessment. This idea is incorporated into the new ABA accreditation standards, which call for multiple assessments. The same is true for regional accreditation standards.

Second, the nationally administered bar examination and the state bar examinations fail to appreciate the distinct mission and student learning outcomes of the various law schools, as well as the distinct student body that each school serves. Assessment requires schools to focus on their unique mission and learning outcomes. To put it simply, what the bar exam tests does not directly correlate with what we teach. For example, the Ohio Bar Exam essays test knowledge of Ohio law. It is not necessarily the role of any law school to teach the specifics of the law of any state.

Where Should Effectiveness Be Measured?

Before we move on to how to begin the assessment process, there is an additional, sometimes challenging, aspect of outcomes assessment with which you should be familiar: its multiple levels. Ideally, assessment of our effectiveness as educators will occur on all levels within an institution: the institution, program, and course.

While this Guide focuses on outcomes assessment at the law school (*i.e.*, institution) level, the basic principles contained herein apply to program-level and course-level assessment as well. The assessment that should be occurring on these various levels is basically the same type of assessment.

It all starts with identifying your desired outcomes. In an institution-level outcomes assessment plan, learning outcomes are identified for graduates of the institution. In a program-level outcomes assessment plan, learning outcomes are identified for graduates of the program (think clinical program, legal writing program, track or concentration, etc.) In a course-level outcomes assessment plan, learning outcomes are identified for students enrolled in the course. The learning outcomes in each plan should correlate, but will be broad in the institution-level plan and narrow in the course-level plan.

Figure 1.D is an example from our school, the University of Dayton. The outcome identified by the Law School, tracks the outcome identified by the University. The outcome identified by the Criminal Law professor tracks the outcome set by the Law School. (There may be additional levels as well. For example, our Legal Profession Program, our research and writing program, has adopted its own outcomes. So, if you are teaching a course in that program, your outcomes will track the program outcomes.)

Note that the identification of outcomes poses no threat to the professor's academic freedom. No one is dictating course content. (Course descriptions are far more directive than institutional outcomes in that regard.) As a professor, setting outcomes is really simply a question of thinking about where your course fits in the bigger picture. It keeps you from living in a silo.

It is vital to understand and communicate to your faculty from the very onset of the assessment planning process that not every law school outcome will, should, or need be addressed in every course. For example, everyone in the building need not teach written communication skills. What you are really evaluating at the institutional level is whether the educational process *as a whole* is producing the learning outcomes.

Course-level assessment is done *by the professor for the professor* (and, of course, for his or her students). We know very few professors

Figure 1.D

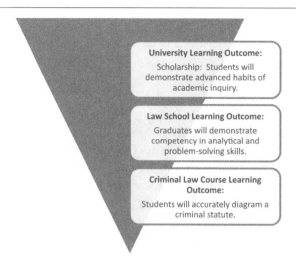

who have not on a given day thought, "Good grief, they didn't get [fill in the blank] at all!" and changed up the next day's lesson plan in response. A course-level assessment plan makes this type of evaluation and response less random and haphazard.

As professors, course-level assessment has made us both more thoughtful about the process involved. We are more systematic in our assessments of our own effectiveness. We give more thought to precisely what it is we want our students to learn (*i.e.,* our outcomes) and whether and how we are actually measuring the outcomes we have identified. ("Hmm, I told the students my course was intended to help build their critical reading skills, but my exam does not test critical reading skills. Houston, we have a problem.")

We do not measure every course outcome every year, but we make sure to measure each periodically. The measures give our teaching efforts direction. And to be honest, it makes you feel good as a teacher when you find a way to fix a problem.

All that having been said, we realize that at least initially, not everyone at your school is going to jump on the assessment bandwagon. Program-level and course-level assessment is something that is likely to develop over time, and that is absolutely fine.

But that does not mean that any member of the faculty can entirely opt out of the assessment process for your law school. The development of your institution-level assessment plan and, ultimately, the achievement of your learning outcomes will require coordination and cooperation among *all* faculty.

Obviously, if a law school's student learning outcome is that graduates will demonstrate analytical and problem-solving skills, this skill will need to be developed in individual courses. That does not mean that every course must address that outcome. What it means is that at least some courses must address it.

This highlights the importance of **alignment** or **curriculum mapping**, which will be discussed in Chapter 4. *Curriculum mapping is defined as a collaborative procedure for determining what knowledge, skills, and values are purportedly being learned in the individual courses within the curriculum and analyzing if and how they correlate to the learning outcomes identified by the school.* It is sheer lunacy to identify a learning outcome for graduates if no one at the school purports to be offering a learning opportunity related to that outcome.

All faculty members need to be able to identify what is being learned in their courses. They also need to recognize that if students are falling short of achieving a particular learning outcome, one or more faculty members may be asked to do more to incorporate that knowledge, skill, or value into an existing course, teach a new course, etc.

The Intersection between Individual Student Assessment and Institutional Outcomes Assessment

Now that you can distinguish between individual student assessment and institutional outcomes assessment, and between formative and summative assessment, let us take a moment to focus on the interplay between the various levels and types of assessment. We would like to share a simple truth we have discovered in our experiences with institutional assessment — while individual student assessment and institutional outcomes assessment are two different things, each serves the other.

The existence of an institutional assessment plan compels individual faculty members to devote more consideration to what students should be learning, how to measure what they have learned, etc. The lessons learned at the institutional level trickle down to benefit students at the individual level.

And the benefits can flow both ways. As discussed above, the outputs gathered as a result of individual student assessment can be repurposed to assist in institutional assessment. A round of oral arguments can serve to both assess the participating students' individual performances and the school's performance at assisting students in developing oral advocacy skills.

As discussed in Chapter 5, ideally, most of the methods/outputs you will use to measure institutional achievement of outcomes are already embedded in a course. It is much easier and more efficient to look to student output/work product that already exists than to create a host of new assessment measures. Further, when you add a measure that does not somehow "count" towards a grade, students' performance may not reflect their true abilities because they may not exert their best effort.

Still, you may well find it beneficial to create a limited number of new outputs. You may discover that no one at your school has actually been measuring some of your outcomes. If you do need to create new outputs, we suggest that you make a conscious effort to use the measures of those outputs to improve individual student assessment as well as institutional assessment. In other words, use them to provide the participating students with formative assessment.

Although institutional assessment is often equated with summative assessment, and individual student assessment is often equated with formative assessment, we eschew such rigid demarcations. There can and should be a substantial overlap between the levels and types of assessment.

While there may be some institutional assessment tools that are summative in nature in that they occur at the end of a law student's course of study, where the student does not have an opportunity to improve his skills, we urge you to adopt formative assessment tools as part of your institutional assessment plan. At least some of your measures should be taken at different points in the students' course of study and participating students should be given feedback that allows them to improve their performance in future courses in the curriculum.

So, for example, a **mini-bar exam**, sometimes known as a **baby bar exam**, *a simulated practice bar examination*, conducted at the end of the first year can both inform individual students where they stand and the institution as a whole where it is succeeding and failing to meet outcomes. If this mini-bar is incorporated into final exams as opposed to being freestanding, no significant additional work is created for professor or student. With careful planning, you can create win/win situations.

More discussion on using formative assessment tools in an institutional plan is provided in Chapter 5.

How to Start Your Outcomes Assessment Planning Process

Now that you have a better idea of what outcomes assessment involves, you are ready to begin the planning process. Before creating your institutional assessment plan, you need a strategy. What will you do? When will you do it? And, who will do it? As illustrated in Figure 1.E, developing and maintaining an institutional assessment plan involves three phases: the Development Stage, the Implementation Stage, and the Evaluation Stage.

Figure 1.E

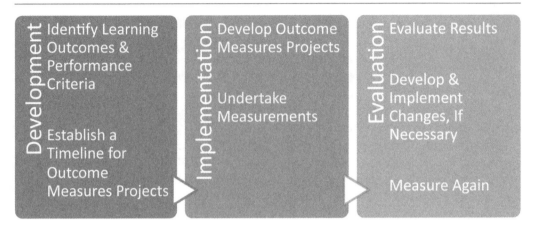

The Development Stage

During the Development Stage, which is discussed in detail in Chapter 4, you will develop the framework for your school's plan. You will identify your school's learning outcomes as well as the **performance criteria** for each outcome. (*The performance criteria state the specific act of performance needed to be able to accomplish the learning outcome.*) You will also establish a preliminary timeline for measuring each outcome. This is your "big picture" stage.

The Implementation Stage

During the Implementation Stage, which is discussed in detail in Chapter 5, you will create and undertake projects designed to measure the achievement of each outcome at least once before your next site visit. Ideally, you will use multiple measures (*i.e.,* undertake multiple projects) in measuring each outcome.

The Evaluation Stage

During the Evaluation Stage, which is discussed in detail in Chapter 6, you will analyze the data gathered during the Implementation Stage to determine whether your students are achieving the outcome. Your school may determine that the outcome is being achieved and no changes are necessary; it may determine that additional measures are needed; or it may determine that the outcome is not being achieved. If the outcome is not being achieved, your school must "close the loop" by implementing changes intended to improve achievement and measuring the impact of any such changes.

The Overlapping Cycle

The assessment process as a whole requires that you keep several balls in the air at once. Assume that your school sought to measure Outcome 1 in Year 1 of your Implementation Stage. During Year 2, you will be evaluating the data you gathered relating to Outcome 1 at the same time you are measuring Outcome 2 and making plans to measure Outcome 3. All of this is infinitely doable, but it requires planning and coordination. More discussion on coordinating your assessment activities is included in Chapter 4.

Having read this Chapter, you are now conversant with the terms and the basic methodology of institutional assessment. There is still much to learn; however, before we get to the actual hands-on of outcomes assessment planning in Chapters 4, 5, and 6, the next two Chapters will give you the background of why we are engaging in institutional assessment and who will be involved.

Action List

Step 1: If your law school is part of a larger university, obtain a list of the university's learning outcomes, if any.

Step 2: Obtain a copy of your school's mission statement.

Step 3: Obtain a copy of your school's latest strategic plan.

Step 4: Ask the dean's office for any other documents that identify your school's goals or objectives.

Keep reading to help you determine the next steps....

Chapter 2

Why?
Outcomes Assessment:
Mandates & Opportunities

Learning Outcome: Readers will explain the reasons for engaging
in outcomes assessment planning.

Readers will demonstrate achievement of this learning outcome
by

✓ Describing the various parties, entities, and standards which
require institutional outcomes assessment.

✓ Exhibiting appreciation for the inherent benefits in assessment
planning.

Having read Chapter 1, you have a basic understanding of how institutional outcomes assessment works and what some of the benefits
are. What may still be baffling you is the abrupt push by your law
school to develop an outcomes assessment plan. Why now? What's
the rush?

Chapter 2 addresses why law schools are suddenly viewing outcomes
assessment planning as an essential task, a mandate. It outlines the
requirements of the regional accreditors generally (the entities who
accredit your university), the ABA, and some law school promotion,
retention, and tenure (PRT) committees. Although law schools will
be required to engage in outcomes assessment planning because of
one, two, or all three of these bodies, that should not be your school's
sole (or even principle) motivator. Outcomes assessment planning
should be done regardless to improve student learning. Furthermore,
outcomes assessment should be seen as an opportunity to reinvent
legal education and to restore its reputation.

**Learn More about
Regional Accreditors
and Assessment**

For an excellent intro-
duction to regional ac-
creditors and
assessment, read:

Staci Provezis, *Regional
Accreditation and Student
Learning Outcomes: Map-
ping the Territory*, Nat'l
Inst. for Learning Out-
comes Assessment (Oct.
2010),
http://www.learningout-
comeassessment.org/do
cuments/provezis.pdf.

To find the regional
accrediting body for your
state, visit the Council for
Higher Education Ac-
creditation Directories,
http://www.chea.org/
Directories/regional.asp.

Assessment as a Mandate

In speaking with faculty from around the country about assessment, the first questions to us have never varied: "Why is legal education suddenly focusing on outcomes assessment? What happened?" Although outcomes assessment practices are grounded in sound pedagogy, which will enhance student learning, the current focus on outcomes assessment is largely being propelled by external pressures to engage in assessment planning for accreditation purposes and/or purposes of tenure and review.

Regional Accreditations

Changing accreditation requirements are the primary reason why legal education is currently focusing on outcomes assessment. In the United States, there are eight regional accrediting bodies, acting under the U.S. Department of Education, which accredit entire institutions of higher learning, such as universities. As a general rule, accreditation reviews are conducted every ten years.

Although the regional accreditors do not accredit individual academic programs, every unit or department within a university is part of the review process for the university as a whole. So, if your law school is affiliated with a larger university, it is subject to the regional accreditation standards. However, just because your school is not affiliated with a larger university doesn't mean that you can ignore the regional accreditors. Even freestanding (also known as standalone or independent) law schools may voluntarily seek regional accreditation and many do.

Each regional accrediting body has its own set of standards by which it evaluates universities. The U.S. Department of Education has the authority to decide which accrediting bodies are officially recognized by the federal government and, thus, wields significant power in terms of the contents of these standards. Federal funding is only available to students at schools that have been accredited by an officially recognized regional accrediting body. This is the main reason that some freestanding law schools are choosing to seek regional accreditation.

In 1988, then Secretary of Education William Bennett issued an order requiring each regional accreditor to include a requirement of institutional outcomes assessment in its accreditation standards. Thus, a direct link now exists between engaging in institutional outcomes assessment and obtaining federal funds.

In 2008, the Secretary of Education sought to go even further, advocating for the implementation of national uniform measures of student learning. Accrediting bodies, colleges, and universities fought the move, and in reauthorizing the Higher Education Opportunities Act (HEOA) the law that governs federal student aid, Congress blocked the new requirements sought by the Secretary. However, the war for control over accreditation is far from over, and battles are likely to flare up each time the HEOA requires reauthorization. Given the often scathing critique by lawmakers and members of the media of the lack of accountability of institutions of higher education, we can expect regulation relating to outcomes assessment to increase in the future.

The current push for law schools to up their assessment game is, at least in part, the result of the tightening of the regional accreditors' standards over the past decade. Universities facing an ever tighter market are promising prospective students a great deal. The question is whether they are delivering on those promises. Failure to properly assess learning outcomes and/or to publicly release assessment data evidences a lack of institutional integrity. To promise something you are not even measuring is quite simply unethical.

We are moving from an era in which schools were expected to engage in some institutional outcomes assessment to an era in which outcomes assessment is driving the accreditation process. In recent years, regional accreditors have toughened their standards out of a desire to avoid greater federal regulation and a concern that many schools' institutional outcomes assessment is deficient.

Failure to develop and execute an effective assessment plan has been among the most common negative findings of regional site visit teams. Too many schools have collected data for the sake of being able to say they assessed, but have not really evaluated or used the data they accumulated.

To make assessment more meaningful, the standards have become more exacting. Today, universally, the regional accreditation standards require that each educational program within a college or university clearly define its learning outcomes, assess achievement of those outcomes, and use the assessment to improve the program. Therefore, all law schools, except for freestanding law schools, *must* engage in outcomes assessment to help their universities satisfy the requirements set out in the regional accreditation process. And, as noted above, freestanding law schools *may* choose to do it, even though not required.

Regional accreditors do not dictate what schools measure (*i.e.*, what they should be teaching) or how schools measure the achievement of outcomes (*i.e.*, what specific tools and instruments should be used). Given the variety of educational programs within a university, that would be an impossible task. Instead, the regional accreditors focus on evaluating the assessment *process*.

Faculty are expected to take the lead in identifying and measuring learning outcomes and in "closing the loop" by making any changes needed to improve student learning.

At the University of Dayton, our accrediting body is the Higher Learning Commission of the North Central Association of Colleges

Isn't institutional outcomes assessment just another name for accreditation?

No. Intuitional outcomes assessment is not synonymous with accreditation.

Are assessment efforts important to obtaining accreditation? Yes. Accreditors expect schools to conduct critical self-assessments of whether their students are learning what they were promised they would learn.

But outcomes assessment's main purpose is to improve student learning regardless of who is watching. Assessment does not involve the mere creation of empirical studies the purpose of which is to provide data to accreditors. Assessment data is to be used to improve programs of education, not merely to create reports.

and Schools (HLC-NCAS). In 2005, the HLC-NCAS dramatically shifted the focus of its accreditation criteria from input measures (*e.g.,* How many volumes do you have in your library?) to outcome measures, asking whether the institution has "demonstrated a commitment to educational achievement and improvement through ongoing assessment of student learning."

Our most recent HLC-NCAS site visit took place in 2007, and as one of the first institutions to be assessed under the new criteria, we could not be certain exactly how the criteria would be interpreted. The University's Assessment Committee worked with the Accreditation Steering Committee in preparing for the site visit and met with the site visit team during its visit to campus.

During the process we learned three important things:

1. Accreditors are looking for a comprehensive and cohesive assessment plan, not scattered, ad hoc assessment efforts.
2. Accreditors are far more interested in the quality of assessment than in the quantity of assessment.
3. Accreditors' principle concern is whether your school is using outcomes assessment to improve student learning.

When faced with a site visit and told that assessment is key, your first instinct may be to start pulling old surveys, studies, etc. from the basement and fill a room with them to demonstrate your school's commitment to assessment. But if you cannot tie the data in these materials back to a learning outcome and you cannot show that you actually used the data to improve your students' educational experience, these stacks of papers have no real value.

Happily, the University of Dayton received a favorable review, but it knew that in ten years, the site team would return and that the expectations regarding assessment would be even greater. So, it mandated that each academic unit, including the School of Law, create a full assessment plan, annually report its assessment activities, and assign a representative to the University's Assessment Committee.

And so, our law school's assessment planning process began.

The American Bar Association

The accrediting body for law schools is the ABA's Section of Legal Education and Admissions to the Bar. Over the past decade, it, too, has slowly begun to embrace the need for outcomes assessment.

Institutional outcomes assessment in some form has been required for ABA accreditation since former Interpretation 301-3 was adopted in August 2004. Former ABA Standard 301(a) mandated, "[a] law school shall maintain an educational program that prepares its students for admission to the bar, and effective and responsible participation in the legal profession." Former Interpretation 301-3 provided "[a]mong the factors to be considered in assessing the extent to which a law school complies with this Standard are the rigor of its academic program, *including its assessment of student performance, and the bar passage rates of its graduates.*" (emphasis added.)

Despite the addition of these interpretations, the real focus of the ABA Standards continued to be on *inputs*, not outcomes. For example, Section 302, devoted to curriculum, required that "each student receive *substantial instruction*" on various areas and that law schools offer "*substantial opportunities*" for certain experiences. What it did not require was proof that students actually learned anything.

Like the early attempts of regional accreditors to incorporate institutional assessment into its standards, the ABA's initial attempts fell short of providing the guidance (and the "teeth") needed to create significant change. Going forward, however, the ABA will actually require concrete evidence of assessment planning and use.

"Why the change?" you might ask. "We're not an elementary school or even an undergraduate department. We're teaching higher-level thinking—something that can't be measured effectively. This type of requirement just doesn't make sense at a professional school. It can't be done."

The reality is that law schools are among the last of the professional schools to face mandated outcomes assessment. (Honesty Check: The truth is that to the best of our knowledge, law schools are THE last of the professional schools to face mandated outcomes assessment.) In 2008, a special Outcome Measures Committee appointed by the ABA's Section on Legal Education and Admissions to the Bar found that accreditation standards for programs in accounting, architecture, dentistry, engineering, medicine, pharmacy, psychology, teaching, and veterinary medicine all required outcomes assessment. (Accreditors of divinity schools require it as well.)

In recommending that the ABA Standards be amended to reflect a greater emphasis on outcomes assessment, the Outcome Measures Committee noted two important trends in professional accreditation. "First, the accrediting body measures a school's performance against its own stated mission." Schools are actually empowered to forge their own identities by the fact that they are no longer required to satisfy "universal," one-size-fits-all input criteria. "Second, accreditation standards are performance based and seek evidence of student learning." A professional school's effectiveness can and should be measured.

The Committee found "the best thinking" of legal educators is reflected in two 2007 publications, *Educating Lawyers: Preparation for the Profession of Law* published by the Carnegie Foundation and Roy Stuckey's *Best Practices for Legal Education: A Vision and a Road Map*

Learn More about the American Bar Association and the Outcomes Assessment Movement

To view the *Report of the Outcome Measures Committee of the American Bar Association Section of Legal Education and Admission to the Bar* (July 27, 2008) visit: http://apps.american bar.org/legaled/commit tees/subcomm/Out come%20Measures%20 Final%20Report.pdf.

The work of the Outcome Measures Committee was greatly influenced by the following works:

Roy Stuckey et al., *Best Practices for Legal Education: A Vision and Road Map* (2007).

William M. Sullivan et al., *Educating Lawyers: Preparation for the Profession of Law* (2007).

The Phase-In Process: Outcome Measures

The ABA has provided the following guidance on the timing of the implementation of the new standards relating to the development of learning outcomes:

"In the initial phases of implementation of the outcome measures Standards set forth in Standards 301(b), 302, 303, and 314, which will begin in the 2016–2017 academic year, compliance will be assessed based upon evaluating the seriousness of the school's efforts to establish and assess student learning outcomes, not upon attainment of a particular level of achievement for each learning outcome. Among factors to consider in assessing compliance with these Standards are whether a school has demonstrated faculty engagement in the identification of the student learning outcomes it seeks for its graduates; whether the school is working effectively to identify how the school's curriculum encompasses the identified outcomes, and to integrate teaching and assessment of those outcomes into its curriculum; and whether the school has identified when and how students receive feedback on their development of the identified outcomes."

ABA Section on Legal Education & Admissions to

published by the Clinical Legal Education Association, both of which support the use of outcomes assessment.

Both publications conclude that competent attorneys possess not only a solid academic knowledge base, but also practice skills and a sense of professional identity. Both further conclude that law schools have not achieved a balance in providing these competencies, often sacrificing practice skills and professional identity to devote time and resources to academic knowledge.

Outcomes assessment is a way to require schools to identify exactly what competencies they seek to provide and to take a hard look at whether they are actually graduating students who possess those competencies.

In 2008, the Council of the Section of Legal Education and Admissions to the Bar's Standards Review Committee undertook a comprehensive review of the ABA Standards. As part of its review, it considered the recommendation of the Outcome Measures Committee. After more than five years of study, including multiple drafts and notice and comment opportunities, the Council approved the most sweeping amendments to the ABA Standards in decades. The ABA House of Delegates concurred in all of the revisions that required outcomes assessment in August of 2014. Although the new standards were effective immediately following the concurrence of the House of Delegates, there will be a phase-in period. More details about the phase in are found in "The Phase-In Process" boxes.

Below are the new ABA Standards for the accreditation of law schools, which specifically reference and require outcomes assessment by law schools.

Standard 301. Objectives Of Program Of Legal Education

(a) A law school shall maintain a rigorous program of legal education that prepares its students, upon graduation, for admission to the bar and for effective, ethical, and responsible participation as members of the legal profession.
(b) A law school shall establish and publish learning outcomes designed to achieve these objectives.

Standard 302. Learning Outcomes

A law school shall establish learning outcomes that shall, at a minimum, include competency in the following:
(a) Knowledge and understanding of substantive and procedural law;
(b) Legal analysis and reasoning, legal research, problem-solving, and written and oral communication in the legal context;

(c) Exercise of proper professional and ethical responsibilities to clients and the legal system; and

(d) Other professional skills needed for competent and ethical participation as a member of the legal profession.

Standard 314. Assessment Of Student Learning

A law school shall utilize both formative and summative assessment methods in its curriculum to measure and improve student learning and provide meaningful feedback to students.

Standard 315. Evaluation Of Program Of Legal Education, Learning Outcomes, And Assessment Methods

The dean and the faculty of a law school shall conduct ongoing evaluation of the law school's program of legal education, learning outcomes, and assessment methods; and shall use the results of this evaluation to determine the degree of student attainment of competency in the learning outcomes and to make appropriate changes to improve the curriculum.

We will detail the requirements of these new standards later in this Guide, but here is a quick overview of the regulatory framework they create.

The new standards create requirements relating to **two different types of assessment, individual student assessment** (also sometimes called "classroom assessment") and **institutional student learning outcomes assessment**. The two types of assessment are not entirely unrelated, but their foci differ.

As discussed in Chapter 1, **individual student assessment** *focuses on measuring the learning of individual students.* In engaging in individual student assessment, you are appraising the academic performance of individual students. Assume Bella is a student in your Torts class. You evaluate Bella's output (exams, papers, etc.) to determine whether she has demonstrated the desired knowledge of tort law. Her grade is based on the evidence of learning provided by her outputs.

Ideally, individual student assessments not only identify the student's level of achievement, but also provide the student with sufficient feedback to understand and correct problems. If Bella has graded, critiqued assignments throughout the semester, she has the opportunity to learn of and from her mistakes, but many law school courses still feature a single assessment at the end of the course.

Legal education has been criticized over the years for its failure to provide sufficient feedback to students. The new standards tackle this perceived weakness of our current system of individual student assessment.

Standard 314, which requires law schools to provide students with "formative assessment," creates a new duty to provide meaningful

the Bar, *Transition to and Implementation of the New Standards and Rules of Procedure for Approval of Law Schools* ¶ 5 (August 13, 2014).

The Phase-In Process: Implementation of the Institutional Outcomes Assessment Plan

The ABA has provided the following guidance on the timing of the implementation of the new standards relating to the implementation of each school's institutional outcomes assessment plan:

"In the initial phases of implementation of the institutional effectiveness standard set forth in Standard 315, compliance will be assessed based on the seriousness of the law school's efforts to engage in an ongoing process of gathering information about its students' progress toward achieving identified outcomes and whether it is using the information gathered to regularly review, assess and adapt its academic program."

Schools will likely be required to "to file a report of some sort at the time those Standards become operative."

ABA Section on Legal Education & Admissions to the Bar, *Transition to and Implementation of the New Standards and Rules of Procedure for Approval of Law Schools* ¶¶ 5, 8 (August 13, 2014).

Distinguishing Among Assessment Types

The new ABA Standards are a call to improve both our assessment of our students' work (*i.e.*, individual student assessment) and our assessment of our own work (*i.e.*, outcomes assessment).

Obviously, there is substantial overlap between the two types of mandated assessment. We use student work/outputs not only to measure their individual achievements, but also the effectiveness of our educational programs at the law-school, program, and course levels. This overlap can sometimes lead to confusion.

You are going to be hearing a lot over the next several years about "classroom assessment." *Classroom assessment is simply another name for individual student assessment.* When someone is talking about classroom assessment, he is talking about how we can satisfy the ABA's mandate to provide more and better formative assessment to our students. So, for example, you might see an article on adding quizzes to a contracts course.

feedback to individual students. Interpretation 314-1 explains, "Formative assessment methods are measurements at different points during a particular course or at different points over the span of a student's education that provide meaningful feedback to improve student learning."

Essentially, this standard is saying that we must look beyond the traditional law-school model of providing a single (summative) assessment at the culmination of a course (the ubiquitous law school final exam) that provides students with little feedback aside from a numerical score or letter grade. Although the new standard does not require multiple assessments in each course, it challenges us to "up our game" in terms of the quantity and quality of feedback we provide to each of our students. The question is whether they are getting the guidance they need to improve. Accreditors are going to be looking to see what kind of feedback the typical student is receiving.

In contrast to individual student assessment, as discussed in Chapter 1, **institutional student learning outcomes assessment** *focuses on the overall effectiveness of your school's program of education.* Institutional student learning outcomes assessment requires you to evaluate your educational program as a whole, to assign a grade to your school as opposed to your individual students. The question is how well your institution is doing at helping students learn. (As is discussed in Chapter 1, outcomes assessment can also be done at the program and course levels to measure the effectiveness of the program or course.)

When you are conducting an institutional outcomes assessment, you are considering the *group* performance of your students. Periodic measures of the performance of sample groups of students provide snapshots of whether your school is achieving its outcomes. Institutional outcomes assessment uses your students' collective performance as a measure of your school's performance.

Legal education has also been criticized over the years for its failure to evaluate the effectiveness of its educational programs. We may teach our law students that evidence is all-important, but our own use of evidence has been woefully inadequate. For instance, we are years behind other disciplines in terms of any empirical study of the pedagogies we employ. The new standards tackle our need to engage in more robust self-assessment.

Standard 315 requires your law school to create and implement a plan for institutional outcomes assessment. It requires accreditors to consider the seriousness of your school's efforts to engage in a process of identifying learning outcomes, gathering information on your students' progress towards achieving those outcomes, and using that information to review, assess, and adapt its academic program.

Standards 301 and 302 flesh out the requirements of the assessment plan. Standard 301 requires your school to establish and publish its learning outcomes. The publication of learning outcomes promotes transparency and fairness to consumers.

Standard 302 requires that the learning outcomes include competency in certain listed essential spheres. After much discussion of and controversy about how specific this listing should be, the ABA settled on a list that differs very little from the list of areas in which students were expected to receive "substantial instruction" under the old Standard 302.

Standard 302 also leaves room for your school to distinguish itself from other law schools, by self-identifying *"[o]ther professional skills needed for competent and ethical participation as a member of the legal profession."* For example, some schools place a much greater emphasis on practice skills than others, and their outcomes should reflect that emphasis.

Finally, Standard 315 requires measurement of student progress. Articulating outcomes is not sufficient to satisfy the accreditation standards — your school needs to measure student performance to determine if the outcomes are being achieved. Institutional outcomes assessment does not require that the progress of every student be tracked as to every outcome. Nor does it require that every outcome be measured every year. That is where the plan comes into play.

In sum, accreditation based on outcomes assessment is here to stay. It is not a fad, which will be replaced by another fad in another decade. Outcomes assessment has been entrenched in K–12 and undergraduate education for the last several decades and is not waning. Law schools are simply a bit late to the dance.

Promotion, Retention, and Tenure Review

Law school faculty may also be required to engage in assessment planning for purposes of promotion, retention, and tenure review (PRT). Universities have already begun to add this requirement to their standard PRT policies.

Some faculty review processes are beginning to look at whether the faculty member has defined learning outcomes for her course, whether she provides assessment activities in the course to assess the achievement of the learning outcomes, and whether and how she uses the evidence of the assessment activities to improve student learning. In sum, they review the professor's course-level outcomes assessment *process*.

Additionally, some faculty review processes are also reviewing a professor's individual student assessment process. As discussed in Chapter 1, the focus of individual student assessment is on measuring

On the other hand, when you hear someone refer to *"course-level outcomes assessment,"* she is talking about how we can satisfy the ABA's mandate to assess our own educational programs. So, for example, you might see an article about how a writing professor used employer and alumni focus groups to shape her course assignments.

Isn't institutional assessment just program review?

No, institutional assessment is more than program review. First, it is systemized, formalized, on-going, and ingrained into the law school's operations. Program review is not mandated and therefore, may be sporadic at best.

Also, program review can be done without regard to concrete evidence on student learning and best pedagogical practices. In contrast, outcomes assessment requires evidence. Note, however, that assessment data can be used to provide such concrete evidence to inform program review decisions.

Scholarship on Assessment

To date, empirical research on the effectiveness of assessment in law schools has been scant. However, scholarship in this area is emerging, and the following articles show the type of work being done:

Carol Springer Sargent & Andrea A. Curcio, *Empirical Evidence that Formative Assessments Improve Final Exams*, 61 J. Legal Educ. 379 (2012).

Andrea A. Curcio, *Assessing Differently and Using Empirical Studies to See If It Makes a Difference: Can Law Schools Do It Better?*, 27 Quinnipiac L. Rev. 899 (2009).

Andrea A. Curcio, *Moving in the Direction of Best Practices and the Carnegie Report: Reflections on Using Multiple Assessments in a Large-Section Doctrinal Course*, 19 Widener L.J. 159 (2009).

Andrea A. Curcio, Gregory Todd Jones, & Tanya M. Washington, *Does Practice Make Perfect? An Empirical Examination of the Impact of Practice Essays on Essay Exam Performance*, 35 Fla. St. U. L. Rev. 217 (2008).

each student's level of achievement and providing the student with constructive feedback. Here, PRT committees are evaluating a professor's individual student assessment process by reviewing her feedback to her students. So, for example, they might review graded exams or papers to assess the quality and quantity of feedback, watch teaching tapes with an eye towards the professor's interaction with students, etc. Given the ABA Standards' new emphasis on individual student assessment, this type of review will likely become even more common.

PRT aside, even in annual performance reviews, some deans ask faculty, in regard to their teaching, what they are doing to improve student learning in their classes. Evidence of assessment activities can be used to provide concrete evidence.

So, to bluntly answer the question of whether the new emphasis on outcomes assessment will affect the way you are evaluated, the answer is "yes." The means by which professors' assessment activities can come into play in performance and other reviews are numerous and varied. Professors may be required to insert their course learning outcomes into their syllabi and then post those syllabi on a common portal. They may be asked to report the formative assessment opportunities each course provides. They may be asked to support bar passage efforts by patterning some assessments on the bar. The list could go on and on.

We feel compelled to address one issue that we know may cause concern to many in the academy. Whether an institution is achieving its learning outcomes is most often going to be measured by looking at the performance of a sample group of students on a class assignment or exam. That measure should **never** be viewed as a reflection of the professor's performance. Outcomes assessment on the institutional level is intended to measure the effect of the educational experience *as a whole* on students.

Assume, for example, students' performance on a Torts assignment at the end of the first semester is being used to measure critical reading skills. If students perform well, it reflects learning that has taken place *across the curriculum*, and if students perform poorly, it reflects a failure that took place *across the curriculum*. A professor should never be made to feel afraid to offer an assignment in his class to be used as an institutional-level outcomes assessment measure.

We would be remiss if we did not address a question that has been raised to us by some faculty members. "What if I teach in a doctrinal area (*e.g.*, Torts) and the assessment shows that students are not meeting expectations in their performance in that area?" As discussed in Chapter 6, what happens is that you and those among your colleagues who were assigned to evaluate the outcome in question work together to analyze what went wrong and develop an action plan to improve student performance. We are all on the same team. Outcomes assessment is about assisting students, not attacking colleagues.

The root problem could be a dozen different things and may not reflect on the abilities of the faculty member at all. For example, it may be that students are struggling in every subject, which may indicate an admissions issue. Or it may be that there are two sections of Criminal Law taught by two professors and both sections are struggling. That might mean that the course is not being allocated sufficient instructional minutes.

If the problem does appear isolated to a single professor, there may be an issue with the measures used. Or that professor may need to reevaluate his coverage or teaching techniques. One poor result should not be the basis for any negative action whatsoever regarding the faculty member.

In sum, the key is to understand that when it comes to outcomes assessment, the focus of PRT and annual performance reviews is on faculty efforts more than student outcomes. Student performance can be affected by a multitude of factors, including the skills and knowledge they had when they started the course. The relevant question for evaluators is whether a professor is actively seeking to improve students' learning experience or simply pulling out the same notes year after year.

Assessment as an Opportunity

Although you may be required to engage in assessment planning for one of the reasons above, you should never engage in assessment for assessment's sake. Such an exercise is an exercise in futility, not utility. As an academy, we should be assessing our work because we want to improve legal education, period.

The last decade has seen unprecedented attacks on legal education by the media, by the public, by alumni, by the bar, and by the bench. We have been criticized on every possible front for failing to provide graduates with the necessary knowledge, skills, and values and for charging too much for too little. Some of those criticisms have been entirely unjust, but some have merit. The outcomes assessment movement provides legal education with a golden opportunity to reinvent itself and to restore its reputation.

Do you believe that your school has mastered the art of legal education? Do you believe that your students are learning all that they can and should? All law professors wish we could answer those questions with a firm, "Yes," but if we are being honest with ourselves, the answer is "No."

Reports such as the Carnegie Foundation's *Educating Lawyers: Preparation for the Profession of Law* highlight the fact that law schools are doing some things very well, and we want to hold on to those strengths, but we have significant room for improvement in many areas. We cannot improve if we do not assess.

Assessment improves student learning. Individual student assessment improves student learning, by motivating students and by providing feedback and multiple chances to develop a skill in a particular course. And, when individual student assessment tools are used as part of an institutional outcomes assessment plan, these tools help the students in those classes learn.

Outcomes assessment can help us as institutions by providing concrete evidence to guide our budgeting, curriculum design, teaching, and strategic planning. It can also provide insight as to new avenues for faculty development.

Institutional outcomes assessment provides every law school with the opportunity to identify its own unique strengths and to provide potential students, current students, and alumni with tangible, empirical evidence of those strengths. It lets us know what aspects of our academic program we should retain as we contemplate change.

But, it also forces us to face up to our failures and do something about them. A fundamental principle underlying outcomes assessment is that teachers and institutions can get better at what they do, but doing so requires self-reflection and a willingness to try something new.

The idea that we are not living up to our potential as teachers and institutions is very hard for many of us to accept. Most law professors have no specialized training as educators, which makes it all too easy to assume that the best we can do is mimic our own law professors and alma maters. We hold on to the past because we do not know what else to do. The system has not encouraged us to do anything more. It's all too easy to think, "I won't get in trouble as long as I simply follow the pack."

But following the pack is not the best we can do. Legal education is not known as a hotbed of pedagogical reform, but there have always been some brave, innovative educators who tried something different in the classroom and succeeded in enhancing learning. Outcomes assessment encourages and even rewards those who are willing to work hard and take risks to improve students' learning experience. It helps all of us discover new and better ways to teach.

With the adoption of the new standards, legal education's follow-the-pack mentality will be turned on its head. Innovation is the new expectation of accreditors.

Assessing where we stand now is a necessary step towards improvement. On some levels, that's a very frightening prospect. We are moving into unfamiliar territory. "What happens if students are not achieving an outcome?" you might wonder. Well, first we need to consider whether we ever should have listed that outcome, whether it was a realistic goal. If the answer is "No," we just learned something about what we should be promising ourselves and our students.

If the answer is "Yes," we work to design a better curriculum and become better teachers. We need to develop a culture where experimentation is not only accepted, but expected. Some experiments will fail, but others will succeed and can be shared.

Another fundamental principle of outcomes assessment is that learning is a journey, not a destination, for student, teacher, and institution. We need to begin taking the path less taken.

Restoring Reputation

The future of legal education has been the subject of much discussion in these difficult economic times. Members of the shrinking pool of prospective students are demanding the best possible benefit of the bargain. "Show me what you can do for me," is their cry.

The law schools that survive and thrive will be those that succeed in becoming student centered, those whose graduates walk away with a firm belief that they take with them the knowledge, skills, and values needed to prosper in the workforce. The data generated by institutional assessment allows your school to show students what it can do for them.

It also creates an alternative to the *U.S. News & World Report* rankings. The validity of the rankings has long been questioned by certain members of the academy. Among the criticisms are that some of the factors used in calculating the rankings are based on purely subjective assessments and that none of the factors used attempts to directly measure the quality of the education being provided.

Publishing your law school's learning outcomes and at least a summary of the results of some of your measures will allow your school to provide evidence to all your constituencies that your school is providing students with a quality education.

Finally, institutional assessment provides a way in which we can distinguish ourselves in the market. The ABA is now making clear that one measure, the bar exam, is not the only measure of student learning. That gives us the freedom to measure (and tout) what we actually seek to produce.

Law schools are as diverse as any other type of school; each with its own inherent mission. Now, with accreditation focusing on non-standardized learning outcomes, we can focus on our law school's unique mission and assess and publicize its successes.

As this Chapter highlights, outcomes based assessment is a new reality for law schools. It is something that will be mandated but has inherent benefits for those who take it seriously.

We sincerely hope this Guide aids your school in embracing this new reality and bringing its benefits to your students.

higher learning should by definition be concerned about learning.

From a human perspective, if you are required to engage in the process, you might as well make it meaningful. Why waste your time and effort? Always remember that the goal is improved student learning. If you engage in the process, make sure it works for you and your students.

Action List

Step 1: Determine the date of your school's next ABA site visit and determine if your school will be reviewed under the new standards.

Step 2: Determine how and to what extent the assessment activities of your faculty are included in promotion, retention, and tenure review and annual reviews.

Step 3: Research: Determine the regional accreditation requirements at your school.

If your school is affiliated with a larger university, engage in the following tasks:

Task 1: Check with your university's central administration to determine what person or body is charged with institutional assessment planning.

Task 2: Ask that person or body what assessment planning requirements, if any, your university imposes on each unit.

Task 3: Determine the date of your university's next regional accreditation site visit.

If your school as a freestanding school has opted to be regionally accredited, engage in the following tasks:

Task 1: Read your regional accreditor's standards and requirements for reporting.

Task 2: Determine the date of your school's next regional accreditation site visit.

Keep reading to determine the next steps....

Chapter 3

Who?
Outcomes Assessment:
The Key Players

Learning Outcome: Readers will identify the parties involved in institutional outcomes assessment planning and explain the roles they play.

Readers will demonstrate achievement of this learning outcome by

✓ Explaining the various roles played by the parties within an institution in assessment planning.

✓ Evaluating the various models for institutional assessment planning and implementation and selecting the model that best fits the needs of their school.

✓ Thoughtfully selecting and carefully educating their schools' assessment actors.

You just set up an appointment with the dean for next week to talk about your new role helping lead the law school's institutional assessment efforts. Having done a bit of research (*i.e.,* having read Chapter 1 and Chapter 2 and taken the action steps listed there), you have a sense of just how significant your new role is.

You're both excited and concerned. You have come to see how institutional outcomes assessment could enhance your students' learning, and as a dedicated teacher, the idea that you have the opportunity to be part of a movement with the potential to create a lasting improvement in legal education resonates with you. However, you realize that you have just been handed a huge job and that you need help.

**Faculty Development
and Assessment**

Although frequently ref-
erenced in this Guide, individual student
assessment and the
"best practices" about individual student assess-
ment are outside the
scope of this Guide.

However, to the extent it
is relevant to your
school's overall strategic
planning on assessment,
some schools are creat-
ing administrative posi-
tions that are charged
with overseeing faculty
development in the area
of teaching. Such posi-
tions, akin to positions
that focus on the devel-
opment of faculty schol-
arship, may have
additional duties such as
coordinating assessment
activities across the curriculum, organizing
teaching workshops, co-
ordinating first-year mid-
term assessments, etc.

Chapter 3 focuses on where you can and should find that help (*i.e.*, who should/will be involved in assessment planning). It addresses the various parties who can be engaged in outcomes assessment on the institutional level and explains the different models for institutional assessment planning and implementation, including an assessment committee, an assessment coordinator, etc.

A key first step in putting together an institutional outcomes as-sessment plan is assembling the proper resources. Having the right people in place can make the difference between success and failure. Three groups are essential: the law school administration, the law faculty, and the university's central administration.

Law School Administration

It will come as no shock to you that nothing moves forward without the genuine support of your dean. Your dean may or may not know a great deal about assessment planning. So, from day one, you need to educate your dean about why institutional outcomes assessment is important, what resources are needed, what needs to be done, and how he or she can help.

Given the numerous and significant amendments to the ABA Stan-dards resulting from the most recent comprehensive review, law school deans (and faculties) may feel somewhat overwhelmed by change. Further, as discussed in Chapters 1 and 2, it is easy and not at all un-common for people to confuse outcomes assessment with individual student assessment. Your mission is to keep institutional outcomes assessment from getting lost in the shuffle.

You are going to need to work closely with your dean from the very beginning. In an ideal world, your dean would read this Guide (or at least Chapters 1 and 2) before your first substantive meeting on insti-tutional assessment. It is unlikely the dean will think to do so without some gentle prompting from you.

The dean should first meet with the person with overall responsibility for developing the plan to clarify the charge and discuss resources. As discussed below, that will most likely be either an institutional assessment coordinator or the chair of an institutional assessment committee. (If the school has appointed both an assessment coordinator and an as-sessment committee, the coordinator typically chairs the committee.)

If an assessment committee has been appointed, the dean should later meet with the committee as a whole to affirm his or her support for this endeavor, to review the committee's charge, and to answer any additional questions. After that, it's a good idea for the dean to meet once a semester or so with the committee to make sure that everyone is still on the same page.

Topic one of the coordinator's/chair's initial meeting with the dean has to be what resources the dean is willing and able to devote to the development of an institutional outcomes assessment plan. Whether you have been asked to coordinate institutional assessment efforts or simply to serve on an assessment committee, you are the first such resource.

Your dean may not fully recognize the scope of the task you are being asked to undertake, so the coordinator's/chair's meeting should begin with a discussion of the dean's goals. The following questions may help you reach a common understanding:

- **Do you want me (or my committee) to focus entirely on institutional outcomes assessment or will I (we) also be asked to coordinate individual student assessment efforts at the law school?**

The importance of the dean's answer to this question cannot be overstated. The new standards call for both institutional assessment and individual student assessment. Developing a plan for each is important, and developing a plan for each will take great time and effort.

If you are being asked to coordinate both types of assessment, you should expect that it will require anywhere from 50–100% of your workday. You should be released from other work accordingly. You have become an administrator, and your title (*e.g.,* director, assistant dean, associate dean) should reflect that fact.

Even if you are being asked to coordinate institutional assessment only, some work release, compensation increase, or other recognition of your efforts may be necessary and appropriate. Be careful to track your time and to make certain the dean is kept apprised of the hours devoted to your assessment duties.

If the dean is proposing that a single committee be charged with overseeing both types of assessment, we strongly urge you to ask that he/she rethink that proposal. The two types of assessment do go hand-in-hand, but there is a steep learning curve for each, and a faculty member serving on such a committee would immediately feel overwhelmed and overburdened.

A better plan would be to create two smaller committees that coordinate efforts. For example, the chair of each might serve as a member on the other, so that the right hand knows what the left is doing. There may also be times when joint meetings are held and/or the two committees jointly sponsor workshops, etc. for the faculty as a whole.

It's vital that the coordinator/chair begin to help the dean understand the workload that will be placed on committee members. We all know that some law school committees involve lots of heavy lifting while others do not. Particularly for the first year or two, an assessment committee will be a heavy lifting committee, and that should be a consideration when assigning its members to additional committees, etc.

The remaining questions assume that your (or your committee's) sole charge is to develop and implement an institutional assessment plan.

- **What is your desired timeline for developing and implementing our new institutional assessment plan?**

Developing your learning outcomes and obtaining any needed approvals will likely take at least one academic year, and that is only the first stage of assessment. It is important that you and the dean be realistic as to how long this process will take.

It is also important to understand you are developing a "plan" that will always be a work in process. Outcomes may change over time, and you will constantly be discovering new ways to measure achievement of outcomes. Thoughtful revision is a good thing.

- **What steps must be taken to obtain approval of the plan as a whole and/or its component parts?**

Institutional assessment plans can be approved in any number of ways. Some schools simply appoint a coordinator, who develops the plan, which is then adopted and implemented by the dean's fiat. Some schools have an assessment committee (or a standing committee, such as academic affairs) develop and approve a plan, which is then implemented by the dean's fiat. Some schools have an assessment committee (or a standing committee, such as academic affairs) develop and approve a plan, which is then approved by the faculty as a whole and implemented by the dean. There are a multitude of variations on these basic themes.

It is unlikely that you will develop a process during your first meeting with the dean, but you should plant the seed that you need to figure out a workable process. Both you and the dean must be realistic in developing the process. For the plan to succeed, to create a situation where key academic decisions, large and small, are guided by outcomes assessment, faculty buy-in is critical. That means that faculty must feel that they are part of the process, that they are being heard.

On the other hand, some of the details of the plan, such as which outcome is measured in a given year and how it is measured, may be better left to an assessment committee, task force, or coordinator. The committee, task force, or coordinator will likely have knowledge and expertise that the faculty as a whole lacks, and even more important, you need to keep the process rolling along. (If a law faculty as a whole had to approve every aspect of the construction of a new law building, the votes on what nails to use could go on for decades!)

We recommend that one aspect of the plan that should be approved by the faculty as a whole is the identification of learning outcomes and performance criteria. The faculty needs to work to develop a shared vision. Doing so may well pose some challenges, but it is essential to obtaining real support for the outcomes from the faculty. The new ABA standards require that the outcomes be published. If you are going to post something this significant on your website or include it in your marketing materials, everyone on the faculty should know what you are promising prospective students and why.

- **What faculty resources are you willing and able to provide towards this endeavor? Will there be a committee assigned? Will that committee be a dedicated committee or an already existing committee?**

Developing an institutional assessment plan is a labor-intensive process that requires a certain level of knowledge and sophistication about outcomes assessment. You must educate the dean about the amount and type of faculty resources that you will require to do the job right.

For the reasons outlined below, we recommend that you ask your dean to form an institutional assessment committee charged with the development of an institutional assessment plan. As discussed later in this Chapter and in Chapter 4, once an assessment plan is in place and your school has moved on to the Implementation and Evaluation Stages, the school will likely find it more practical to disband the assessment committee and form separate, smaller assessment task forces for each outcome.

- **What financial support are you willing to offer? What type of funding might be available?**

The development and implementation of an assessment plan will invariably require some funding. It need not break the bank, but it cannot be done for free. Again, everything will not be settled at this first meeting, but it is important for the dean to start thinking about this piece of the puzzle.

During all stages of the process, there may be years when the assessment coordinator is asked to do significant work over the summer. If so, he or she should be compensated in the form of a stipend, 10- or 12-month contract, etc. He or she may also benefit from having a research assistant or additional administrative support staff.

As noted above, education of faculty will be essential to the success of any institutional assessment plan. Some resources will be free. For example, you may bring in assessment experts from other units within your university to consult, conduct faculty workshops, etc.

But some important resources are not free. The assessment coordinator should certainly attend and present at the national assessment conferences that are beginning to sprout up around the country. Attending this type of conference can also be beneficial to committee members. The dean may also wish to use stipends to encourage and support scholarship in this area.

The Financial Cost of Assessment

Isn't assessment expensive? Where is the money going to come from to support an assessment culture at a law school when it is already strapped financially?

Simply answered, yes, there will be costs associated with assessment. However, the costs should not be overstated, and the value added to your students' learning experience by engaging in institutional outcomes assessment must be considered.

Administrators must make the hard decisions of allocations and budget. That may mean moving some funds away from scholarship to teaching. Such a move will no doubt trouble some faculty members, but it may be necessary to ensure the continued success of your law school. At most schools, tuition pays the bills, and schools that fail to keep pace with advancements in law teaching may find it increasingly difficult to attract students.

The entire faculty can benefit from bringing in national experts to conduct faculty workshops on assessment. Hearing about the exciting things that are happening at peer institutions can inspire faculty to become more involved.

Once you reach the Implementation and Evaluation Stages, you may need funding to support the creation and/or administration of assessment tools. For example, you may wish to use a tool, such as the Law School Survey of Student Engagement (LSSSE) or the Intercultural Development Inventory (IDI), for which you must pay on a per student basis. Similarly, you may wish to hire outside (or inside) evaluators to review a particular student work product to measure achievement of an outcome.

Do not leave your dean with the impression that all of this is going to be wildly expensive—you can develop and implement a very effective institutional assessment plan on a limited budget—but do educate your dean of the fact that there should be a budget line for institutional assessment.

And here is the question we hope your dean asks you.

- **Besides providing human and financial resources, how can I help promote the development of an effective institutional assessment plan?**

Nothing is more essential to creating a culture of assessment than the public support of the dean. The dean's words and actions relating to outcomes assessment provide both motivation and legitimacy.

He or she should make frequent public statements in support of assessment to faculty, students, and the public. Support can be voiced at faculty meetings, in the school newsletter, at orientation, at alumni events, and on the school website to name a few. If the dean becomes excited about assessment, others will follow.

The dean should also show support for assessment (both institutional and individual) by valuing assessment activities in the faculty review process and valuing teaching in hiring decisions (*i.e.,* hiring teachers as well as scholars).

Most importantly, the dean should set an example by not only using the results to satisfy accreditors, but to inform strategic planning, budgeting, etc.

Law School Faculty

Law faculty will play a variety of roles, major and supporting, in institutional outcomes assessment planning and implementation. We will first describe the responsibilities of key faculty assessment actors, and then describe those of the faculty as a whole.

Faculty Assessment Actors

The institutional assessment coordinator, the institutional assessment committee, the individual assessment task forces, or some combination of the three are charged with actually developing and implementing the institutional assessment plan. These faculty assessment actors are asked to assume significant responsibilities and undertake a wide number of tasks. Putting together the right team is essential.

The Institutional Assessment Coordinator

A growing number of schools are appointing a faculty member to serve in the administrative or quasi-administrative role of institutional assessment coordinator. The title varies from one school to another (*e.g.*, assistant dean for institutional assessment, associate dean for institutional assessment, director of institutional assessment, assessment coordinator, etc.), but the function is the same. This individual oversees the development and implementation of the institutional outcomes assessment plan and serves as a resource for faculty, staff, and administrators. In short, she is the person charged with making sure that all of the balls being juggled stay in the air.

While not absolutely necessary, we believe that the appointment of an institutional assessment coordinator is a smart move. You need someone in the building with expertise. You need someone in the building who is accountable for making certain things get done. You need someone in the building who sees the big picture, including the need to work within any parameters set by the university. And you need someone in the building who is in it for the long haul—institutional assessment has become a permanent fixture—a dedicated leader will provide stability to the process.

In schools that lack a coordinator, but have appointed an institutional assessment committee, the committee chair essentially takes on the responsibilities of the coordinator by default. If you are serving as a chair, it is particularly important to document your efforts and your hours. They may far exceed those of other chairs and warrant a work release or other adjustment to your terms of employment.

The bottom line is that your school needs someone willing and able to run the show.

The Institutional Assessment Committee

A growing number of schools are also coming to see the value of a dedicated institutional assessment committee. At this point, you may be wondering what value a committee may have, particularly if your school has opted to appoint a coordinator. You may also be questioning

---

The Human Resources Cost of Assessment

Won't assessment create extra work for faculty members who are already over-worked?

Simply answered, yes, when an institution starts institutional outcomes assessment planning, there will be "extra work" for those responsible for assessment planning, implementation, etc. (*e.g.*, involvement in assessment committee, task force, etc.). However, this work constitutes service on a law school committee and should be given the same credit afforded work on comparably demanding committees.

Any extra work involved in individual student assessment or course-level assessment is outside the scope of this Guide. However, we believe that with sufficient education and guidance, faculty members will come to see that a more formalized assessment process can be incorporated into their classrooms with minimal extra time or effort on their parts.

why a new committee is needed or why work cannot simply be farmed out to an existing committee or committees.

While it is certainly possible to assign the coordinator complete responsibility for and control over assessment planning and some schools do just that, we believe that using a committee to help lead your school's outcomes assessment efforts has some very real benefits.

One benefit is that the development of a plan that reflects your school's unique mission and identity requires the kind of broad perspective that can only be provided by a faculty committee. No matter how talented and dedicated your coordinator is, he or she can only represent the views of one person.

A cross-section of the faculty can provide tremendous insights into what types of outcomes might be desired by different components of the faculty, what types of tools might be available to measure those outcomes, etc.

The committee need not and should not be huge. At most schools, a group of four to six faculty members, including the chair, will be sufficient to provide the needed diversity of perspective. A committee that is too large can get so bogged down in allowing everyone to speak that nothing ever gets done.

We carefully handpicked our first committee to make sure it had the diversity we felt we needed. We asked our dean to appoint certain faculty members because of what we knew each could bring to the table. (Thankfully, our dean understood the importance and complexity of our endeavor and was more than willing to support our desire to cherry pick.)

We deliberately created a mix of skills faculty (legal writing, clinical, etc.) and doctrinal faculty. We included people who had taught for decades and those at the very beginning of their teaching careers. And by including a faculty member who was also an administrator, we were able to bring in yet another perspective.

The mix provided more than a few surprises. For example, there were times when some committee members were absolutely floored that another would passionately object to a draft outcome that seemed perfectly innocuous to them. The healthy discussion spurred by this type of objection was invaluable.

We also consciously chose to appoint a committee that reflected different views on the value of outcomes assessment. Some members of our committee voiced strong support for outcomes assessment, some voiced healthy skepticism, and some were in the middle. The committee welcomed any voicing of doubts because it allowed us to address those doubts at the committee level and not in the middle of a faculty meeting. (Okay, we didn't always "welcome" it, but we all knew it was a necessary evil.)

Make no mistake about it—outcomes assessment is controversial among faculty and administrators and likely will be for some time. For the plan to develop as it should, we truly needed someone on our committee to ask the tough questions. The meetings were not always fun and tempers sometimes flared, but the small size of the committee and the hard-won expertise of its members ultimately allowed us to look for areas of common ground.

Another benefit is that the members of the committee can become the plan's best ambassadors. It is difficult, if not impossible, for an assessment plan developed by one person to gain acceptance by the faculty as a whole. We selected committee members who were respected by (and hung out with) different groups within the faculty. We encouraged them to talk about what we were doing and listen to the reactions of our colleagues.

A law school is not Oz, and we did not want assessment to be perceived as being controlled by "the man behind the curtain." We are not going to lie and say there has been no push back on our efforts, but the credibility of the process is so much greater than it would have been had we not included such respected colleagues.

Although it is entirely possible to "farm out" all or part of the assessment planning process to an existing committee, we believe that doing so is not a best practice. Under some outcomes assessment planning models, the task of developing an assessment plan is assigned to a standing committee, such as academic affairs. Our concern about this type of model is that the members of a standing committee are inevitably charged with additional tasks that will prevent them from developing the necessary expertise and devoting the necessary time to develop an effective plan.

For example, trying to create an outcomes assessment plan while also charged with approving new courses, taking a look at the curve, and developing a new attendance policy is simply not a good idea.

Especially now, when outcomes assessment is a new concept for most faculty, educating committee members is essential. On every law school committee, there will be one or two new members who need to get up to speed, but on this committee, almost every member will be a novice.

As evidenced by the publication of this Guide, committee members are going to be asked to learn a great deal. They will need more than a general understanding of assessment planning. This group needs to learn to build a clock, while the rest of the faculty simply needs to learn to tell time.

Committee members not only require expertise to create the plan, they need it to sell the plan to other members of the faculty. The move to outcomes assessment is a sea change in legal education. Building the faith of the faculty as a whole will be no small task. If there is even the slightest sense that those charged with assessment planning lack expertise (*i.e.,* don't know what they are doing), faculty buy-in will be that much more difficult to achieve.

Committee members are also going to be asked to spend countless hours in and out of the meeting room working on the end product. Institutional assessment requires a "working committee" that will likely need to meet an hour or more each week. Whether it is researching what other schools have done, surveying the faculty, or drafting a part of the plan, homework is required of every member.

We recommend that the composition of the assessment committee remain largely the same for at least two years. After that, if the committee remains in existence, the dean can rotate members of the committee every several years. This rotation will allow new members to learn more about assessment while keeping enough "guiding members" to keep the process going.

Once the plan has been fully developed and the Implementation Stage is reached, it may be possible to eliminate the institutional assessment committee. The committee has served its function of laying the foundation of the school's assessment strategy in the Development Stage.

If you think of the tasks to be performed in the Development Stage as being on the macro level, the tasks to be completed in the Implementation and Evaluation Stages should be considered tasks on the micro level. These tasks are very focused and deal with one learning outcome at a time. Therefore, these tasks are better performed by smaller individual assessment task forces with oversight by an institutional assessment coordinator.

If the committee continues to exist into the Implementation and Evaluation Stages, its workload will be less demanding at this point and will likely involve updates and revisions to the institutional learning outcomes and periodic curriculum mapping. However, the individual members of the committee will have an additional duty: the chairing of the individual assessment task forces.

The Assessment Task Forces

We recommend that a small task force be assigned to each learning outcome for the Implementation and Evaluation Stages. Once the assessment plan is up and running, the required assessment activities will actually increase. Someone will need to develop assessment tools/measures, evaluate results, create action plans for needed change, etc.

As will be discussed in Chapter 4, *some assessment activity will be undertaken for each outcome each year*. That is a lot for one committee to juggle, which is why it makes sense to create the individual task forces. At this juncture, you will quite simply need more members of the faculty to play a role in the assessment process.

Let's say that your school has adopted 8 desired student learning outcomes. A task force comprised of 3–4 faculty members should be assigned to each outcome by the dean or her representative. These members should have some recognized expertise relating to the learning outcome to which they are assigned. For example, legal writing professors, trial advocacy professors, and other skills professors should be on the task force that focuses on communication, whereas doctrinal professors should be on the task force that focuses on substantive knowledge of the law.

Additionally, the first chair of each task force should ideally be a member (or former member) of the institutional assessment committee, who can impart the committee's vision and knowledge of institutional assessment to the task force. The actual tasks to be accomplished by these task forces are outlined in detail in Chapter 4 and charted in Table 4.8 in Chapter 4.

The Tasks to Be Accomplished by Assessment Actors

As you think about how best to allocate assessment planning responsibilities at your school, it is useful to consider the tasks to be accomplished one by one. Think about what model would work best at your school. In other words, would it better for this particular task to be assigned to a committee, a coordinator, a task force, or all three?

1. Education of the Dean, the Assessment Actors, and the Faculty

All of the assessment actors should play some role in educating the dean and the faculty about institutional assessment. But someone, usually the coordinator or chair, must assume a lead role.

During the Development Stage, the coordinator's/chair's first task is to educate himself on the best practices for institutional assessment. Someone must become the law school's expert, the go-to person.

The chair/coordinator will serve as the first and primary educator of the dean and the assessment committee (if any) on institutional assessment generally. He will provide them with background readings, explain the basics of assessment planning, and answer questions. (And if he does not know the answers, he will consult with someone who does.)

However, all of the assessment actors should assume some responsibility for educating the faculty. Again, this is all new, so it is vital to make a conscious effort to help faculty members understand the "who, what, where, when, why, and how" of institutional assessment generally. That might mean developing workshops, bringing in experts, creating a resource website, etc.

The task of keeping faculty up to date on what you are doing at your school and why is equally important. You cannot succeed without transparency. Appropriate reporting might involve frequent emails, faculty meeting discussions, formal reports, etc.

2. Development of the Institutional Assessment Plan

As explained in Chapter 4, developing the institutional assessment plan will require multiple steps. The assessment actors, typically the members of the assessment committee, must identify the learning outcomes and performance criteria, map the outcomes and criteria to the existing curriculum, obtain the needed approval of the plan (or at least the outcomes and criteria) from the dean and/or faculty, and create a timetable for the measurement of each outcome.

The first two steps in creating the plan are to identify and to draft the outcomes and performance criteria. Doing so will require the assessment actors to research ABA requirements, university requirements, law school requirements (as expressed in mission and strategic planning statements), etc. They will also need to consult with the dean, the faculty, and other constituencies.

Creating outcomes and criteria that truly reflect your school's mission and identity requires a tremendous amount of thought and discussion. Multiple drafts are to be expected. Like any writing project, there is some good, old-fashioned grunt work involved.

The third step is to map the proposed outcomes and criteria back to your existing curriculum by creating a curriculum map. If they do not match, either the outcomes or the curriculum must be changed. This step may require lots of knocking on the doors of faculty members who forgot to respond to your multiple requests for information. The map must be complete.

The fourth step is to revise the learning outcomes in light of the information gained from the faculty and from the curriculum mapping exercise.

The fifth step is to obtain approval of the plan so that it may be published and implemented.

And, lastly, the sixth step is creating the "plan for the plan." Here you will create a timetable for the data collection on all learning outcomes and a timetable for measuring each outcome with the goal of measuring one or two outcomes a year, analyzing the results and making needed changes the following year, and measuring again, if necessary, the year after that. The basic idea is to measure each outcome at least once before your next accreditation review. Working with the dean or her designee, you will also assign implementation and evaluation duties.

3. Implementation of the Plan

As explained in detail in Chapter 5, once the plan has been developed and adopted, the real work begins. The Implementation Stage requires the assessment actors, typically the members of the assessment task force for each outcome, to pin down *exactly* what they seek to measure; where it will be measured; how it will be measured, and who will be responsible for the measurement.

It must determine through what courses or other activities relevant data may be collected (*e.g.,* to measure oral advocacy skills, you might collect videos from an internal moot court competition); develop and/ or review assessment tools; decide what rubric, if any, will be used in evaluating the data; determine what sample size is needed; decide how to select the sample; and collect the data (*i.e.,* use the tools).

Ideally multiple measures/tools are used to determine what level of competency your students have achieved with regard to each outcome. Creating even one assessment tool to collect data is a significant undertaking, and the task force will likely be creating three.

Additionally, in this stage, the assessment actors will need to determine who will score or tabulate the data (*e.g.,* apply the rubric), what the desired performance threshold for each tool is, and who will evaluate the data to determine if the outcome in question has been achieved. Obtaining scorers and evaluators (and the funds to pay them, if necessary) can be a job in and of itself.

4. Evaluation and Use of the Results (i.e., "Closing the Loop")

The Evaluation Stage poses its own challenges. As explained in Chapter 6, the assessment actors, again typically the members of the assessment task force, must evaluate the data collected, including finding the root cause or causes of any failure to achieve an outcome; communicate key findings to stakeholders; and, if the findings warrant change, close the loop by developing and implementing an action plan and making any needed permanent improvements to educational programs.

If the measures for a given outcome indicate that it is not being achieved, action must be taken. The question is not so much whether improvement is immediately achieved, but rather whether your school is taking steps to improve. Change may come in a multitude of forms, including, but not limited to, adding an additional required class, teaching a topic in a different way, and providing more formative assessment (*i.e.,* critique) to students in a course or courses.

These are obviously not steps that the assessment actors can take on their own. Again, some or all faculty must be the agents of change. And the dean must make clear that maintaining the status quo is not an option.

The Faculty as a Whole

Even with the support of your dean and the efforts of a dedicated team of assessment actors, your institutional assessment plan will not succeed without the cooperation and involvement of your faculty. The faculty's participation will be required during every stage of the assessment process.

The Development Stage

Your first request of the faculty will be for its time. As you ramp up your assessment efforts, you should be providing presentations, workshops, etc. that introduce faculty members to the basics of outcomes assessment.

You may wish to use this Guide (or selected chapters) to provide faculty with needed background. Additionally, consider preparing a one-page handout for your first faculty presentation that summarizes general information about institutional outcomes assessment as well as the responsibilities of the faculty.

During the Development Stage, faculty members should be provided with formal and informal opportunities to comment on proposed learning outcomes and performance criteria long before they come to a vote. They should also be encouraged to share their thoughts with assessment actors informally at lunch and in the hallways.

Look for every way possible to make your faculty a part of the conversation. For example, we conducted electronic surveys inviting comment on each of our outcomes, which allowed for anonymous posting. The beauty of that tool was that no one voice could dominate the conversation.

Curriculum maps cannot be completed without faculty participation, so you should make every attempt to make the mapping process as quick and painless as possible. You should also make clear that no expectation exists that all or even most of the institutional outcomes will be covered in every course. Make it a point to share the results as soon as possible. Be transparent in all that you do.

The Implementation Stage

Given how new we all are to outcomes assessment, law schools are still scrambling to find ways to effectively measure certain outcomes. As you develop your assessment projects, make it a point to actively solicit the faculty for ideas.

It is also important to make faculty aware that you will need their help to collect data. Most outcomes assessment projects will involve using information that faculty members are already collecting in a different way. So, for instance, you may ask to have access to exam answers or papers from one of their classes. You may also ask them to help you create the rubric for measuring what that work says about students' achievement of a particular outcome.

Educating faculty members about institutional assessment is essential to eliciting this type of assistance. They need to be confident that in using their materials, you will not be measuring the professor's performance. Rather, the results will be used to look at the big picture of how the school as a whole is doing on this outcome.

The Evaluation Stage

You will need the faculty's help in analyzing what the data means. Does it indicate that students are achieving the learning outcome or not? If not, why not? And if not, what can your school do to try to address the root cause of the problem?

The loop cannot be closed, improvements in students' academic performance cannot be made or even attempted, without faculty participation. On some levels, this stage provides the toughest challenges. For instance, where change is needed, faculty members must be willing to step up to the plate and undertake pilot projects to test the efficacy of possible actions.

It may take years, but every law school needs to develop a culture that embraces pedagogical experimentation and change. Deans need to constantly reassure faculty members that they will not be penalized for trying something that does not work, that their attempt at improvement whether successful or not will be viewed as a positive on performance evaluations. We need to get past the fear of change.

We also need to do much more to provide faculty with the tools they need to enhance the student learning experience. Obtaining the data provided by outcomes assessment is a huge step towards helping us all understand where our programs are succeeding and where they are failing. But knowing that we are failing at something does not tell us how to fix the problem.

Law schools need to work together to create real change. The authors of this Guide both came up through the legal research and writing ranks, a place where you can find a workshop or conference on pedagogy every month of the year and where scholarly writing is largely devoted to how to be better teachers. We believe that the achievement of learning outcomes can be improved because we have seen it, and we have done it.

If legal education can find a way to provide those same resources to every professor, regardless of subject matter, every professor and every institution can improve their students' learning experience.

University Central Administration

Your university likely offers a wealth of possible resources, most of which are available at absolutely no cost. Three are worthy of particular note: the university assessment committee, the office of institutional research, and the learning and teaching center.

The University Assessment Committee

Participating in a university assessment committee is a terrific way to make certain that your assessment planning is consistent with university requirements and to learn from the experiences of other units. If your university has such a committee, reach out to it and make the law school's interest in having a place at the committee table known.

One of this Guide's authors was appointed to our University Assessment Committee even before assessment efforts at our Law School began in earnest. She left her first meeting with knowledge that she had hitherto lacked, knowledge that the University actually had its own list of learning outcomes (known as the "Habits of Inquiry"). She also left with an armload of resources on the basics of institutional assessment. To this day, she receives a constant flow of help and information from the committee.

As noted in Chapter 2, law schools are at the tail end of the assessment parade. Our colleagues in units like engineering have been engaging in institutional assessment for years. Our School of Engineering's representative on the University Assessment Committee was willing and able to provide advice on every aspect of the assessment process as well as to share rubrics, planning charts, and other materials. Members from other units were equally gracious.

If you have the opportunity to spend some time with others engaged in assessment at your university, you will discover that we are tackling the same issues. There is no need to reinvent the wheel.

The Office of Institutional Research

While they are referred to by a multitude of different names, almost every university has someone who plays the role of director of institutional research. This person is charged with providing leadership in the collection and analysis of data for things like strategic planning, accreditation, institutional studies, etc.

As an expert in the area of assessment, the director of institutional research can help assist you at virtually every stage of the institutional assessment planning process. We found her assistance to be particularly valuable when we were engaging in projects to measure various outcomes. Among other things, she could tell us what sample size was needed for a valid and reliable study and what the data we gathered meant (*e.g.*, whether a difference in performance was statistically significant). She had the expertise in statistical analysis that we lacked, and her services were provided for free.

Seek out your director and make him or her part of your team.

The Learning and Teaching Center

Again, while they are referred to by a multitude of different names, almost every university has a **Learning and Teaching Center** (*also known as Center for Excellence in Teaching, Center for Teaching and Learning, etc.*), *a facility and/or program devoted to providing resources and opportunities for faculty development in the area of teaching.* The center is typically populated by professors with a proven track record for excellence and with expertise in both teaching and assessment.

The center can serve as a wonderful source of speakers for faculty workshops, etc. It can also be a resource to which you turn as you seek to close the assessment loop. If an outcome is not what you desire, and you are seeking ideas on how a topic might be more effectively taught, why not turn to the teaching experts? Good teaching is good teaching, and successful methods can transfer from one subject area to another.

Moving Forward

Having completed the first three chapters of this Guide, you are now equipped to answer the basic questions about institutional assessment: What is it? Why are we talking about it? and Who will be involved? In the upcoming chapters, we move from theory to practice and actually start explaining the most challenging question of all, "How do you do it?"

Action List

If you are the coordinator/chair ...

Step 1: Meet with your dean and pose the questions provided in this Chapter:

- *Do you want me (or my committee) to focus entirely on institutional outcomes assessment or will I (we) also be asked to coordinate individual student assessment efforts at the law school?*

The remaining questions assume that your (or your committee's) sole charge is to develop and implement an institutional assessment plan.

- *What is your desired timeline for developing and implementing our new institutional assessment plan?*

- *What steps must be taken to obtain approval of the plan as a whole and/or its component parts?*

- *What faculty resources are you willing and able to provide towards this endeavor? Will there be a committee assigned? Will that committee be a dedicated committee or an already existing committee?*

- *What financial support are you willing to offer? What type of funding might be available?*

Step 2: If your dean has yet to appoint a committee, but plans to do so, consider which members of your faculty would make effective members. Do not forget to seek as diverse a representation as possible.

Step 3: Finish reading this Guide. You need to know where you are going before your first committee meeting!

Step 4: Once the committee is in place, begin the process of educating its members. Provide each member with a copy of this Guide and/or other background materials.

Step 5: Schedule your first meeting. At the meeting, you should review the committee's charge, answer questions about institutional assessment, and schedule weekly meetings for the remainder of the term.

Step 6: Contact the head of the university assessment committee to make him/her aware of your new role and seek guidance on university protocols and resources.

Step 7: Identify good contact people within the office of institutional research and the learning and teaching center.

If you are a dean, a member of the assessment committee (or simply someone interested in assessment), keep reading....

Chapter 4

How?
Outcomes Assessment:
The Development Stage

Learning Outcome: Readers will develop a well-reasoned, comprehensive institutional assessment plan.

Readers will demonstrate achievement of this learning outcome by

✓ Creating a comprehensive list of institutional learning outcomes that accurately reflect the knowledge, skills, and values their schools' graduates should possess.

✓ Creating institutional performance criteria for each learning outcome that express in specific and measurable/observable terms what must be shown to establish the outcome.

✓ Creating a curriculum map that identifies which learning outcomes and performance criteria are addressed and assessed in each course.

✓ Developing a timeline for assessment that establishes the sequence and schedule of key assessment activities for each learning outcome.

✓ Assigning implementation and evaluation duties for each learning outcome to faculty members with expertise in the relevant area.

You've met with your dean, who has decided to appoint an institutional assessment committee to begin the task of creating your school's institutional assessment plan. Your first committee meeting is scheduled for next week.

Figure 4.A

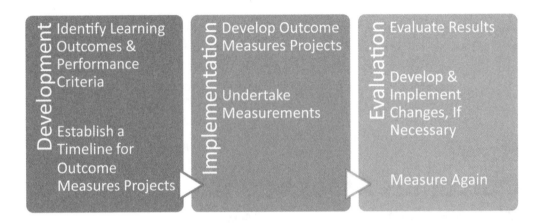

As discussed in Chapter 1, developing and maintaining an institutional assessment plan involves three stages: the Development Stage, the Implementation Stage, and the Evaluation Stage. You know that your committee's first task will be to develop the framework for your institutional assessment plan, but what will that take in terms of time, thought, and resources? You need a plan for developing your plan.

And when we say "plan," we actually mean that you will create a physical document called an institutional assessment plan. In this Chapter, you will be introduced to the various lists, maps, and tables that will make up your institutional assessment plan, and we will help you fill them out.

Think of this Chapter as providing the plan for your plan. It is your "how-to" guide to developing and documenting an outcomes assessment plan framework. Chapter 4 addresses the various steps of the Development Stage, providing examples and notes about best practices, and is tailored to the unique pedagogy of legal education, incorporating examples that are directly tied to law schools.

Documenting Your Institutional Assessment Plan

As mentioned above, an assessment "plan" is both a strategy and a document that details that strategy. Imagine you were constructing a binder with all of the materials needed for your plan. What might that table of contents look like? What components will you need to move forward to the Implementation Stage? What components will stakeholders, such as faculty, expect to see?

We believe that Table 4.1 provides a useful model.

Table 4.1. University of _____ School of Law Institutional Assessment Plan

Table of Contents		
Tab	**Document**	**Date Adopted or Completed**
1	List of Learning Outcomes and Performance Criteria	___/___/___
2	Curriculum Map	___/___/___
3	Data Collection Cycle for ___ Outcomes (Table 4.5)	___/___/___
4	Three Year Cycle of Implementation and Evaluation Activity (Table 4.7)	___/___/___
5	Outcome 1 Documents (Note: Devote a separate tab to each outcome) Assessment Cycle for Learning Outcome (Table 4.6) Parties Responsible for Implementation & Evaluation (Table 4.8) Assessment Blueprint Form & Appendices (*See* Chapter 5) Triangulated Analysis Form & Appendices (*See* Chapter 6) Specific Action Plan, If Needed, & Appendices (*See* Chapter 6)	___/___/___
6	Communication Archive (Note: Include emails and reports to faculty, relevant faculty minutes, etc.)	N/A

This binder contains every piece of information relating to your plan that your key stakeholders (*i.e.*, assessment actors, faculty, administrators, and accreditors) might desire. It begins with its centerpiece, the list of learning outcomes and performance criteria that the assessment committee has created and the law school has adopted. (*See* Steps 1–5 in Figure 4.B.) The list of outcomes is followed by a curriculum map, which identifies where and how those outcomes are being addressed in your educational program. (*See* Step 3 in Figure 4.B.)

Next come the tables that bring your "plan" to life, that identify what assessment activities will be undertaken, when they will be undertaken, and who will undertake them. (*See* Step 6 in Figure 4.B.)

In describing the plan, the binder first provides information relating to institutional assessment on a macroscopic scale. Table 4.5 sets forth

Outcomes Assessment and the Need for Flexibility

Learning outcomes are organic and are subject to revision based upon alignment, experience, and further reflection. Therefore, although you will identify an initial list of learning outcomes during the Development Stage, you will definitely revisit this issue over the years.

the data collection timeline for *all* of your school's learning outcomes, providing you and your stakeholders with a bird's-eye view of the data collection cycle of your plan. Table 4.7 goes a step further, looking at all assessment activities, not just data collection, for all outcomes. It creates a template for a three-year plan, outlining what activities your school will undertake with regard to each outcome in each year.

The binder next provides specific information on the individual outcomes, devoting a separate tab to each. Table 4.6 sets forth the assessment cycle timeline for each individual outcome, outlining what you will do with regard to that outcome in each year over a seven-year period. But when we say "you," we don't mean you the reader as an individual. Assessment is a large job, never to be done by one person alone (as you will see once you fill out Table 4.7). So, in Table 4.8, the law school assigns implementation and evaluation duties for each outcome.

Again, we will walk you through the purpose of each table and how to fill them out later in this Chapter, so don't worry. We will also provide examples of what each table looks like when completed. And, to provide further assistance, we have blank forms in Appendix B.

Take note that even after your assessment plan is complete, you will continue to use this binder to document the Implementation and Evaluation Stages of each outcome. You will be introduced to the Assessment Blueprint Form in Chapter 5 and the Triangulated Analysis Form and Specific Action Plan in Chapter 6. These documents, along with their appendices will be added to Tab 5 by the assessment coordinator as they are completed.

The binder's final tab documents communication relating to the plan's creation and implementation. So, for example, if the assessment committee surveyed the faculty about what outcomes should be adopted, the survey results would be included under this tab. Similarly, emails to the faculty about the plan and faculty meeting minutes relating to the plan would be found here.

Over the next three chapters, we are going to stress the importance of documentation over and over again. It's so easy to document something at the moment it takes place and so hard to document something years later. When accreditors come knocking at your door or a faculty member says, "I don't even remember discussing that," you really don't want to have to try to remember at what faculty meeting six years ago the faculty approved an aspect of your plan. When in doubt, put it in the binder!

The Process: An Overview

As illustrated in Figure 4.B, the development of your outcomes assessment plan will involve a stepped process.

Figure 4.B

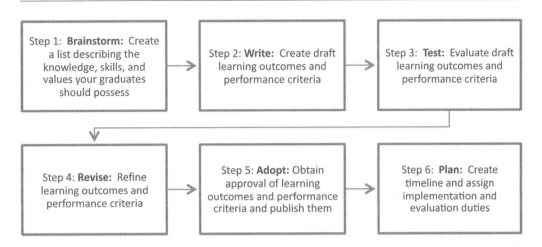

Within the six steps, there are a number of smaller tasks that must be accomplished and questions that must be answered. Where necessary, we have divided each step into the various tasks that must be accomplished to complete that step.

To begin your institutional assessment plan, you must first create institutional learning outcomes and performance criteria. The first five steps address how to make that happen. Step 6 will address how to prepare for the Implementation Stage. Your assessment process can easily come to a screeching halt if your plan fails to create a timeline for assessment and/or to assign responsibilities for each assessment project. Creating accountability will be a key to success.

Don't worry if this all sounds a little overwhelming. The process is not nearly as complicated as it sounds. Simply take things step by step, and soon you will have an institutional outcomes assessment plan in hand.

Step 1: Brainstorm: Create a list of knowledge, skills, and values but don't recreate the wheel

Your first assessment committee meeting should focus on the basics (*i.e.*, making sure that every member understands the committee's charge, setting up meeting times, etc.), but by your second meeting, you should be ready to begin what we think of as the brainstorming step. The first task in this brainstorming step is to create a draft of your school's learning outcomes.

To get started, a good homework assignment for the second meeting is to ask each committee member to review the ABA Standards and other resources described below and come to the next meeting with a

Key to Success: Engage your Faculty

As you make your way through the brainstorming phase, try to make a point of seeking input from all members of the faculty, not just those on the assessment committee. At this point in the process, we are most definitely not talking about something like calling for a faculty vote on the learning outcomes. Instead, we are simply suggesting that a casual discussion over coffee or in the hallway can help educate the faculty about where you are in the process and provide you with valuable insights about your colleagues' vision of your school and its students. This can also be a good time to begin holding (or at least planning) faculty workshops on the basics of institutional outcomes assessment.

Keep in mind that your faculty may be apprehensive about the changes and challenges law schools and law faculty are now facing. You can lessen fears about (and opposition to) outcomes assessment by making it a known quantity. Transparency and openness now can help win votes when you seek final approval of the outcomes.

list of five to twelve attributes (knowledge, skills, or values) your school should expect its graduates to possess. This process is the initial plunge into the drafting of the learning outcomes.

Learning outcomes *identify the knowledge, skills, and values that you want your graduates to have upon completion of their studies.* Put another way, creating learning outcomes requires you to reflect on the following questions. What does the successful law school graduate know? What can the successful law school graduate do? And what does the successful law school graduate value?

Warn your committee members that now is not the time for great specificity. You are shooting for 6 to 12 outcomes, not 132. So, for example, if a committee member believes a graduate should be able to draft a clear and effective brief, that member should include something like "effective written communication" on his/her list.

These lists need not (and will not) be in perfect learning outcome form or language at this point. They are simply intended to spur conversation. Ideally, the lists can be submitted to the committee chair in advance of the meeting so that she can develop a master list of areas of agreement and difference. You may be surprised as to how much agreement actually exists.

Over the next few meetings, the committee should focus on refining the list. Again, you should be concerned about substance, not form, at this point. You can focus on drafting later. (Law professors can and do argue for hours over comma placement!) Right now, your committee is answering the fundamental question of what the "value added" of an education at your school should be.

As you work to refine your list, bear in mind that the list as a whole should set forth the knowledge, skills, and values that the committee believes are *essential* to a graduate. A graduate who fails to achieve even one of the listed outcomes is not prepared for the practice of law. If the committee is at odds over a particular outcome, ask each member to consider whether the achievement of that outcome is truly essential or merely aspirational. Use the list to set a threshold for achievement for your graduates.

Once you have a refined list from the committee, you can then work on ensuring that the list includes other essential components.

The tasks set forth in Figure 4.C are crucial to developing the content of your outcomes.

Task 1: Incorporate All Outcomes Mandated by the ABA

Identifying the core competencies or knowledge, skills, and values of a law graduate is simple in the sense that there are plenty of resources to guide you. Because the ABA will be accrediting institutions based upon its accreditation standards, your list of desired knowledge, skills,

Figure 4.C

 Task 1

Start with the basics

Incorporate all outcomes mandated by the ABA .

 Task 2

Look inward

Include outcomes reflecting your school's unique mission and any public promises it has made.

 Task 3

Get specifiic

Identify performance criteria for each outcome.

and values must reflect the learning outcomes identified by the ABA. The ABA lists the following learning outcomes.

Standard 302. LEARNING OUTCOMES

A law school shall establish learning outcomes that shall, at a minimum, include competency in the following:

(a) Knowledge and understanding of substantive and procedural law;
(b) Legal analysis and reasoning, legal research, problem-solving, and written and oral communication in the legal context;
(c) Exercise of proper professional and ethical responsibilities to clients and the legal system; and
(d) Other professional skills needed for competent and ethical participation as a member of the legal profession.

Interpretation 302-1

For the purposes of Standard 302(d), other professional skills are determined by the law school and may include skills such as, interviewing, counseling, negotiation, fact development and analysis, trial practice, document drafting, conflict resolution, organization and management of legal work, collaboration, cultural competency, and self-evaluation.

Interpretation 302-2

A law school may also identify any additional learning outcomes pertinent to its program of legal education.

As you can see, the mandatory outcomes list adopted by the ABA does not contain any real surprises. For instance, the fact that a lawyer should demonstrate competency at written and oral communication in the legal context is obvious. When we compared the ABA's list to our school's outcomes, it did not require us to change or add anything.

Nonetheless, it is important to note that the ABA also calls upon schools to do some soul-searching—to determine what "other professional skills" its graduates should possess. Simply cutting and pasting the language from Standard 302 should not be your goal.

To inspire you a bit, we have included examples of what other law schools are doing with their learning outcomes in Appendix C.

Task 2: Include Outcomes Reflecting Your School's Unique Mission

After ensuring that your list incorporates the basic knowledge, skills, and values identified by the ABA, you should then flesh out the list by looking inward. Although you need not recreate the wheel, your learning outcomes should clearly reflect the knowledge, skills, and values that are important for your students at *your* institution. You need to "own" your outcomes.

Take the time to review your school's mission statement. Look at your school's website, catalog, etc. to see what types of promises your school is making to others. All the while, talk to your faculty and other key constituencies. Find out what they think is important. This is your chance to embrace who you are as an institution.

Mission Statements

As noted by Interpretation 302-2, another consideration in drafting outcomes is determining whether there are outcomes that are particularly pertinent to your school's program of legal education. A good place to begin this task is by reviewing your school's mission statement. An institution's **mission statement** *describes the essence of an institution and outlines the guiding principles, aspirations, and values of the institution. Mission statements are usually stated in broad, abstract terms, not in learning outcome language.* An institution's mission statement can usually be found in the institution's charter, its handbook, and/or its self-study materials.

If your law school is affiliated with a larger university, the law school's learning outcomes should be aligned with the university's mission and learning outcomes, if any, as well. Regional accreditors may look to see if your law school's learning outcomes align with those articulated by the university.

For example, the University of Dayton is a Catholic, Marianist institution. The University's mission statement (and learning outcomes) as well as the School of Law's mission statement reflect Catholic, Marianist ideals. Therefore, in creating the School of Law's learning outcomes, we needed to incorporate this mission in our learning outcomes. Specifically, one of our learning outcomes states:

> *Learning Outcome 9: Graduates will exemplify the Marianist charism of service, community, and inclusivity.*

We initially had some concerns about aligning our outcomes with those of the University. We feared that the task would be difficult because its outcomes were largely drafted with the undergraduate population in mind. But once we actually started, those concerns were quickly put to rest. We discovered that a good education is a good education at any level. We all want our students to gain knowledge, to problem solve, and to communicate well. All of the outcomes required by the ABA could be tied in neatly to one or more of our University's outcomes.

We also discovered that thinking about questions like what it means to be a Catholic, Marianist law school is a beneficial exercise in and of itself. As educators, we make choices every day about what we teach and how we teach. Pondering what we hope to achieve helps inform those decisions.

Aligning your institutional learning outcomes with the missions of your university and law school is ultimately rather simple. All you need to do is to tailor your learning outcomes to your specific institution—to spell out what makes your program and your graduates special.

Marketing Materials

Because your institutional learning outcomes are specific to your institution, they should reflect, and not contradict, public statements about the institution. At this point in the process you should take a "top-down approach," where you look at documents that describe your school's curriculum—catalogs, brochures, and your institution's website.

For example, at our School, we advertise ourselves as producing problem solvers with extensive practice experience. All of our students must take both an externship or clinic course as well as a capstone course prior to graduation. Therefore, to incorporate these curricular promises and requirements, one of our learning outcomes is as follows:

> *Learning Outcome 6: Graduates will demonstrate competency in legal practice skills.*

By adopting this outcome, we are guaranteeing that we will actually measure how well we are keeping this promise to prospective students. It's called, "truth in advertising."

Task 3: Get Specific — Identify Performance Criteria for Each Outcome

By the time you have completed tasks one and two, you should have a list of items that describe the knowledge, skills, and values you desire for your graduates in very broad terms. That's a good beginning, but your committee still has some important decisions to make before it is ready to move on to the writing step.

Learning outcomes are always described in broad terms for good reason—they are intended to identify and encapsulate *all* of the learning that is desired of a graduate in a way that is easy to understand. However, those broad terms can make it far too easy to create a list of outcomes that mean absolutely nothing. For instance, of course a law graduate should be able to communicate, but what does that mean in real terms?

If your committee stopped at drafting learning outcomes and failed to provide guidance as to what each outcome actually requires students to learn, World War III might well break out when the time came to measure those outcomes. For example, assume your school adopted the following outcome: "Graduates will demonstrate competency in legal practice skills." Can you imagine all the different faculty views on what legal practice skills should be encompassed by this statement? It is essential to reach some level of consensus on what this outcome requires now, long before you reach the measurement stage.

To avoid future confusion and conflict, for each learning outcome, you will also draft approximately three to seven **performance criteria** (sometimes referred to as "assessment criteria," "performance elements," or "performance indicators"), which are *the more specific characteristics students must demonstrate to establish a particular outcome has been satisfied. The performance criteria are intended to address the ambiguities found in the learning outcomes. They force you to describe in concrete terms what each outcome requires.*

We like to think of the performance criteria as the bridge between a learning outcome and the assessment task/tool used to measure that outcome. When you are creating the performance criteria, you are essentially creating the foundation for the rubric you will use to evaluate students' performance on whatever task or tasks are being used to measure achievement of the outcome.

The following example may help you better understand the crucial role played by performance criteria.

Learning Outcome 3: Graduates will demonstrate competency in analytical and problem-solving skills.

Graduates will demonstrate achievement of this learning outcome by

- critically reading the applicable authority, including identifying the key rules within each authority.

- synthesizing the relevant rules of law into a logical framework for analysis.

- where rules conflict, thoroughly analyzing which rule a court is likely to apply.

- meticulously applying the identified rules to the facts, including evaluating potential counterarguments, to determine the likely outcome of the case.

- when appropriate, analogizing the facts to and distinguishing the facts from those of precedent cases in specific and helpful ways to determine the likely outcome of the case.

- accurately identifying practical considerations, such as cost and effects on other people.

Note that the performance criteria express in specific and measurable/observable terms what must be shown to establish the learning outcome. They state the specific acts of performance required to be able to conclude that a graduate has achieved the learning outcome.

Performance criteria are really where the rubber meets the road in terms of creating a shared faculty vision of the characteristics of your graduates. It is typically easy to obtain agreement on broad learning outcomes like "Graduates will demonstrate effective communication skills" and "Graduates will demonstrate analytical and problem-solving skills."

However, it can be difficult to drill down and obtain agreement on specific performance criteria. The first challenge for faculty members is forcing themselves to engage in reverse engineering. For example, exactly what processes are required to formulate an effective analysis of a legal issue? Asking a law professor to break down the steps in which he or she engages in analyzing a legal issue is not unlike asking a big league homerun hitter to describe the mechanics of his swing. It's just something you do without thinking.

But students need to know exactly what we are asking them to do, and we need to know exactly where they are succeeding and failing. We will never be able to improve their learning if we cannot identify where their process is letting them down and help them learn to improve it.

For example, one student may fail to properly articulate the applicable rule because his critical reading skills are weak, and he did not see the rule when he read the relevant authorities. Another may struggle to articulate the same rule because she struggles with the concept of synthesizing rules from different cases. A third may fail to articulate the same rule because she ran out of time on an exam or improperly edited a paper to fit within the page limits. We need to know where to focus our efforts as teachers.

The second challenge for faculty members is reaching a consensus. Reasonable minds can differ over what skills, etc. must be acquired to achieve learning outcomes. For example, one of our learning outcomes states, "Graduates will demonstrate competency in legal practice skills." Some of our faculty members believe passionately that every law graduate should have some minimal competency in trial advocacy while others believe with every bit as much passion that not every graduate needs the skills of a trial lawyer.

As was the case with the learning outcomes, you can resolve some conflicts simply by asking each member to consider whether the achievement of a particular criterion is truly essential or merely aspirational. It's also important to keep in mind that we are talking about the knowledge base and skill set needed for someone just entering the profession, not an experienced practitioner. Use the list of criteria for each outcome to set a threshold for achievement for your graduates.

Step 2: Write: Create Draft Learning Outcomes & Performance Criteria

By the time you have completed Step 1, you will have a laundry list of essential knowledge, skills, and values. Step 2 requires you to use that list to create a clear, concise statement of what you expect your students to have learned by graduation day.

In drafting learning outcomes and performance criteria, the first rule of thumb is to keep it simple. Effective learning outcomes and performance criteria are written in easy to understand language. You want people to understand your learning outcomes and performance criteria, and those "people" include students and even prospective students. Therefore, it is necessary to use plain English. Avoid any abstract terms, acronyms, or educational jargon. Just keep it simple.

In terms of substance, effective learning outcomes and performance criteria have three essential characteristics. One, they are student centered. Two, they require some observable action by the student. Three, they include a learning statement that specifies what learning will be demonstrated by observable action.

The examples in Figure 4.D demonstrate how the three parts fit together.

Figure 4.D

Learning Outcome: "Graduates will demonstrate competency in analytical and problem-solving skills."	**Student Centered:** *Graduates* **Observable Action Required:** *will demonstrate* **Learning Statement:** *competency in analytical and problem-solving skills*
Performance Criterion: "Graduates will demonstrate this outcome by synthesizing the relevant rules of law into a logical framework for analysis."	**Student Centered:** *Graduates* **Observable Action Required:** *synthesizing* **Learning Statement:** *the relevant rules of law into a logical framework for analysis*

Making Your Outcomes & Criteria "Student Centered": Whose Behaviors Are You Assessing?

Learning outcomes and performance criteria should always begin with a stem that identifies the group whose behaviors are being assessed. Remember. The idea is to measure what is being learned, not what is being taught.

In drafting institutional outcomes you should assess the behaviors of "graduates," rather than "students," because institutional assessment focuses on the end product. In contrast, if you were drafting course-level outcomes and criteria, you would use the word "students."

Poor Learning Outcome: Faculty will teach students to use fundamental legal research tools.

Poor Learning Outcome: The curriculum will include components devoted to effective legal research.

Good Learning Outcome: Graduates will research effectively and efficiently.

Requiring Observable Action: What Should a Graduate Be Able to Do?

Because you will ultimately be measuring achievement of outcomes and criteria, it is critical that outcomes and criteria require a student to "do" something that you can observe and measure. So, for example, even when you are looking at what knowledge or attitude/value a student may have acquired, you should be thinking about how a student might demonstrate that knowledge or attitude. Ultimately, every outcome and criterion should require that a graduate somehow *show* you what he or she has learned.

Because institutional learning outcomes are written in broad terms, it is fine to use a verb that is itself a bit broad. Institution-level outcomes frequently incorporate the language, "will be able to demonstrate." Instead of saying, "Graduates will know X," a well-written outcome will say something like, "Graduates will be able to demonstrate knowledge of X." This distinction, while small, is significant. It foreshadows the measurement that is to come.

The verbs used in performance criteria (as well as learning outcomes at the course level) tend to be more precise. They are simple, specific action verbs, which delineate behavior.

Action Verbs and Cognitive Learning

The majority of law school learning outcomes and performance criteria relate to cognitive learning (*i.e.*, knowledge recall and various intellectual skills, such as comprehending and organizing information). The mantra of many a law professor is "I am teaching you to think like a lawyer."

Bloom's Taxonomy is often used to link the various levels of cognitive learning to a set of action verbs, which allows you to create outcomes and criteria that are tied to the desired ability level. **Bloom's Taxonomy** *is a foundational theory of learning often relied on in higher education. It consists of a framework for categorizing educational goals created by Benjamin Bloom with collaborators in 1956. The six categories recognized in ascending level of difficulty are knowledge, comprehension, application, analysis, synthesis, and evaluation.* The six categories are illustrated in Figure 4.E. In drafting your outcomes and criteria, you really want to think about how high up on Bloom's Taxonomy you desire a student to climb.

The practice of law involves higher order thinking skills, not just knowledge. Of course, we want our students to possess substantive knowledge about particular foundational areas of the law. But, in some ways, that is the least important thing we ask our students to learn. The law is constantly changing; therefore, our purpose in legal education is not to just impart knowledge but to impart the skills that

Figure 4.E. Bloom's Taxonomy

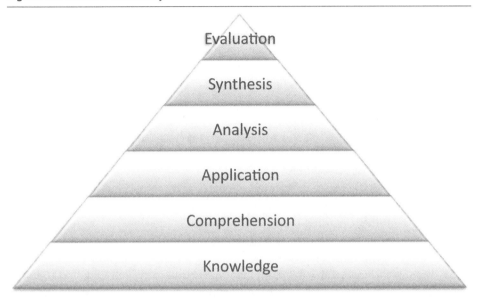

will allow our graduates to identify, interpret, and properly use the applicable law. Our students need more than what they can learn in a book; they need skills that will help them in the future. The action verbs used in your outcomes and criteria should reflect the expectation that graduates will be able to do something more than simply regurgitate information.

Table 4.2 provides a helpful list of action verbs tied to Bloom's Taxonomy. We gathered this list from various sources and made an effort to include verbs that are commonly used within our discipline.

Table 4.2. Action Verbs

Knowledge	Comprehension	Application	Analysis	Synthesis	Evaluation
Articulate	Classify	Apply	Analogize	Arrange	Appraise
Define	Compare	Employ	Analyze	Combine	Assess
Identify	Contrast	Engage	Criticize	Construct	Conclude
Label	Discuss	Extend	Discriminate	Create	Decide
List	Explain	Illustrate	Discriminate	Develop	Evaluate
Match	Give Examples	Relate	Examine	Formulate	Issue Spot
Name	Interpret	Solve	Infer	Organize	Judge
State	Summarize	Use	Question	Synthesize	Recommend

Action Verbs and Practice Skills

Over the past three decades, law schools have placed a growing emphasis on practical or practice skills. When writing a learning outcome relating to practice skills, such as legal research and writing, the skill often becomes the action verb. To illustrate, an outcome might read, "Graduates will be able to research a legal issue effectively and efficiently." Just know that there is no magic incantation that must be used — there is no set list of action verbs that must be used in every situation. We are providing you with suggestions here, but you should feel free to select other verbs, particularly those that reflect actions that are unique to our discipline.

Law school learning outcomes also typically reflect the particular importance of communication skills. Whether he or she is reading them, writing them, hearing them, or speaking them, words are the lawyer's stock in trade. Lawyers also need to be able to work well with multiple constituencies, including the bench, the bar, and, of course, clients. Table 4.3 contains some action verbs you may find useful in describing desired communication, interaction, and group skills.

Table 4.3. Communication, Interaction & Group Skills

Communication, Interaction & Group Skills			
Advise	Connect	Express	Observe
Answer	Counsel	Facilitate	Persuade
Arbitrate	Defend	Inform	Read
Argue	Draft	Interact	Rebut
Articulate	Educate	Listen	Respond
Collaborate	Empathize	Mediate	Speak
Communicate	Explain	Negotiate	Write

Action Verbs and Values and Attitudes

Perhaps the most difficult learning outcomes and performance criteria to identify and draft are those relating to the values and attitudes that we desire our graduates to possess. We have heard some members of the academy express concern over how one can ever measure values and attitudes. We will discuss the issue of measurement more fully in Chapter 5, but the necessity to develop an outcome or criterion capable of measurement must be considered even during the drafting stage.

It is imperative to choose verbs that involve observable actions. As discussed above, in drafting your institutional learning outcomes, it is fine to simply say something like, "Graduates will demonstrate an appreciation of" a particular value. But in drafting your performance criteria, you want to give some thought to what specific types of behaviors/actions can be used to establish attitudes and values. The example below provides an example from our school.

> ***Learning Outcome 9:*** *Graduates will exemplify the Marianist charism of service, community, and inclusivity.*

Graduates will demonstrate achievement of this learning outcome by

- exhibiting civility and treating others with respect.

- displaying diversity skills, including sensitivity to social and cultural difference.

- contributing to the profession's fulfillment of its responsibility to ensure that adequate legal services are provided to those who cannot afford to pay for them.

Table 4.4 contains some action verbs that you might find useful in describing desired attitudes and values.

Table 4.4. Attitudes and Values

Attitudes and Values			
Act	Contribute	Follow	Select
Adhere	Display	Participate	Serve
Choose	Exemplify	Perform	Share
Comply	Exhibit	Practice	Volunteer

Creating a Learning Statement: What learning will take place?

The learning statement is the very essence of the learning outcome or performance criterion. It describes the essential knowledge, skill, or value that has been learned. In drafting the learning statement, you will use the lists that your committee has developed.

Keep in mind that your school's learning statements should reflect what students will learn from any set of professors and any sequence of courses in any given year. As you draft your statements, think in terms of the language used in your course catalog, which incorporates broad language that reflects generally what is learned without delineating specific concepts or terms.

Poor Performance Criterion: Students will be able to effectively use Westlaw and Lexis.

Good Performance Criterion: Students will be able to identify and effectively employ the fundamental tools of legal research.

Learning Statements and Knowledge

When your outcome or criterion refers to knowledge, the learning statement will identify exactly *what* knowledge must be demonstrated. The following examples illustrate the components of learning outcomes and performance criteria focused on knowledge.

Learning Outcome: *Graduates will demonstrate knowledge and understanding of the law and the American legal system.*

Who?	Graduates
Will engage in what behavior?	will demonstrate
Evidencing what?	knowledge and understanding of the law and the American legal system

Performance Criterion: *Graduates will demonstrate achievement of this learning outcome by identifying, describing, and interpreting the fundamental terms, rules, and principles of law, including significant alternative formulations, such as minority rules.*

Who?	Graduates
Will engage in what behavior?	identifying, describing, and interpreting
Evidencing what?	[knowledge and understanding of] the fundamental terms, rules, and principles of law, including significant alternative formulations, such as minority rules

Learning Statements and Skills

When your outcome or criterion refers to skills, the learning statement will identify exactly *how* (*i.e.*, the manner in which) the skill must be performed. The following examples illustrate the components of learning outcomes and performance criteria focused on skills.

Learning Outcome: Graduates will communicate effectively and efficiently to individuals and groups.

Who?	Graduates
Will engage in what behavior?	will communicate to individuals and groups
How (*i.e.*, in what manner)?	effectively and efficiently

Performance Criterion: Graduates will demonstrate achievement of this learning outcome by writing legal documents that are clear, concise, well-reasoned, organized, professional in tone, appropriate to the audience and the circumstances, and if appropriate, contain proper citation to authority.

Who?	Graduates
Will engage in what behavior?	writing legal documents
How (*i.e.*, in what manner)?	[in a manner that is] clear, concise, well-reasoned, organized, professional in tone, appropriate to the audience and the circumstances, and if appropriate, contain proper citation to authority

Learning Statements and Attitudes or Values

When your outcome or criterion refers to attitudes or values, the learning statement will identify exactly **what** attitudes or values must be demonstrated. The following examples illustrate the components of learning outcomes and performance criteria focused on attitudes or values.

Learning Outcome: Graduates will exemplify the Marianist charism of, service, community, and inclusivity.

Who?	Graduates
Will engage in what behavior?	will exemplify
Evidencing what?	[adoption of] the Marianist charism of service, community, and inclusivity

Performance Criterion: Graduates will demonstrate achievement of this learning outcome by contributing to the profession's fulfillment of its responsibility to ensure that adequate legal services are provided to those who cannot afford to pay for them.

Who?	Graduates
Will engage in what behavior?	contributing to
Evidencing what?	[recognition of] the profession's responsibility to ensure that adequate legal services are provided to those who cannot afford to pay for them

Tying It All Together — Learning Outcome & Performance Criterion Template

You now know everything necessary to draft your learning outcomes and performance criteria. The template that follows walks you through the process we just described.

Learning Outcome & Performance Criteria Template
Learning Outcome Number _____

Who?	
Will engage in what behavior? Select an action verb from the lists provided in the Guide for cognitive learning, practice skills, or values/attitudes	
Evidencing what? (Learning statement relating to knowledge or attitude) *OR* How (*i.e.*, in what manner)? (Learning statement relating to skill)	

Completed Learning Outcome: Graduates will:

_____

_____

_____

Related Performance Criteria
Using the same template, create 3 to 7 performance criteria

Graduates will demonstrate achievement of this learning outcome by....

1._____
_____

2._____
_____

3._____
_____

4._____
_____

5._____
_____

6._____
_____

7._____
_____

Step 3: Test: Evaluate Draft Learning Outcomes & Performance Criteria

By the time you have completed Step 2, you will have a draft list of learning outcomes and performance criteria in hand. You are well on your way to completing your assessment plan. However, before you even think about proposing adoption of these learning outcomes and performance criteria, you need to take a step back and ask two tough questions:

1. Have we identified the *essential* learning outcomes and performance criteria?
2. Are these learning outcomes and performance criteria *achievable*?

In answering these questions, it is wise to involve a broad number of law school constituencies. Faculty and administrators must be consulted, but there is also much to learn from alumni and potential employers. The sections that follow provide some practical advice on the evaluation process.

Have we identified the essential learning outcomes and performance criteria?

A fundamental question to be posed to your core constituencies is whether the assessment committee has captured the essence of what you want your students to have learned by graduation. Are the outcomes and criteria that you have identified truly essential? Have you missed anything essential? Does the list as a whole reflect what you believe to be the proper mix of knowledge, skills, and values? The time to ask these questions is now. The following tasks will help you with this evaluation.

Task 1: Get the Faculty Involved

Institutional learning outcomes should be created through developing a consensus among faculty members. Although an assessment committee may propose a set of institutional learning outcomes, the learning outcomes should be presented to the full faculty for input and (and ultimately) approval. Such consensus ensures acceptance and permanence. Additionally, consensus on the institutional learning outcomes assists in alignment throughout the curriculum.

So how can you best involve your faculty at this stage? As discussed in Chapter 3, before handing faculty members your draft list of outcomes and criteria, the committee first needs to educate faculty about institutional assessment. They need not be experts on the topic, but they need foundational knowledge.

Such knowledge can be promoted by asking faculty members to read all or part of this Guide. It can also be promoted by sponsoring lunchtime workshops conducted by the institutional assessment coordinator, the assessment committee, assessment experts from elsewhere within your university community, and/or outside experts. Simply providing a twenty-minute report of some type at a faculty meeting is not going to get the faculty where it needs to be in terms of understanding.

Once you are comfortable that the faculty understands the basics of institutional outcomes assessment, you should distribute the draft list of learning outcomes and performance criteria for notice and comment purposes. You could certainly introduce it at a faculty meeting, but we do not believe that a faculty meeting provides the best venue for obtaining meaningful feedback from faculty members. You need to hear from everyone, and unless your faculty meetings are very different from those to which the authors have been exposed, the conversation is often dominated by a few, who may or may not represent the views of the majority.

In order to obtain meaningful input from each member of our faculty, we surveyed them as to the extent to which they agreed each draft outcome and criterion was advisable. We also asked for suggestions as to any outcomes and criteria we may have missed. We used SurveyMonkey, but there are countless other applications that could perform the same function. A copy of our outcomes survey is found in Appendix D.

After surveying the faculty, the assessment committee met, reviewed the comments, and revised the outcomes accordingly. Ultimately, the outcomes required very little revision. A supermajority of the faculty agreed or strongly agreed as to the advisability of each outcome. We believe that providing faculty with the opportunity to review and reflect on the outcomes in peace allowed members to develop a better understanding of why we had proposed each outcome.

Believing that we had found a consensus on the outcomes, we used the same process to survey the faculty about the performance criteria for each outcome. We opted to cover only the outcomes in the first survey because we wanted to provide faculty with a "big picture" perspective, but there might also have been advantages to including the criteria at that stage. Doing so might have enhanced the depth of faculty members' understanding of each outcome. In the end, there is no right or wrong choice on this issue.

As we expected, there was less consensus on the proposed performance criteria. Although a majority of the faculty supported almost all of the proposed criteria, we needed to tweak the language of a number of the criteria. After the revisions, we circulated the outcomes and criteria to the faculty a second time, providing the survey results and explaining the revisions. We then provided a notice and comment period. Thereafter, we felt that we had a workable list of outcomes and criteria.

Task 2: Beyond the Faculty: Get Others Involved

While your faculty is a key constituency, a thoughtful evaluation requires you to look beyond the ivory tower. The majority of your faculty is likely not currently engaged in the practice of law. Particularly given the rapidly changing legal landscape of the last decade, law schools should be actively seeking the advice of the legal community on what knowledge, skills, and values its graduates should possess.

Collaboration with the bench, bar, advisory boards, and employers of your students creates accountability to the law school's core constituencies and also ensures that the outcomes and performance criteria meet the current demands of practice. Such collaboration also has the added benefit of creating a bond between the law school, its alumni, and the legal community in which it operates.

So, how do you reach out to these groups? One way is through the use of surveys or focus groups. Ask these groups what they expect new graduates to know, to be able to do, and to value. That can either be done as part of the assessment process or an independent endeavor.

At our School, the Assessment Committee was able to pull on evidence gathered from several of our colleagues in the Legal Profession Program (our research and writing program), who had formed a Bar Outreach Project and used surveys and focus groups to gather such evidence for use in their skills courses.

Bar Outreach Project Information

To learn more about our colleagues' Bar Outreach Project read:

Sheila Miller, *Are We Teaching What They Will Use? Surveying Alumni to Assess Whether Skills Teaching Aligns with Alumni Practice*, 32 Miss. C. L. Rev. 419 (2014).

Susan C. Wawrose, *What Do Legal Employers Want to See in New Graduates?: Using Focus Groups to Find Out*, 39 Ohio N.U. L. Rev. 505 (2013).

Victoria L. VanZandt & Susan C. Wawrose, *Using a Bar Outreach Project to Learn about Today's Law Practice*, The Second Draft 11 (Spring 2011).

Reaching out to these groups provides credibility and practicality to your learning outcomes. As an additional benefit, your students will be pleased to know that they are learning what their future employers want.

Two last groups that you should consult when evaluating your learning outcomes are your alumni and current students. Both groups can be reached through surveys and focus groups, asking them what knowledge, skills, and values are important as they engage in their current positions as clerks, externs, or practicing attorneys. You can also ask them to review the learning outcomes for clarity and comprehension.

Are these learning outcomes and performance criteria achievable?

A second fundamental question to consider in evaluating your outcomes and criteria is whether they are achievable. The mere fact that faculty, bench, bar, and students agree that it would be a wonderful thing for graduates to know X, be able to do Y, or believe Z does not automatically mean that that outcome is achievable. A law school should not "over promise" when it comes to learning outcomes. Learning outcomes should reflect what can *reasonably* be accomplished during a course of study.

Reasonableness in Light of Student Abilities: The Need to Prioritize

The assessment committee (and indeed the faculty as a whole) should seek to ensure that outcomes and criteria are reasonable in light of the time and abilities of students. You must look at each outcome and criteria and ask, "Is this something a recent graduate should really be able to do?"

In doing so, it is vital to consider its reasonableness in light of the full list of outcomes and criteria. As discussed above, a law school should typically limit itself to 6 to 12 outcomes and 3 to 7 criteria per outcome. We must be realistic about the demands being placed on students.

Law schools and law students are being pressured on all sides. There is more pressure than ever before to produce students who pass the bar on the first attempt, and at the same time, employers are screaming for students with more practice skills than ever before. (It really was not that long ago that few schools even employed full-time research and writing faculty and not much longer ago that the idea of a law clinic was considered radical.) In whittling the list of outcomes and criteria down to a reasonable number, faculty must prioritize.

Reasonableness in Light of Faculty Resources: The Need for Curriculum Mapping

Reasonableness must also be considered in light of the faculty resources available at your law school. It is easy for faculty to agree that outcomes "X," "Y," and "Z" are highly desirable, but it may not be so easy to agree on where within the curriculum we will create opportunities for students to learn them.

In the law school setting, the right hand often does not know what the left hand is doing. Course descriptions typically identify the broad subject matters covered but make little or no mention of the cognitive and other skills we seek to teach. Think about your own school. Do you really know what learning opportunities the average student is provided over the course of his or her time there?

It is absolutely essential that your outcomes and criteria align with your curriculum and teaching methodologies. We cannot expect students to learn that which we do not teach.

The beauty of identifying learning objectives and specific performance criteria is that it can make us more thoughtful educators. For example, if we say, our graduates will be able to critically read cases, we need to be able to say where (*i.e.,* in what course(s)) we believe we are helping students learn; how we believe we are helping students learn; and when and how we are measuring whether students have learned to critically read cases.

We use the example of critical reading because it is such a fundamental skill for any attorney and because one of our discipline's key justifications for using the case method is developing this skill. Yet, when empirical studies, such as the LSAC's study on "Developing an Assessment of First-Year Law Students' Critical Case Reading and Reasoning Ability" have been undertaken, they have found little support for the idea that students' critical reading skills improve over the course of their time in law school. We say we are teaching students to read critically, we think we are teaching students to read critically, but are we? Engaging in outcomes assessment compels us to do something that should come naturally for a group of lawyers, rely on evidence, not assumptions, in our decision making.

One way to obtain a handle on whether your proposed outcomes and criteria are consistent with what your faculty is currently seeking to teach is to create what is known as a curriculum map. We start this discussion off with a caveat. Curriculum mapping, also known as alignment, is not "really" assessment. It focuses on inputs (what our curriculum provides) as opposed to outputs (what our students learn).

However, we feel that it is a necessary step in assessment planning because it aids assessment planning in two ways: (1) it tests the validity of your proposed learning outcomes and performance criteria and (2) it helps identify possible tools that you can use in your assessment plan. Therefore, we are putting it here as the third task that you should engage in as you evaluate your learning outcomes and performance criteria.

A Jurisdictional Issue

The creation of a curriculum map may be the province of your school's curriculum or academic affairs committee. We believe that efforts should not be duplicated; however, in order to help with your school's assessment planning, the map must be organized around your learning outcomes and performance criteria, whatever committee chooses to undertake the task.

Task 3: Create a Curriculum Map

Now, what is it? A **curriculum map** *is a grid of the courses in your curriculum that identifies which learning outcomes and performance criteria are addressed and assessed in each course.* You can choose to map the entire curriculum or to focus only on required courses. It is wonderful to have a map based on the entire curriculum, but constructing such a map can be a huge undertaking. For instance, obtaining information from every adjunct is a chore. Focusing on required courses lightens the burden and allows you to focus on the common learning opportunities afforded each student. A sample of a curriculum map is provided in Appendix E.

It is important to take note of the distinction between "addressed" and "assessed" here. For example, a professor may state that she addresses legal, ethical, and professional standards in her Administrative Law class; however, she may never assess students' knowledge of or attitudes toward those standards in her course. In other words, she brings up ethical issues in class discussion but does not incorporate them in exams, etc. Therefore, the skill is addressed, not assessed.

That's not necessarily a bad thing — every professor need not assess (or even address) every outcome or criterion, but it is something you need to know for planning purposes. If your school adopts outcomes or criteria that are not addressed or assessed by anyone, it will ultimately result in the loss of credibility with students and others, including accreditors.

You can try to create a curriculum map by reviewing your school's course catalog or a collection of syllabi and guessing what learning outcomes and performance criteria are addressed and assessed. However, we would suggest the much better route is to survey the faculty directly and use their data to fill in the grid. A sample survey, which we adapted from a survey created by Dean Andrea Funk at Whittier Law School, is included in Appendix F.

The survey should not only ask faculty to indicate whether each outcome and criterion is being addressed, but the level to which the knowledge, skill, or value is being developed. We asked our faculty to use the following scale, which is designed to indicate both whether it is being addressed and assessed in one fell swoop.

- "Introduced"—Students are introduced to this knowledge, skill, or value, but are not tested or otherwise assessed as to what they have learned. (This knowledge, skill, or value may be developed in another course in more depth.)
- "Competent"—Students are instructed and assessed on this knowledge, skill, or value and are expected to demonstrate basic competency by the end of the course.

- "Proficient"—Students have advanced instruction in and/or additional practice with and are assessed on this knowledge, skill, or value and are expected to demonstrate proficiency by the end of the course. ("Proficiency" means that a student demonstrates a mastery of the subject matter that goes beyond basic competency. However, it does not require that a student demonstrate the expertise that would be expected of an experienced practitioner.)

We also asked faculty members to identify the assessment tools used where assessment takes place and to indicate whether they provided written feedback (W), oral feedback (O), group feedback (G), or individual feedback (I) or any combination of the above. Requiring this information has a way of making faculty think about exactly what they are assessing when they assign a paper or create an exam.

Once completed, the curriculum map will show if your institution is actually providing students with the opportunity to learn the knowledge, skill, or value featured in each outcome and criterion. It also shows progression—are skills just introduced and never practiced and achieved? Is there too much focus on one learning outcome in the curriculum? It reveals gaps and patterns. Ultimately, it should demonstrate how core courses provide competency in all learning outcomes. Additionally, it can help the assessment committee locate assessment tools embedded in the curriculum.

If no class actually addresses an outcome or criterion, you need to go back to the drawing board. Maybe that knowledge, skill, or value is not a learning outcome that you want to keep. If it is, then, the faculty will need to ensure that it is somehow addressed. That could mean adding a required course or it could mean incorporating it within existing courses.

Similarly, you need to go back to the drawing board if you discover that the outcome or criterion is not addressed in any *required* course or courses. If you are saying that the outcomes and criteria set a threshold for achievement of your graduates, *all* of your students should be provided with the opportunity to learn the knowledge, skill, or value featured in each. It should be part of the core curriculum. Again, going back to the drawing board could mean dropping the outcome or criterion or it could mean changing your curriculum or teaching methods.

We do have one proviso on this point: it could be the case that although an outcome or criterion is not covered in the required courses, it is covered by other activities in the law school in which all or almost all students engage, like pro bono requirements, etc. Not every educational activity takes place in the classroom.

Finally, you need to go back to the drawing board if you discover that no one is assessing the outcome or criterion. Generally, the ABA

Curriculum Mapping: An Added Benefit

In addition to the assessment planning benefits, curriculum mapping helps to validate the curriculum and helps law schools be accountable to public criticism that they are not providing education that is tied to practice. A curriculum map can highlight the learning activities that students have throughout the curriculum.

and other accreditors will look to see whether your school is seeking to graduate students who have achieved a basic competency in the areas covered by the outcomes and criteria. If an outcome or criterion is never measured, it is hard to argue that your students have achieved a basic competency.

You can certainly institute something like a standardized law-school-wide test, such as a mini bar exam to address this issue, but an even better solution is to find a way to measure it within a class or classes that actually counts towards a grade. You are sending a mixed message to students when you say something is a "desired" outcome, but achievement of that outcome is not deemed sufficiently important to count towards a grade or otherwise be recognized.

The creation of a curriculum map tied to learning outcomes and performance criteria is a truly fascinating exercise in that it forces the faculty and administration to take a hard look at the allocation of faculty time and resources. It provides hard data that can be used in making a multitude of critical decisions. You can ensure that this valuable data is not lost by placing a copy of your curriculum map in your Institutional Assessment Plan binder.

Step 4: Revise: Refine Learning Outcomes & Performance Criteria

Having obtained input from your key constituencies, your committee can now refine your draft learning outcomes and performance criteria and prepare a final proposal for the person or body charged with their adoption. The following checklist will assist you in your task.

Individual Learning Outcome & Performance Criterion Checklist

- ❏ Is the outcome/criterion essential?
    - ❏ Is it a skill, a value, or knowledge that every graduate must possess as opposed to something aspirational?
    - ❏ Has the faculty reached a consensus as to its value?
- ❏ Is the outcome/criterion achievable?
    - ❏ Can the relevant knowledge/skill/value be acquired in the period of time a student is in law school?
    - ❏ Can we point to exactly where in our curriculum every student is provided with the opportunity to acquire the relevant knowledge/skill/value?
- ❏ Is the outcome/criterion observable/measurable?
    - ❏ Is the outcome/criterion described in terms that require the graduate to demonstrate something (*i.e.,* is an appropriate action verb used)?

❏ Is the school currently measuring every student's acquisition of the relevant knowledge/skill/value?

❏ If not, are there ways that the relevant knowledge/skill/value could be measured and is the school willing to commit to undertaking the necessary measurements?

❏ Is the outcome/criterion written in explicit, clear terms?

❏ Does it specify exactly what knowledge or attitude must be demonstrated or how (in what manner) the relevant skill must be performed?

❏ Is the language sufficiently simple that a student or prospective student can understand it?

Once you are comfortable with your revisions of the individual outcomes and criteria, you should take one last look at the collection as a whole. Does it reflect the mission and identity of your school? Does it contain a proper mix of outcomes relating to knowledge, skills, and values? Does it satisfy the ABA Standards? If you can say "yes" to all of these questions, you are ready to move on to Step 5.

Step 5: Adopt: Obtain Approval of Learning Outcomes & Performance Criteria and Publish Them

Step 5 is to obtain formal approval of the learning outcomes and performance criteria in whatever manner your school requires. At some schools that means a vote by the full faculty; at some it means a vote by the assessment committee after a notice and comment period for the faculty, and at some, it means authorization by the dean. There is no one-size-fits-all approval process.

That having been said, we strongly suggest that approval be by a vote of the full faculty. The outcomes and criteria are going to be put into action, not into a file drawer. Faculty buy-in is going to be crucial to the implementation of your institutional assessment plan.

Once approval has been obtained, the learning outcomes and performance criteria should be placed in your Institutional Assessment Plan binder and published by the institution via its catalog, its website, its handbook, etc. The public display shows prospective students, students, and the general public what a graduate will get out of a degree from your institution.

We would be remiss if we did not add that as teachers, we have found referencing our institution's outcomes and criteria to be incredibly helpful in course design. Thinking about the "big picture" of what the law school is trying to achieve has made us more mindful of the possibilities our courses create for assisting in the desired student learning. We know that no course will or should address every outcome and criterion, but we have each discovered knowledge, skills, etc. on which we could place more emphasis. It has also compelled us to be more thoughtful in designing our assessments, questioning ourselves as to whether we actually assess that which we claim to teach.

In the future, we hope to get more faculty to engage in this thought process. (We cheerfully confess that we are both assessment geeks, and we still have miles to go to convert the faculty as a whole.) We need to continue our work educating the faculty. For example, we plan to begin sending out an annual reminder to the faculty of what our outcomes and criteria are. Publication should not mean simply popping the information onto a webpage that no one ever visits. It should mean actively reminding the various law school constituencies (faculty, students, alums, etc.) of what the end game is.

Step 6: Plan: Create Timeline and Assign Implementation and Evaluation Duties

Now that the learning outcomes and performance criteria are created and approved, you want to use them as the foundation of your assessment plan. But what is this "plan" of which we speak?

As you may recall from Chapter 1, outcomes assessment is an ongoing, formalized, and systematic process to improve something, in which outcomes are created; data is gathered to measure the achievement of the outcomes; the data is analyzed; and then, the data is used to improve the achievement of the outcomes.

Identifying learning outcomes and performance criteria are merely the first step in the assessment process. Ultimately, your law school must measure student achievement of the learning outcomes using data collected from student outputs (*See* Chapter 5); analyze the data obtained from such measurements (*See* Chapter 6); and use the data gathered to improve student learning (*i.e.*, "close the loop") (*See* Chapter 6).

As shown in Figure 4.F, these steps are often represented as a circular process.

As will be discussed below, the assessment committee may or may not become a standing committee. However, even if it is viewed as an ad hoc committee, its work is not completed until an assessment plan is in place. The new ABA Standard 315 requires law schools to "determine the degree of student attainment of competency in the learning outcomes and to make appropriate changes to improve the curriculum." Drafting outcomes is not enough. Your school must actually make use of them, and that will not happen without a plan.

The assessment plan serves two key functions. One, it provides a sequence and schedule for the key assessment activities. Two, it allocates responsibility for undertaking these activities.

Figure 4.F

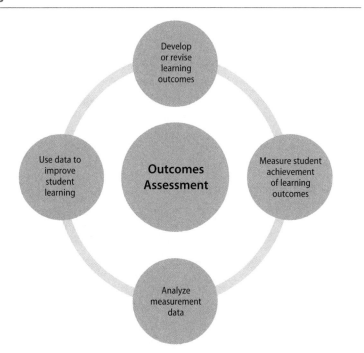

Task 1: Sequence and Schedule Key Assessment Activities

The first task in developing the plan is to determine the sequence in which the different learning outcomes will be measured and evaluated. You will not be gathering data on every outcome every year. Doing so would quickly overwhelm the resources your school can devote to assessment.

Instead, your goal should be to *complete the assessment cycle for each outcome* once or twice during the seven-year period between ABA site visits. When the ABA comes to town, you want to be able to say that you have thoughtfully evaluated the degree of student attainment of competency as to each outcome. What that means is that you will be collecting data for (*i.e.,* measuring) one to two outcomes per year.

During the first seven-year period, prioritizing your assessment of the outcomes will be an important task. You can make that decision from seeking input from others, including the dean, the advisory board, or the faculty. Also, you can use evidence of low student performance gathered from bar results, LESSEE, etc. It really requires you to ask, "What is our biggest concern at this moment?"

Your assessment plan should begin with a timeline that shows the data collection cycle. Table 4.5 shows how the timeline might look if you have adopted eight outcomes. Note that this table assumes that you wish to measure each outcome once every four years, but you could elect to collect data more or less often. We think four years is a good standard cycle. It guarantees that each outcome will be assessed at least once (and usually twice) between accreditation site visits, and it allows time for a thoughtful assessment. The four-year cycle gives your school a year to develop the measurement strategy and tools, a year to collect the data, a year to evaluate the data collected, and a year to implement any needed changes before you begin the cycle again. (And if, as may often be the case, no changes are needed, your task force can get a jump start on developing your strategy for the next cycle.)

Table 4.5. Data Collection Cycle for Eight Learning Outcomes

Learning Outcomes (each with measurable performance criteria)	2017–2018	2018–2019	2019–2020	2020–2021	2021–2022	2022–2023	2023–2024
1. Graduates will...	•				•		
2. Graduates will...		•				•	
3. Graduates will...			•				•
4. Graduates will...				•			
5. Graduates will...	•				•		
6. Graduates will...		•				•	
7. Graduates will...			•				•
8. Graduates will...				•			

* Table adapted from *Assessment Planning Flow Chart* ©2004 Gloria M. Rogers, PH.D., ABET, Inc. (grogers@abet.org) Copyright 2005.

Table 4.5 provides a bird's-eye view of the data-collection cycle, but it is important to remember that data collection is only one phase of the assessment cycle for each outcome. You will be doing something with each outcome each year. Thus, your assessment plan should also contain a timeline for *each* outcome that reflects the assessment cycle for that outcome. Table 4.6 provides a template for your assessment cycle timeline for each outcome.

Once you have created a table showing the assessment cycle for each outcome, you can easily compile the information found in each to create an overview of your school's planned assessment activities for the next few years. Table 4.7 provides a template for a three-year period.

Remember to place your completed tables in your Institutional Assessment Plan binder.

Table 4.6. Assessment Cycle for Learning Outcome 1

Implementation & Evaluation Activity	2016–2017	2017–2018	2018–2019	2019–2020	2020–2021	2021–2022	2022–2023
Review performance criteria that define the outcome	•				•		
Map (or review map of) where your school addresses and assesses these criteria	•				•		
Use map to identify where data will be collected	•				•		
Develop a measurement strategy and the needed assessment tools for the performance criterion or criteria under review	•				•		
Collect data		•				•	
Evaluate assessment data, including processes			•				•
Report findings			•				•
Take action where necessary				•			

* Table adapted from *Assessment Planning Flow Chart* ©2004 Gloria M. Rogers, PH.D., ABET, Inc. (grogers@abet.org) Copyright 2005.

It is important to remember that your assessment plan should be a living document. Nothing about the schedules outlined in the provided tables should be viewed as etched in stone. For example, suppose that in the course of evaluating the achievement of Learning Outcome 1, you discover some real problems, and in the course of evaluating the achievement of Learning Outcome 2, you discover everything is just fine. If that is the case, you may opt to measure Learning Outcome 1 more frequently to see how well any actions taken are working, and you may opt to measure Learning Outcome 2 once every seven years instead of twice every seven years. Your plan should be updated based on changing circumstances.

Table 4.7. Three-Year Cycle of Implementation and Evaluation Activity

Implementation & Evaluation Activity	Year 2020–21 Outcome								Year 2021–22 Outcome								Year 2022–23 Outcome							
	1	2	3	4	5	6	7	8	1	2	3	4	5	6	7	8	1	2	3	4	5	6	7	8
Review performance criteria that define the outcome	•				•					•				•					•				•	
Map (or review map of) where your school addresses and assesses these criteria	•				•					•				•					•				•	
Use map to identify where data will be collected	•				•					•				•					•				•	
Develop a measurement strategy and the needed assessment tools for the performance criterion or criteria under review	•				•					•				•					•				•	
Collect data			•				•		•				•						•				•	
Evaluate assessment data, including processes		•				•					•				•	•		•				•		
Report findings		•				•					•				•	•		•				•		
Take action where necessary		•			•						•				•				•					•

* Table adapted from *Assessment Planning Flow Chart* ©2004 Gloria M. Rogers, PH.D., ABET, Inc. (grogers@abet.org) Copyright 2005.

Task 2: Assign Implementation and Evaluation Duties

The final task in developing the plan is to determine who will be responsible for implementing the assessment plan. This is no small task. As the tables above indicate, there is much to be done. The efforts of the entire faculty, not just the assessment committee or coordinator, will be needed.

The dean must be a key player in the decision-making process. She has several crucial decisions to make. First, the dean must decide what person and/or body is going to provide the oversight required to make certain that all of the trains are running on time, that *all* the activities shown in Table 4.7 are taking place. In other words, what assessment actors are going to supervise the Implementation and Evaluation Stages? This role may be played by the assessment coordinator and/or the assessment committee.

Some schools opt to disband the assessment committee once the assessment plan is in place. That is doable, but it leaves the assessment coordinator with a tremendous amount of work, which should be reflected in his or her course load and other assignments. The dean might also consider appointing co-coordinators or keeping a streamlined assessment committee.

Second, the dean must decide who is going to be responsible for devising measurements and evaluating results with regard to each outcome. As discussed in Chapter 3, an assessment task force should be appointed for each outcome. Ideally, every member of the faculty will be assigned to one task force. Members of the assessment committee (whether it is still in place or has been disbanded) should be spread throughout the different task forces to provide expertise on institutional assessment.

The faculty selected to evaluate results should be faculty with expertise in the outcome being studied. So, for example, if written communication skills are being evaluated, it makes sense to make research and writing faculty and faculty teaching courses which satisfy the upper-level writing requirement a part of the task force. And if a faculty member is going to be charged with evaluating results, he or she should also be involved in the design of the assessment methods/tools used to measure achievement. Ideally, the task force for each outcome will see it through the entire assessment cycle.

Table 4.8 shows how the responsibilities for each outcome might be allocated. Note that you should complete one table for each outcome and that the members appointed to the task force for that outcome should be listed on its top row. The completed tables should be placed in the Institutional Assessment Plan binder.

Table 4.8. Parties Responsible for Implementation & Evaluation

Learning Outcome: (List the learning outcome here.) Assesment Task Force Members: (List the persons assigned to the task force for this learning outcome here.)	
Implementation & Evaluation Activity	**Responsibility for Activity**
Review performance criteria that define the outcome	Assessment Task Force and Assessment Committee and/or Assessment Coordinator
Map (or review map of) where your school addresses and assesses these criteria	Assessment Committee and/or Assessment Coordinator and/or Assessment Task Force with the assistance of All Faculty
Use map to identify where data will be collected	Assessment Task Force with the assistance of Assessment Committee and/or Assessment Coordinator
Develop a measurement strategy and the needed assessment tools for the performance criterion or criteria under review	Assessment Task Force with the assistance of Assessment Committee and/or Assessment Coordinator
Collect data	Assessment Task Force
Evaluate assessment data, including processes	Assessment Task Force with the assistance of any needed experts
Report findings	Assessment Task Force
Take action where necessary	Assessment Task Force with the assistance of All Faculty

Having completed this Chapter, you now have all the tools to complete the Development Stage—you can create learning outcomes and performance criteria, create a curriculum map, develop a timeline for assessment, and assign the various implementation and evaluation duties. You are now ready to move on to the Implementation Stage!

Action List

Step 1: Brainstorm: Create a list of knowledge, skills, and values but don't recreate the wheel.

- Have committee members (or whoever are your initial assessment actors) create a list of 5–12 attributes (knowledge, skills, or values) your school should expect its graduates to possess.

- After the list is created, review it and engage in the following tasks:

Task 1: Ensure that your list incorporates all outcomes mandated by the ABA. Compare your list to the list published in ABA Standard 302.

Task 2: Ensure that your list includes outcomes reflecting your school's unique mission and reflects public statements about your institution. Remember to review catalogs, brochures, and your institution's website.

Task 3: Then, get specific—Identify 3–7 performance criteria for each outcome.

Step 2: Write: Create draft learning outcomes & performance criteria.

- **Ensure that they are student-centered, require some observable action, and include a learning statement.**

Step 3: Test: Evaluate draft learning outcomes & performance criteria.

Task 1: Get faculty involved.

- Educate faculty on institutional assessment by holding training sessions or having them read portions of this Guide.

- Create survey on learning outcomes and performance criteria to distribute to the faculty.

Task 2: Get input on learning outcomes and performance criteria from other constituents.

- Survey students, alumni, local bench, bar or hold informal meetings or focus groups.

Task 3: Create a Curriculum Map.

- Develop and distribute curriculum mapping survey to faculty.

- Create curriculum map after receiving faculty survey responses.

Step 4: Revise: Refine learning outcomes & performance criteria after input and curriculum mapping.

- **Fill out the Individual Learning Outcome and Performance Criterion Checklist.**

Step 5: Adopt: Obtain approval of learning outcomes & performance criteria and publish them.

- **Decide the manner by which approval will be obtained and get it.**

Step 6: Plan: Create timeline and assign implementation and evaluation duties.

Task 1: Sequence and schedule key assessment activities.

- Fill out Table 4.5: Data Collection Cycle for Learning Outcomes.

- Fill out Table 4.6 for each outcome: Assessment Cycle for each Learning Outcome.

- Fill out Table 4.7: Three-Year Cycle of Implementation and Evaluation Activity.

Task 2: Assign implementation and evaluation duties.

- Fill out Table 4.8: Parties Responsible for Implementation and Evaluation for Each Outcome.

Then, keep working … your plan is now a living document!

Chapter 5

How?
Outcomes Assessment:
The Implementation Stage

Learning Outcome: Readers will develop a logical, comprehensive assessment strategy for each outcome and undertake measurements.

Readers will demonstrate achievement of this learning outcome by

✓ Explaining the various types of measurement tools, benchmarks, performance standards, and sampling methods used in collecting and evaluating assessment data.

✓ Formulating and implementing a thoughtful triangulated measurement strategy for each performance criterion that includes multiple measures of different types (direct and indirect, qualitative and quantitative), takes advantage of existing tools, establishes appropriate performance thresholds, and collects only the data that the school can and will use.

✓ Designing and employing assessment tools that provide valid and reliable data.

✓ Meticulously documenting their strategy in an Assessment Blueprint Form.

You now have your institutional assessment plan in hand, and you are set to begin the Implementation Stage. Completing your institutional assessment plan is a huge accomplishment, but the truth is that the real work has just begun. This is the stage that never ends.

Figure 5.A

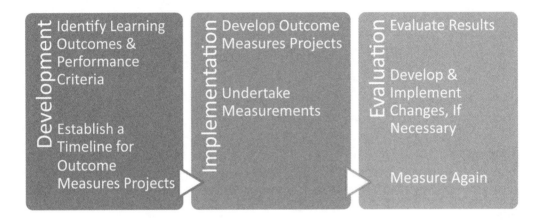

Don't panic! What we mean is that from here on out you will be gathering evidence of the attainment of the various learning outcomes identified in your plan. In other words, you will be taking the measures that will be used in evaluating how your students are doing. You will not measure every outcome every year, but you will measure at least one outcome every year.

This Chapter focuses on how to develop and undertake meaningful measurement.

A Word on Measurements

The idea of measuring something sounds simple, but there are some hidden complexities. For instance, if we were making bread and asked you to measure the flour for us, your first question to us might well be "By weight or by volume?" or "With a scale or a measuring cup?" Measurement essentially involves the use of some standard/unit/benchmark that allows you to compare one thing to another. If our recipe calls for 5 cups of flour, and all you have to measure the flour is a scale, our baking project is in deep trouble. You need to know what standard of measure will be used before you begin a baking project.

The same principle holds true for an assessment project. You cannot develop meaningful assessment methods/tools without knowing what type of **benchmark** will be used in evaluating the results. As used in this Guide, a **benchmark** is *the standard against which an individual student's performance is being compared.* We will discuss the development of an appropriate benchmark in more detail in Chapter 6, but for now, let's focus on some basics.

There are many different types of possible benchmarks. Benchmarks can be **norm-referenced**, which means that *competency is measured by comparing the student or students' performance to the performance of other students. Grading on a curve is a form of norm-referenced assessment.*

Norm-referenced assessment is **not** employed when undertaking an institutional assessment because no matter how well or how poorly the students do as a group, the performance numbers will look the same. For example, if your school's curve is based on a requirement that the overall GPA for the class is 3.00, the mean will be 3.00 in years when your students are brilliant and in years when your students are mediocre.

Benchmarks can also be **value-added/longitudinal**, which means *performance is measured by comparing students' performance on a test (or other instrument) after some period in law school to their performance on the same instrument when they began law school. The idea is to determine whether there has been value added by the students' progression through the curriculum.*

Value-added benchmarks are rarely employed when undertaking an institutional assessment. The key reason is because accreditors, potential employers, prospective students, and other "outside" constituencies really do not care whether graduates have learned "something." Rather, they are interested in whether graduates have learned "enough" to be competent lawyers.

The benchmarks used for institutional assessment are almost always **criterion-referenced**, which means that *competency is measured based on whether a student satisfies certain the prerequisites set by the assessor* (*e.g.,* gets at least 35 out of 50 questions on a multiple-choice test right). When a criterion-referenced benchmark is used, at least theoretically, every student could be found to be competent or every student could be found to be incompetent.

Criterion-referenced benchmarks can rely on *criterion set by experts outside the law school* (*i.e.,* use an **external standard**). The ABA mandates this type of comparison in Standard 316, which requires that a law school's bar passage rate meets certain standards.

Institutional assessment rarely involves the use of external standards in large part because schools generally do not share common assessment instruments. For example, it would be impossible to compare the Torts exam scores of Dayton students to those of another law school. Still, there are few opportunities for the use of external standards. For example, most schools today have students complete the Law School Survey of Student Engagement (LSSSE) on a periodic basis. It would certainly be possible for the ABA, the AALS, or even a consortium of law schools to develop benchmark scores for at least some of the LSSSE questions.

Institutional assessment typically involves the use of an **internal (local) standard** that is *based on criteria established by faculty for identifying a competent graduate.* As discussed later in this Chapter,

Learn More About It

For a comprehensive discussion of the various types of benchmarks, we highly recommend the following guide:

Linda Suskie, *Assessing Student Learning: A Common Sense Guide* (2009).

the faculty involved develop a **rubric** (*i.e., scoring guide*) to describe the criteria under which a student's performance is to be evaluated.

The Implementation Stage: What? Where? How? And Who?

As described in Chapter 4 and shown in Figure 5.B, the assessment of **each** outcome has a natural cycle that can last anywhere from three to seven years and then begins anew. Your school should **not** be collecting data on every outcome every year; ideally, no more than two (or at most three) outcomes will be in the data collection phase of the cycle in any given year. Also, ideally, a different assessment task force is working on each outcome—as the saying goes, "Many hands make light work."

This section focuses on describing the activities required during the Implementation Stage: reviewing performance criteria (Activity 1); developing or reviewing a curriculum map (Activity 2); using the curriculum map to determine where the data will be collected (Activity 3); selecting appropriate assessment methods/tools (Activity 4); and collecting data (Activity 5).

Figure 5.B

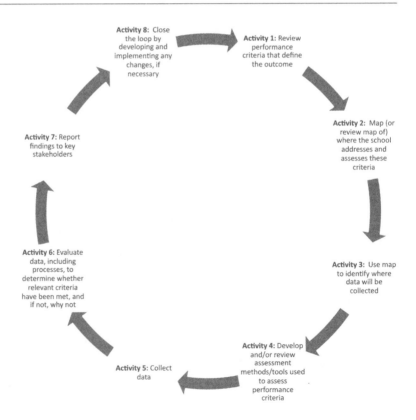

Activity 8: Close the loop by developing and implementing any changes, if necessary

Activity 1: Review performance criteria that define the outcome

Activity 2: Map (or review map of) where the school addresses and assesses these criteria

Activity 3: Use map to identify where data will be collected

Activity 4: Develop and/or review assessment methods/tools used to assess performance criteria

Activity 5: Collect data

Activity 6: Evaluate data, including processes, to determine whether relevant criteria have been met, and if not, why not

Activity 7: Report findings to key stakeholders

Each of these activities is best understood when considered in light of the ultimate goal of the Implementation Stage, **getting as honest and accurate a measure as possible of the knowledge, skills, and values that your faculty has identified as essential to a graduate.**

Practical Example A: As we walk you through the Implementation Stage, we will use the outcome shown below to provide practical examples of the types of decisions you will face along the way.

Learning Outcome: Graduates will demonstrate competency in analytical and problem-solving skills.

Graduates will demonstrate achievement of this learning outcome by

- Critically reading the applicable authority, including identifying the key rules within each authority.

- Synthesizing the relevant rules of law into a logical framework for analysis.

- Where rules conflict, thoroughly analyzing which rule a court is likely to apply.

- Meticulously applying the identified rules to the facts, including evaluating potential counterarguments, to determine the likely outcome of the case.

- When appropriate, analogizing the facts to and distinguishing the facts from those of precedent cases in specific and helpful ways to determine the likely outcome of the case.

- Accurately identifying practical considerations, such as cost and effects on other people.

Getting (and Staying!) on Track: The Assessment Blueprint

Every successful assessment effort requires thoughtful planning, strong organization, and good record keeping. Since law faculty members are new to the institutional assessment game, we understand that it is going to take time to master the assessment process.

To make life just a bit easier, we recommend that you use the Assessment Blueprint Form in Table 5.1 to keep your assessment task force on track. The Assessment Blueprint, adapted from a form created by the American Physical Therapy Association, serves three important functions.

One, it provides the assessment task force with needed structure. By completing the form, you are ensuring that you have engaged in all of the required activities and have developed a comprehensive measurement strategy.

Two, it provides faculty, administrators, and accreditors with a complete, detailed record of the process employed by the assessment task force. By completing the form and attaching the required appendices, you are ensuring that you have properly documented your Implementation Stage efforts.

Three, it creates consistency in reporting. Remember your law school will have multiple task forces in action. Having each adopt its own reporting content and format standards could be a nightmare—vital information could be omitted, readers could struggle to follow the process, etc. It is important that everyone develop a common language and understanding of the institutional assessment process. Using the same form will create that commonality.

In Chapter 6, we will introduce you to two additional forms, the Triangulated Analysis Form and the Specific Action Plan Form, which will serve the same functions for the Evaluation Stage. The three forms are designed to be used together.

In time, your school may adopt its own version of these forms. In fact, we hope it does. That will be a sign of growing comfort with and sophistication as to the institutional assessment process, but for now, we suggest that you keep everyone on the same page.

Make sure that one member of the task force is made responsible for completing the necessary forms and otherwise documenting the progress of the task force. It is easy to assume that someone is keeping track of documentation only to discover that nothing has been done. You may want to designate this person as the "secretary" or "recorder."

And as you progress through the Implementation and Evaluation Stages, make a point of providing your school's assessment coordinator with copies of the relevant forms and their appendices. (If your school does not have an assessment coordinator, the dean should appoint someone else to be the archivist for assessment materials.) In the short term, these documents can be placed behind the appropriate tab of the Institutional Assessment Plan binder.

As the stack of documents grows, the assessment coordinator will need to create an archive. This archive can consist of hard copy or electronic files, depending on the preference of your school.

The authors of this Guide believe that the archive should be permanent. We store student records forever, so we certainly have the capability to do the same for institutional assessment records. Someone who is conducting an assessment fifteen years from now may find the work done today to be a helpful guide. At a minimum, the records should be kept until your next regional accreditation site visit and law school accreditation site visit have been completed.

We will provide details on how to complete each column in the form later in this Chapter.

Table 5.1. Assessment Blueprint Form

Outcome: Criterion: Assessment Cycle: 20__–20__ Assessment Task Force Members:					
Column A	Column B	Column C	Column D	Column E	Column F
Tools/ Measures	Tool Type (Direct or Indirect; Objective or Subjective; Quantitative or Qualitative)	Where and when will data be collected (*i.e.*, in what class or other setting)?	What is the performance threshold?	Who will score/tabulate the data?	Who will evaluate the data?
Tool 1					
Tool 2					
Tool 3					

* Adapted from http://www.apta.org/outcomesassessment/, with permission of the American Physical Therapy Association. Copyright © 2006 American Physical Therapy Association.

Settling on the "What"

Having articulated the learning outcomes and performance criteria in your institutional assessment plan, you may think that the question of what you seek to measure has been settled. But as is often the case in life, the devil is in the details. Activity 1 requires the assessment task force to resolve any ambiguity as to what is required to satisfy an outcome and to select the performance criterion or criteria on which to focus attention during this particular review cycle.

Activity 1: Review performance criteria that define the outcome

The first activity an assessment task force must undertake is to review the performance criteria that define the outcome. The review can serve three functions.

First, it can be used to ensure that everyone on the task force is on the same page as to the meaning of each criterion. (It's amazing how many different ways a room full of law professors can interpret a one-sentence criterion!) You need to agree as to what exactly is being measured before you even think about collecting data.

Depending on the process your school adopts, you may or may not need to suggest a formal amendment to the criterion at that moment in time, but you should at the very least make clear in your Assessment Blueprint Form documentation what interpretation those charged with measurement employed.

Practical Example A (Analytical Skills): Scenario A-1:

Assume that your school has adopted the learning outcome "Graduates will demonstrate competency in analytical and problem-solving skills" and performance criterion "Graduates will demonstrate achievement of this learning outcome by critically reading applicable authority."

At the beginning of the Implementation Stage, the assessment task force sits down to review this criterion. We seriously doubt that anyone at the table will dispute the idea that critical reading is essential to the practice of law, but a dispute may well arise as to what critical reading requires. What would achievement of this criterion look like? Being asked to measure achievement of a criterion forces you to look at it with a more critical eye than you may have used during the Development Stage.

At our school, we ultimately added a further descriptor to the criterion, making it "Graduates will demonstrate achievement of this learning outcome by critically reading applicable authority, identifying the key rules within each authority." Could critical reading entail something more than identifying the key rules of law? Certainly. But this descriptor provided us with something measurable/visible upon which we could all agree. Perfect? No. Good? Yes.

Second, the review can be used to determine if the existing criteria still reflect the faculty's view of the specific acts of performance required to be able to conclude that a graduate has achieved the learning outcome. While outcomes tend to largely remain the same over time, performance criteria may change.

For example, when one of the authors, who shall remain nameless, attended law school back in the Dark Ages, there was a very real, albeit unwritten, expectation that "Graduates will demonstrate competency in legal research." However, there was no expectation that "Graduates will demonstrate achievement of this learning outcome by effectively and efficiently finding relevant legal authority using computer-assisted legal research methods." (At that time, our computer-assisted legal research training consisted of spending an hour in a former broom closet watching a teaching assistant type dot commands into a dedicated terminal!) In the current era, we certainly expect our students to engage in effective and efficient computer-assisted legal research. Times change!

During the first assessment cycle for an outcome, the assessment task force will have newly minted performance criteria in hand, so it is unlikely that a need will exist for significant additions or deletions. In subsequent cycles, the task force may discover legitimate reasons for change.

Third, the review must be used to select which performance criterion or criteria will be the focus of this assessment cycle. In sum, the task force must determine **exactly** what needs to be investigated now. Because learning outcomes are by necessity written in broad terms, the performance criteria for each outcome cover lots of ground.

Instead of trying to cover every criterion every time you look at a particular outcome, make it your goal to cover every criterion at least once over three or four assessment cycles. Doing so will allow you to really focus on the criterion at issue. It also makes it infinitely easier to find an assessment activity to measure its achievement.

For example, most schools will adopt an outcome that reads something like this, "Graduates will communicate effectively and efficiently to individuals and groups," and performance criteria that read something like this, "Graduates will demonstrate achievement of this learning outcome by writing legal documents that are clear, concise, well-reasoned, organized, professional in tone, appropriate to the audience and the circumstances, and if appropriate, contain proper citation to authority," and "Graduates will demonstrate achievement of this learning outcome by speaking in a clear, concise, well-reasoned, organized, and professional manner that is appropriate to the audience and the circumstances."

Measuring the achievement of these two criteria will require different tools. For instance, you might use legal research and writing course memoranda in evaluating the former and trial practice arguments in evaluating the latter. There is no need to try to look at both at the same time. Doing so merely complicates the assessment process.

So, how might you choose the order in which you attack criteria? All of the criteria are important—otherwise, they would not be listed as criteria. But as we all learned from reading "Animal Farm," "All animals are equal, but some animals are more equal than others." Some skills are building blocks for others. For instance, in drafting an exam answer, students can rarely identify the relevant facts if they have yet to master the skill of identifying the applicable rules. So, it might make sense to investigate their ability to identify the rules before you investigate their ability to use the facts.

You should also take advantage of the instincts of your faculty. If your colleagues are saying, "These students just don't know how to read!" that suggests that reading skills should be investigated sooner rather than later. And of course, if student performance failed to meet expectations during one assessment cycle and changes to your educational program have been made in response, you might opt to revisit the criterion in question sooner rather than later to see if the changes made a positive difference.

The bottom line is that there is no absolute right or wrong plan, but you should have a plan.

Settling on the "Where"

Once you have settled on what you need to measure, you need to determine where you might undertake to measure it. Assessment activities can be either **embedded activities** or **add-on activities** — *the distinction being whether the activity is a part of the student's course work* or *is provided outside of the context of a class.* For example, to assess a learning outcome addressing issue spotting, an assessment activity could be reviewing exam answers from a course, specifically focusing on the students' ability to issue spot: an embedded activity. Conversely, a mini-bar exam could be provided to all students after the completion of their first year to assess issue spotting skills: an add-on activity.

Add-on activities may not only take place outside of the context of a class, they may take place outside of the law school, and they may take place years after a student has graduated. For example, you could send a survey to alumni and/or employers seeking information on alumni attitudes and/or behaviors.

When you can use an embedded assessment, do. Using embedded tools is preferable because students tend to take assignments more seriously (and hence perform better) in the context of a class. Therefore, embedded tools may provide better evidence of student learning.

Students are motivated to perform because it is part of their class work, even if a grade is not attached. They are, of course, most motivated to perform when a grade is attached to an assessment. But be careful not to assume that grading an assignment is all that is needed to ensure motivation. If a grade is attached, it is essential that the grading rubric given to students actually reflects the criterion being assessed.

For instance, if you are assessing students' ability to spot ethical issues, the assignment should make clear that the professor will be evaluating whether the student identified the relevant ethical issues.

If students believe something will not count towards the grade, they will likely direct their efforts and attention elsewhere, which will give you a less than accurate picture of the work they are capable of doing.

Another advantage of embedded tools is that they often already exist; therefore, it may take little or no time, money, or effort for the assessment task force to use them. It may be as simple as looking at the product of an activity (*e.g.,* an exam answer) in a different way.

There are likewise benefits and drawbacks to using add-on tools. A common add-on tool would be a standardized test, such as a practice mini-bar exam. Usually, such tests are fine to use, particularly if used in combination with other embedded tools. However, you must make sure the standardized test is actually measuring the knowledge, skills, etc. encompassed in your learning outcomes. If not, the results will not provide you with any meaningful information.

For example, if your school buys a standardized mini-bar exam from a commercial vendor to measure your students' acquisition of knowledge, you need to think about whether it covers the topics actually addressed in your school's courses. To illustrate, many of today's criminal law casebooks focus on helping students understand the basics of the elements of every crime (*e.g.,* conduct, mental state, etc.) as opposed to learning the specific elements of individual crimes (*e.g.,* battery, arson, etc.). As a result, criminal law professors often expect students to pick up the elements of individual crimes when they study for the bar in their own state.

If your criminal law professors have this expectation, a mini-bar exam that contains questions relating to knowledge of the elements of individual crimes would not be an effective measure of student learning. Instead, you should work with the vendor to prepare a custom mini-bar that measures whether students are learning the materials that are actually being covered.

A benefit of standardized tests, surveys, etc. is that they are typically easy to administer and allow you to take advantage of the expertise of commercial vendors in creating meaningful assessments (*i.e.,* in psychometrics). An important question is whether your school wishes to devote the necessary financial resources to purchasing such tools.

If you choose to use any add-on tools, realize that you will need to find a way to motivate students to put forth their best effort. Here are some tips on how you might do so:

1. Most important, provide educational incentives by giving them meaningful feedback where appropriate. (Turn an otherwise summative assessment tool into a formative assessment tool. Give each student his or her results, and whether it is in the form of a handout, a lunchtime review session, or something else, provide

(a) Exceeds Expectations
(b) Meets Expectations
(c) Below Expectations
(d) No Opinion

For more information
visit: http://www.ee.ucla.edu/academics/accreditation/assessment-procedure.

Embedded Assessments Outside the Classroom

Most embedded assessments will be linked to courses, which is one reason why curriculum mapping is so important. However, embedded assessments may also be linked to activities outside the classroom. For instance, your school might measure attitudes relating to the obligation to engage in pro bono activities using volunteer hours already being tracked as part of a pro bono service award program.

an explanation of the results and suggestions for how to improve areas of weakness.)

2. Provide financial incentives, like lunch or a small gift card to a local coffee shop. (Financial incentives can be particularly important when you are asking students to complete a survey because that type of activity has no direct educational benefit to the individual student.)

3. Beware of survey fatigue. (Someone at your school should be assigned as a gatekeeper to ensure that students are not being overwhelmed with survey requests, etc.)

4. Try to find a convenient time in the students' schedules to administer the tool. (In doing so, consider both your class schedule and your academic calendar.)

5. Make use of technology where appropriate. (Students are much more apt to complete an instrument if all they need to do is "point and click.")

6. Keep it simple when possible. (Whether it is an exam or a survey, longer is not necessarily better.)

Don't be afraid to mix things up a bit. As discussed later in this Chapter, it is a best practice to use multiple assessments. Coupling an embedded assessment with an add-on can create a dynamite combination that allows you to assess achievement from multiple perspectives.

Practical Example A (Analytical Skills): Scenario A-2:

Assume that your school has adopted the following learning outcome, "Graduates will demonstrate competency in analytical and problem-solving skills," and performance criterion, "Graduates will demonstrate achievement of this learning outcome by critically reading applicable authority, identifying the key rules within each authority."

It would be entirely possible to embed an assessment tool into an existing course. For example, students in a course could be asked to take a brief quiz (in or out of class) over an assigned case or could be asked to read a case and identify the key rules of law as part of a final exam.

It would also be possible to use an add-on assignment. For example, in recent years, researchers have developed multiple-choice instruments geared towards assessing case reading and reasoning. Dorothy H. Evensen et. al., *Developing an Assessment of First-year Law Students' Critical Case Reasoning and Reasoning Ability: Phase 2* (2008) (available at http://www.lsac.org/docs/default-source/ research-(lsac-resources)/gr-08-02.pdf). As discussed above, the challenge of such assessments is obtaining student participation. You will need a carrot or a stick to ensure that the students who participate are representative of your student body as a whole.

Activity 2: Map (or review map of) where your school addresses and assesses these criteria

During the first assessment cycle for an outcome, the assessment task force should have the curriculum map created as part of the assessment plan in hand. However, in subsequent cycles, the task force (or someone else within the law school) will almost certainly need to update the map. New courses may have been added to the curriculum, new professors may be teaching existing courses, and/or long-time professors may have changed their teaching or assessment methodologies. For more on curriculum mapping, see Chapter 4.

Activity 3: Use the map to determine where data will/can be collected

The curriculum map is where you begin your search for a course or courses in which to embed an assessment. Ideally, it will point you to one or more courses in which the achievement of the criteria at issue is already being measured. If no one is currently measuring achievement, look for courses in which the professor at least purports to be teaching the knowledge, skill, or value involved.

Finding the right course(s) is only the first step in the process. You must next convince the professor(s) involved to participate in the process. Doing so might be as simple as providing you with access to assignments, exams, etc.

However, it will most likely involve some tweaking of the design of an assignment or exam question to ensure that it provides a meaningful measure. The professor may also be involved in the creation of a scoring rubric, which is described below. In other words, participating in the process usually involves some effort on the part of the professor.

The dean's help will be essential to obtaining the needed faculty participation. She will need to make clear the expectation that at some point, every professor will "host" the assessment in one course or another. (And a small stipend certainly would not hurt!)

It will also be vital to communicate to the faculty as a whole that these institutional assessments will not be used to evaluate individual faculty members. The school may be using a second-semester Torts exam to measure critical reading skills, but the results of the assessment demonstrate how the program in legal education as a whole is doing in helping students learn to read critically. The results will not be considered in any evaluation of the Torts professor. What will be considered is that he or she performed a valuable service to the law school in hosting the assessment.

Settling on the "How"

Once you know what you seek to measure and where it will be measured, you must determine exactly how it will be measured. In other words, you must select the appropriate assessment tools. Our choice to use the plural in the preceding sentence was a conscious one. In undertaking any assessment it is a best practice to use multiple measures of different types.

There are a variety of **assessment tools, activities, or measures** *(the terms being used interchangeably) that can be used to gather evidence of learning. Think of them as indicators of performance.* In addressing the "how" of measurement, what you are really doing is developing a measurement strategy. Before we address how to create an effective measurement strategy, an introduction to some basic terminology, the types of tools available, and the essentials of creating meaningful measures is needed.

Basic Terminology

Assessment activities can be **direct** or **indirect**. As discussed more fully below, **direct measures** *are based on actual student work or performance*, whereas **indirect measures** *are based upon opinion, either the student's opinion or any other observer's opinion.* Direct data or evidence of student learning comes closer to fulfilling the demands of assessment. Examples of direct assessment methods include: tests, quizzes, exams, legal memoranda, and other checks of performance, such as one-sentence summaries and portfolios. Examples of indirect assessment methods include: reflection papers, surveys, interviews, and focus groups.

Assessment tools can be **formative** or **summative**. As discussed more fully in Chapter 1, **formative assessment** is traditionally defined as *assessment conducted throughout the course of study through which students are provided feedback to improve their learning.* In contrast, **summative assessment** is traditionally defined as *"assessment after the fact,"* assessment that occurs after a course of study. It typically provides *no opportunity for individual students to improve their learning and little or no feedback to the students.*

Types of Assessment Tools

With the basic terminology in mind, now we turn to the various types of tools available. This list does not include every possible tool as any tool that provides evidence about student learning would qualify. Our goal is to provide sufficient examples to help you recognize potential tools at your school. We focus on a few tools that are most familiar and adaptable to the law school environment.

Direct Assessment Tools

Any tool where the student actually produces work product in some form is known as a **direct assessment tool**. Direct assessments allow the assessor to examine or observe student work product to determine what specific learning has taken place. For example, legal memoranda and briefs, oral or written reports, exams, quizzes, and oral arguments are all potential direct assessment tools.

Direct assessment tools tend to be viewed with great favor because they do not involve guesswork. What the students can and cannot do or do and do not know is right there in front of the assessor and any "outside" constituency, such as an accreditor, who wishes to review the work product.

In developing direct assessment tools, think about assignments that your students already do either in class or outside of class as part of the curriculum—any such assignment is a potential direct assessment tool. Do not forget that some fabulous direct tools for assessment purposes can be found in penultimate courses, such as capstones and other simulation-based courses, which ask students to engage in practical application of what they have learned over their three years in law school.

Additionally, assignments completed as part of student externships and clinics may highlight skills and knowledge that are not tested in doctrinal courses. They also provide you with the opportunity to receive assessment/feedback from external sources (*e.g.,* externship supervisors and clinic clients). Clinicians also frequently record student performances to allow for formative assessment. Those same recordings can be repurposed for institutional assessment.

A less frequently used tool in the law school setting, but one with great potential as an assessment tool, is the portfolio. There are two basic types of portfolios: **showcase portfolios** and **developmental portfolios**. *A showcase portfolio demonstrates the extent of a student's mastery of learning outcomes by "showcasing" his best work product. A*

The Challenge of Assessing Attitudes and Values

Assessing attitudes and values is more difficult than assessing knowledge and skills. Since the ABA says they must be included, you need to think creatively about how they might be measured.

While law schools measure students' knowledge of the law of lawyering in Professional Responsibility courses and the bar measures this knowledge with the MPRE, attempts to measure students' critical thinking skills with regard to ethical issues and their core attitudes have been minimal. The good news is that our colleagues in medicine and engineering have been developing direct assessment tools that we can use as models. *See, e.g.,* J. Savulescu, et al., *Evaluating Ethics Competence in Medical Education,* J. Med. Ethics 367-74 (1999); Larry J. Shuman et al., *Can Our Students Recognize and Resolve Ethical Dilemmas?,* Proceedings of the 2004 American Society for Engineering Education Annual Conference & Exposition (2004).

With a little thought, we can also develop useful indirect assessment tools

developmental portfolio demonstrates the extent of a student's mastery of learning outcomes by showing the student's progress, including samples of the student's early work product and later work product throughout the student's academic career. Portfolios can be embedded into systems like legal research and writing programs, capstones and other simulation-based courses, externships, and clinics.

And don't forget what's happening in the classroom every day. Lori has used classroom response systems ("clickers") in her classes at various times. Posting a multiple-choice or true-false question for a "vote" takes all of fifteen seconds and can serve a dual role. It can be used both to assess student learning and to promote class discussion. (Depending on how you use the clickers, the results can be tied to individual students or simply provide you with the performance of the group as a whole.) To have a valid assessment, the professor and the assessment task force will need to craft the questions with some care, but that task is far from difficult.

And the more old school members of the faculty who favor the traditional Socratic Method will be happy to hear that the Socratic Method can also provide opportunities for individual assessment. An assessor could systematically observe student performance in the classroom (either live or recorded) and use a rubric to evaluate it. This process would not be unlike what we do with moot court competitions. It would not require the evaluation of every student—a sampling would do. This tool would require more resources than the clicker system described above, but if the resources are there, it is doable.

The bottom line is that we have a multitude of direct assessment tools from which we can choose.

Indirect Assessment Tools

In addition to direct assessment tools, indirect assessment tools can be used to assess learning outcomes. **Indirect assessment tools** *allow an assessor to infer that learning has (or has not) taken place, but do not allow for the direct examination of work product.*

Indirect assessment tools tend to focus on what students, alumni, employers, and other constituencies *perceive* students have learned. They often involve self-assessment.

Indirect assessment tools also sometimes look to what behaviors are being exhibited by students/graduates. The idea is that a person's behaviors reflect his or her values and attitudes. For example, there may be an assumption that if alumni are taking more CLE classes than required by the bar, they value lifetime learning or if they are donating more pro bono hours than required, they believe attorneys have an ethical obligation to promote access to justice.

Because indirect assessment tools require the assessor to make some assumptions, which may or may not be correct, they are typically viewed with less favor than direct assessment tools. For instance, alums might be donating more pro bono hours than the bar requires because their firms require them to do so.

That having been said, indirect assessment tools still have value. Indirect assessment may be the only assessment method available for some outcomes, particularly those involving attitudes. Indirect assessment can also be a valuable complement to direct assessment, often providing a deeper insight into what aspects of your educational program students perceived as being the most helpful.

Unlike direct assessment tools, indirect tools typically are not em-bedded in a course and typically do not serve the dual purpose of grading and assessment. A few examples of indirect assessment methods include: reflection papers, surveys, interviews, focus groups, and in-stitutional data.

First, reflective essays are a viable indirect assessment tool and can be embedded in open-ended survey questions, course journals, as part of a developmental portfolio, and in a multitude of other ways. Reflective essays can assess a variety of learning outcomes. For example, they can be used to assess students' ability to recognize moral and ethical dimensions to problems and to assess communication skills. Developmental portfolios often include a requirement that students write reflective essays or reviews, where a student is asked to review all of the documents in the portfolio and reflect on his development of the learning outcomes.

Reflective essays can be used as both a direct assessment tool and an indirect assessment tool. They allow you to directly assess writing competency and at the same time collect data on selected issues, such as a student's reflection on his own learning (*i.e.,* metacognition). **Metacognition** *or student self-assessment* is important for a student's future professional life. You can assess and teach a valuable life skill at the same time.

Second, surveys can make excellent assessment tools. Surveys can provide data on both perceptions and behaviors. They can seek in-formation on very discrete topics or can seek more wide ranging data. Surveys can also be periodically repeated to track the impact of program changes resulting from assessment.

Surveys can be sent to various stakeholders to gather important data. Stakeholders' perceptions as to the effectiveness of our educational programs are important, regardless of whether they are accurate.

As we mentioned before, surveys to alumni and the bench and bar can be used at the outset of the assessment process when defining learning outcomes, asking the question "what do graduates need to know, do, and value?" Exit surveys to students can gather information

(*e.g.,* reflective essays and attitudinal surveys, etc.). Measuring atti-tudes and values will take some work, but it is not the impossible dream.

on students' perceptions of their attainment of the learning outcomes. Surveys can also be used to elicit information from alumni and/or employers as to the attainment of the learning outcomes. Finally, surveys to faculty members can be used to assess the attainment of learning outcomes within an institution, and/or specific programs or departments, like an externship program.

A real challenge with surveys that are not embedded in a course can be getting those surveyed to respond. It can be particularly challenging to obtain data from alumni and employers. In attempting to survey these groups, it is wise to work closely with your alumni relations and career services offices. You should have an articulated strategy for maximizing the response rate of every survey.

We would be remiss if we did not mention a survey that almost every law school is currently administering, the Law School Survey of Student Engagement (LSSSE). LSSSE provides a wealth of data— much of which we believe is going unused. Some of the questions go directly to student attitudes/perceptions of what they have learned. For example, LSSSE specifically asks whether students' experience at the law school has contributed to their ability to write clearly and effectively. Some of the questions go directly to behaviors that may relate to whether a particular outcome has been achieved. For example, LSSSE specifically asks how many hours the student devotes to legal pro bono work. The LSSSE data is sitting on a computer somewhere at your school. All you need to do is use it.

Third, focus groups consisting of students, alumni, employers, and other stakeholders can be used as an indirect tool. The major drawback to the use of focus groups is that they can be costly and time consuming.

To be done well, focus groups require a lot of preparation and a neutral facilitator. They typically involve six to twelve participants and last one to two hours. Prior to the focus group, the assessment task force should compose an "interview guide," consisting of the three to six questions relating to the outcome/criterion under discussion.

A best practice to maintain neutrality is to use a facilitator from outside the law school. Using a skilled neutral is essential. The neutral needs to keep the discussion on topic without being overly controlling. An unskilled neutral can lead the participants to seemingly support the view that the "neutral" takes. The facilitator also needs to be able to get everyone involved in the discussion.

Along with the neutral, a note-taker who is not part of the focus group is required. The note-taker may either transcribe the entire session or attempt to summarize the responses to each question. The reliability of this measure can be improved by allowing participants to review and comment upon the accuracy of the notes. Additionally, with the knowledge and permission of the focus group participants, we suggest recording the sessions—audio-recording, video-recording, or both. These recordings should also be transcribed. The reliability of the measure can also be improved by asking participants to complete a very short (3-to 5-question) survey covering the key questions addressed by the group and requiring participants to provide a scaled response (*e.g.*, "On a scale of 1 to 5 ....").

The notes, transcript, and survey are used by the facilitator to help generate a report that describes the responses to each question, including things like whether there was a consensus view, how strongly held that view appeared to be, any major and minor themes, etc.

Fourth, one-on-one structured interviews of students, alumni, employers, and other stakeholders by trained interviewers can serve as a valuable indirect assessment tool. Like surveys and focus groups, interviews can serve numerous purposes and seek a variety of data from the same stakeholders. Unlike surveys and like focus groups, they allow for follow-up questions that may take you in unexpected directions.

Like focus groups, the major drawback to the use of interviews is their time- and resource-consuming nature. They require the same careful preparation, facilitation, note-taking, and reporting as do focus groups. The benefit of one-on-one interviews is that participants may be more open than if they were sitting with their peers in a focus group. The cost is that instead of one- to two-hour focus group, someone must facilitate six to twelve 1- to 2-hour interviews.

Fifth, institutional data already in hand can be invaluable as an indirect measurement tool. For example, the ABA already requires us to collect and report placement rates, salaries, and other employment information nine months after graduation. Placements rates, salaries, etc. provide some indication of how graduates of your school are perceived by employers. You can dig even deeper by surveying employers who interviewed on campus.

A good way to begin the process of finding indirect assessment tools is to question faculty and staff as to the work that is already being done. You may be surprised by the data that is already being collected. You may also discover that you can save resources and increase participation by piggybacking a few assessment questions on to existing instruments and processes.

Ensuring the Effectiveness of Your Measurement

Once you have selected what you believe to be an appropriate tool, you will need to turn your attention to ensuring that the measure provided by that tool is meaningful. There is no point in undertaking a measurement that will not provide you with good quality data. The necessary components of effective assessment are validity and reliability.

Ethical Assessment

When collecting information from human subjects, ethical and legal responsibility comes into play. Some types of research require approval by federally mandated institutional review boards (IRBs). Typically, IRBs provide an exemption for internal research and reporting on the effectiveness of educational programs, 45 C.F.R. § 46.101(b)(1), but before you begin your first assessment project, you should contact your school's IRB for clarification of its policies.

If you wish to publish the results of any studies to an outside audience (other than an accrediting body), IRB approval is likely necessary. To obtain such approval, you must seek it before you begin collecting data and obtain the informed consent of the student subjects of the study.

Even if an assessment project does not have go through the IRB process, the school bears ethical responsibilities to those involved. You should respect and protect anonymity, confidentiality, and privacy. Always report results in the aggregate and take all necessary steps to maintain individual student's anonymity.

We are going to provide you with a brief explanation of each of these concepts, but before we do, we have one very simple piece of advice for you: **In designing any assessment tool, run, do not walk, to your school's institutional researcher.** Trust us. If your school is affiliated with a university, there is an office of institutional research somewhere on campus. It has been our experience that institutional researchers are not only willing to help but excited about the prospect of working with the law school.

The assessment task force and the faculty involved in a project have the expertise to identify what the outcomes and criteria are, what rubrics should be employed in evaluating projects, what a "competent" performance looks like, etc. What they likely lack is the expertise in things like what sample size is required and how to structure survey questions. If help is available in these areas, it is foolish not to take advantage of it.

"Validity" relates to *the degree to which a tool measures what it is supposed to measure.* The assessment must accomplish the purpose for which it was intended and provide useful information, measuring what has actually been learned by the students.

For example, a typical law school essay exam question would provide a valid measure of students' ability to spot the relevant issues, articulate the applicable rules, and identify the legally significant facts. Each is something a student would be expected to do to produce a satisfactory answer. Designing a rubric that identifies the key issues, rules, and facts that the student should articulate would be easy.

In contrast, a typical law school essay exam question would not provide a valid measure of students' case-reading skills. There is simply nothing on an answer that you could point to that would identify someone as a good, fair, or poor case reader. (You might assume that if a student does a great job of articulating the relevant rules, she must be a good reader, but it could just as easily be because someone gave her a wonderful outline.) If you are struggling to design a rubric that specifically identifies what would be observed in a sophisticated, competent, or not yet competent answer, you need to go back to the drawing board because your tool likely does not provide a valid measure.

Even where there is validity as to the content of the tool (*i.e.,* it measures what it is supposed to measure), its validity may be brought into question if its instructions are unclear. For instance, if there is ambiguity as to the depth to which students should discuss the applicable rules on an exam and you are assessing their ability to articulate the rules, your results will be less valid. Similarly providing inadequate time limits could bring the results into question. It is vital to construct each tool with care, anticipating anything that might bring the validity of its measure into question.

Reliability refers to *the degree to which the tool yields the same results on repeated trials (i.e., demonstrates consistent results). Reliability depends in large part on representative sampling and scoring consistency.*

Institutional assessment typically involves assessing the work of a sampling of your students, not the entire student body. It's neither practical nor necessary to assess every student on every outcome. When we say that reliability depends in part on representative sampling, we mean that results can be skewed (made less reliable) when your sample does not represent the characteristics of the student body as a whole.

This point seems obvious, and we doubt that you had planned to limit your samples to law review members. But we raise it because there is an art to obtaining a representative sample. This is one of the times when even a brief consultation with your school's institutional researcher can pay big dividends.

It's also important to bear in mind that tools which involve self-selection of participants are also less reliable. The students who respond to your call for survey takers within five minutes may not represent your student body as a whole. Again, your institutional researcher may have some very useful advice on how to address the challenges of self-selection.

When we say that scoring consistency is important, we mean that there should be what is known as **scorer reliability**. *Scorer reliability refers to the need for consistency in the assessments made by different scorers and by the same scorer at different points in time.*

The need to have consistency among different scorers arises all of the time in the context of moot court competitions. And every law professor who has ever sat with a stack of 100 bluebooks knows the struggle that even one scorer can face in trying to be consistent over two or three days.

Developing and following a detailed grading rubric helps assure both types of consistency. It is also helpful to review a sampling of answers before scoring any answer to norm/calibrate expectations. The development of rubrics is discussed later in this Chapter and norming is discussed in Chapter 6.

Do bear in mind that some scorer variation is inevitable. Reliability falls on a spectrum. Your goal is to make your measures as reliable as possible. No one expects perfection.

Our Advice: Developing Your Measurement Strategy

Now that we have discussed the various pieces of the measurement puzzle, it's time to consider how to put them together to formulate a measurement strategy. We believe that there are three keys to developing an effective measurement strategy:

1. Use multiple measures to maximize the reliability of your measures.
2. Take advantage of the tools you already have to minimize the drain on resources.
3. Collect only the data that you can and will use to make your measures meaningful.

Use Multiple Measures

A huge component of your strategy is determining how to make your results as valid and reliable as possible. As discussed above, no tool provides a perfect measure. Even if it is extremely well designed and well executed, no single tool/assessment activity can provide the comprehensive view needed to determine whether a criterion is being achieved. Therefore, it is essential to use multiple tools.

The use of several different tools validates your conclusions as to whether learning outcomes are being obtained. We suggest using what is known as **methodological triangulation**, *employing multiple tools, in this case, two direct tools and one indirect tool, to assess a criterion in an institutional plan.* That may not be possible in every instance—for example, it can be difficult to find direct tools that measure attitudes—but where possible, you should make an effort to use both direct and indirect measures.

We also suggest that of those three tools, each be a different type of tool (for example, you should not use two multiple-choice exams) because you want your assessment to be accessible to different learning styles and strengths. For instance, we have all had students who excelled on essay exams but struggled with multiple-choice exams. The greater the variety of tools, the more you take this type of difference out of the mix.

Multiple tools also allow you to bring in a wider range of evaluators. An employer may have a very different view of what constitutes competent work than does a law professor. Where this type of discrepancy is found to exist, your school needs to at least think about whether its program of legal education is meeting the needs of the bar.

As you are choosing your tools, make a conscious effort to identify the flaws of each. In other words, consider what it may *not* measure well. Then make a conscious effort to select another tool that you believe may "fill in the blanks" left by the first.

Use the Tools You Have

Before you run around trying to create a dozen new assessment tools, take a long hard look at the assessment already taking place at your school. Use your curriculum map. Look at what professors say they do to assess certain learning outcomes in their courses. Roam the halls of the law school and talk to your colleagues. (We are willing to bet that they neglected to mention some of the tools that they use when the curriculum map was created.) You may be shocked to learn that there is an embedded assessment tool just waiting to be used. In addition to professors, think about others who evaluate students: peers, alumni, externship field supervisors, and employers, to name a few.

Using the tools you have is important for several reasons. First, the entire purpose of institutional assessment is to enhance legal education, not get in its way. The more we take advantage of tools that are already in place, the less risk of disruption.

Second, when you use an existing tool, the professor involved has essentially already said that this knowledge, skill, or value is worthy of assessment. Are you going to tweak that assessment a bit? Very probably yes. But we know few professors who would reject the opportunity to better assess their students, particularly if they are part of the improvement process.

Third, in this era of tightened belts and shrinking faculties, using resources wisely is essential. Faculty buy-in will increase as our colleagues recognize that they will not be asked to radically change what they do. Legal education is already changing. We don't need to ram assessment down anyone's throat. Law faculty are already adding more assessment to courses. As more professors start assessing in their courses, embedded assessment tools will only become more readily available.

We do not mean to imply that a new tool is never going to be a good idea. And some members of your faculty will happily volunteer to try something new. All we are suggesting is to start things slowly.

Collect Only the Data You Need

Finally, get a little data, not a lot. One of the biggest problems with assessment planning is that you can get tied up in gathering the data and then do absolutely nothing with it. All that succeeds in doing is undermining your credibility with faculty, students, and other stakeholders and creating assessment fatigue. Therefore, although there may be a temptation to obtain a lot of data, only obtain the data that you can and will use. Keep it simple.

First whatever you do, do not create a project simply for purposes of taking a measure. If you are going to track the number of students entering the library each day, do it for a reason! And if you are going to ask your students to take their time to complete the LSSSE, do something with the results and share that something with faculty and students alike.

Second, when you do create an assessment project, think long and hard about how many student performances to measure. As noted throughout this Guide, institutional assessment does not require that you measure the performance of every student—the focus is on student performance generally. **Sampling,** *assessing a representative group,* is acceptable.

Sometimes, sampling is not necessary. You can conduct what is called a **census,** *an assessment of the entire population of a unit.* For instance, if you administer a multiple-choice, mini-bar to the entire second-year class, you can measure the results of the entire class. Obviously, more is better in this instance as scoring is a breeze and a smaller sample size would create a larger margin of error. The same holds true when you are conducting a survey.

However, at times, sampling is not only acceptable but actually preferable. For instance, if you decide to use an essay question from the first-year Torts exam to measure students' issue spotting skills, scoring the essay will require both time and specialized expertise. As discussed in detail below, we recommend that each essay be scored by three scorers. How many members of your faculty would volunteer (or at least grudgingly agree) to review 200 essays? A representative sample of 20 to 25 essays would provide the same information and still have an acceptable margin of error. (In fact, the scoring may actually be more consistent with the smaller sample.)

If you do need to gather a sample, what is the proper size? The sample must be representative and complete. Sounds simple enough, but what is the magic number? Unfortunately, there is no hard and fast rule about the size of the sample, but the following questions may guide you.

1. **What is the size of the general population?** The larger the size the larger the sample needed. A rule of thumb is that **at a minimum** your sample should be **the greater of 10 students or 10 percent of the student population being measured.** So, if 50 students are taking the essay exam in question, you would assess at least 10 of the essays, but if 200 students are taking the essay exam in question, you would assess at least 20 of the essays.
2. **How long and complex is the project being assessed?** If scoring the project will be quick and easy, adjust your sample size **up** accordingly, but never go below the minimum described in question 1 above.
3. **As a practical matter, how much in the way of resources (time, money, etc.) can you devote to scoring?** The larger the sample, the more confident you may be in the results, but you must be

realistic about your resources. You need to weigh the cost of adding to the sample size against the benefits. If you have a dedicated group of Emeritus professors who will cheerfully donate their time to scoring, you can afford to adjust your sample size **up**, but you will rarely have that luxury. Again, you should never go below the minimum described above, but your available resources will dictate by how much you can exceed the minimum.

While these questions provide some guidance, it is always a good idea to seek assistance from the institutional researcher at your institution or a statistician. And while you are questioning the researcher about the best size for your sample, you should also ask about its composition.

It is essential that your sample be representative of your school's general population, and the institutional researcher can help you identify a random selection method. Among the most commonly used random selection methods are simple random sampling, cluster random sampling, and stratified random sampling.

1. **Simple random sampling** *requires that everyone in the population have an equal chance to be selected for the sample.* Drawing names from a hat is a classic example of random sampling, but using a random number generator (don't worry, your registrar has one) is how it is typically done today.
2. **Cluster random sampling** *involves randomly selecting subgroups/ sections and assessing everyone in that section.* So, for example, if you have eight legal writing sections, you might choose two to sample and look at all of the briefs from those two sections.
3. **Stratified random sampling** *involves dividing the population into subgroups based on significant characteristics that are of interest to the institution, such as gender or race, and selecting a representative sample from each subgroup.* So, for example, if women compose 45% of your general population of 1,000 students, and you wish a sample size of 10% of the population, you would randomly select 45 women from the pool of 450, and then 55 men from the pool of 550. Stratified sampling is used when you have concerns about how a particular segment of the population is faring. It helps you evaluate whether your program of legal education is adequately serving that segment of the population.

All of this sounds complex and is complex to mere law professors — just writing this section has made our heads spin — but to an expert like an institutional researcher it is simple. Again, never hesitate to ask for help.

Learn More about Drafting Multiple-Choice Questions

There are many helpful books, book chapters, articles, and other resources devoted to the art of drafting multiple-choice questions. Here are just a few we recommend:

Susan M. Case & Beth E. Donahue, *Developing High-Quality Multiple-Choice Questions for Assessment in Legal Education*, 58 J. Legal Educ. 372 (2008).

Victoria L. Clegg & William E. Cashin, *Improving Multiple-Choice Tests*. IDEA Paper No. 16. (1986)http://ideaedu.org/sites/default/files/Idea_Paper_16.pdf.

Linda Suskie, *Assessing Student Learning: A Common Sense Guide,* Ch. 11 (2009).

Activity 4: Develop and/or review assessment methods/tools used to assess performance criteria

The time has come to move from theory to practice. You are ready to develop and/or review the specific tools you will use to assess the criterion or criteria under consideration. When we say that you may "review" the tool, we are referring to the fact that even if the tool is an existing assessment already embedded in a course, you may need to fine-tune it to ensure the validity of your measure (*i.e.,* to ensure that it measures what you want it to measure) and to ensure that it is reliable (*i.e.,* demonstrates consistent results). For tools that provide quantifiable data, you must also adopt a performance threshold, which establishes the desired collective level of achievement for your students.

Developing Direct Assessments

You must carefully design your tool to align with the criterion/criteria you seek to assess. As discussed above, direct assessments are favored because of their reliability. There are two types of direct assessment tools, objective and subjective, each of which poses its own unique challenges.

Objective tools, such as multiple-choice and true/false questions, *require no specialized expertise to score correctly*. Because scoring is consistent, when correctly designed, these tools provide reliable measures. They allow you to test a wide breadth of topics, and they can be compiled into a single exam or spread throughout the semester in weekly quizzes, midterms, etc. They provide good measures of knowledge of subject matter, such as legal standards. As shown by their use in tests like the MPRE and MBE, objective tools also provide insight into students' basic ability to apply the rules to the facts.

As anyone who has ever attempted to write a good multiple-choice question will attest, the challenge is in writing the questions. Two basic problems tend to arise. First, if questions are drafted on an ad hoc basis, the mix of questions may not match the subject matter covered in the course. There may be five questions on a relatively unimportant topic that received little attention and only two on something that was central to the course. A good way to promote validity is to create what is known as a "**test blueprint**," which *forces the tool's author to map the knowledge, skills, or values that an assessment tool is intended to measure.* Ideally, the map is created before the tool, but a map can also be used as a check before finalizing the tool.

Second, if questions are poorly drafted, they may not measure students' actual knowledge. One good way to make certain that the multiple-choice questions used in an assessment provide good measures is to do a test run of those questions the semester or year before. This practice is standard among professionals in the testing business. For example, only 50 of the 60 questions on the MPRE actually count. The other 10 are being tested for future use.

If you are taking advantage of an existing test, there is a good chance that you will be able to pull statistics on each question from the results of prior years. (Our IT department provides a statistical analysis of every question on a multiple-choice test.) Your institutional research office can help you review the statistics to help identify any problems.

Another way to help ensure validity is to review the individual questions, looking for common errors. A full review of the rules of writing multiple-choice questions is a bit beyond the scope of this work, but the sources cited in the "Learn More about Drafting Multiple-Choice Questions" box should provide you with an excellent start.

Subjective tools, such as essay exams, memoranda, and oral arguments, *require specialized expertise to score correctly*. The fact that the scoring is subjective by its nature creates some degree of inconsistency. Different scorers may score the same paper differently, and even the same scorer might score it differently at a different time. Thus, the scoring of subjective tools is by its very nature less consistent than the scoring of objective tools.

Nonetheless, they still have great value. Some skills, like oral advocacy and legal writing, simply cannot be adequately tested using a multiple-choice format. The scorer needs to observe the work product. Subjective tools also allow you to assess depth of knowledge and understanding in a way that is impossible with a multiple-choice format. There is something to be said for not having the correct answer appear somewhere on a page.

So, your goal with subjective tools should be to make them as valid and reliable as possible, knowing that they will never be perfect. As with objective tools, well-drafted questions are essential to valid results. The author of the assignment must identify *exactly* what knowledge, skill, or value the assignment is intended to measure and must carefully craft the **prompt** (i.e., *the call of the question), to allow students to understand exactly what the author wants them to do*.

For example, in drafting an essay exam, some professors want students to review every element of a potential claim using the IRAC (issue, rule, application, and conclusion) format. Other professors want students to focus only on the elements that appear to be at issue or only on factual analysis. If you are seeking to assess students' knowledge and understanding of the applicable rules, you should state that fact in the prompt. In other words, tell the students exactly what is being assessed.

A Word on the Use of Exams as Assessment Tools

As you ponder using exams as assessment tools, always bear in mind that you need not use the entire exam. For example, a Torts exam may include three one-hour essay questions. If you are using the exam to measure something like issue-spotting skills, you almost certainly do not need all three questions to do so. In fact, your measure is likely to be more valid and reliable if you simply pick one essay and focus on creating the most effective assessment of it that you can.

Just remember that if you are going to single out a question, you need to take steps to ensure that students' work on the other essay questions does not detract from their attention to that question. What law student hasn't spent too much time on one question at one point or another?

If you can make that question the first to be answered and collect it separately upon completion of the time limit, you can improve the reliability of your measure.

We both provide students with the cold rubrics described below as part of (or even before making) the assignment. Vicki provides students with cold rubrics for various legal writing assignments as the assignment is made. Lori posts the cold rubric she uses to grade essay exams on her course web page. Whether you are measuring for institutional assessment purposes or grading purposes, why hide the ball from students?

To ensure that results are as reliable as possible, the author of the assignment should create a rubric, a scoring guide, as part of the process of creating the assignment. Once students have submitted the completed assignment, the assessment task force working with the assignment's author and the scorer or scorers will create what we like to call a **hot rubric**, *which will include the **dimensions** of the assigned task, the relevant components of the task (i.e., the specific knowledge, skills, and or values involved), a scale of the varying levels of achievement, and a description of what each level of achievement looks like.* We will talk much more about the hot rubric and what it looks like in Chapter 6, but Table 5.2 serves as a quick preview.

Table 5.2. Hot Rubric Format

Task Description: _____ *(What task is the student expected to complete?)*			
Dimensions *(What components are needed to successfully complete the assigned task?)*	**Scale Level 1** *(What is the quality level of the work?)* Sophisticated	**Scale Level 2** *(What is the quality level of the work?)* Competent	**Scale Level 3** *(What is the quality level of the work?)* Not Yet Competent
Dimension 1	Description—*Sets forth the observable evidence that would establish this quality level for this dimension.*	Description	Description
Dimension 2	Description	Description	Description
Dimension 3	Description	Description	Description
Dimension 4	Description	Description	Description
Dimension 5	Description	Description	Description

In creating an assignment, its author, working with the assessment task force, needs to develop what we like to call a **cold rubric**, which is simply *a list of the dimensions of the assignment.* What components must you be able to observe in a student's performance for you to consider it to be successful? As the author is creating the assignment, he or she double-checks it against this list to make certain that the assignment's content is sufficient to allow measurement of each dimension. In other words, the author runs a validity check.

For example, some essay exam questions are simply more fact-rich than others. Some questions require relatively little factual analysis— they are more geared to assessing a student's understanding of some intricacy of the law (*e.g.,* the existence of a majority and minority rule). If the items listed in the rubric focus on your students' understanding of some intricacy of the law, your validity check will allow you to quickly see this question is not the right question for an assessment of students' ability to use the facts effectively.

The more task-specific (*i.e., dimension*-specific) you can make your rubric, the more valid your measure will be. When a scorer is forced to consciously assess whether the student accomplished each identified task, it keeps him or her from drifting away from the assessment's purpose. And when multiple scorers are involved, it keeps them from putting individual spins on what is required to satisfy the criterion or criteria at issue.

That having been said, we strongly advise against providing a laundry list of dimensions. The rubrics you create for purposes of institutional assessment are typically far more narrow and limited than those you may create to provide students with formative assessment on an assignment. For instance, drafting a memo takes a multitude of skill sets, each of which should be touched upon to one degree or another in providing students with a formative assessment of their work.

You may use exactly the same memo as an institutional assessment tool, but the rubric used would not touch on every necessary skill-set. If you are using the memo to evaluate students' issue-spotting skills, you would not list citation as a dimension. In contrast, citation would likely appear on the grading rubric.

Keeping the list of dimensions short simplifies the task for those asked to score and enhances the reliability of the measure.

Developing Indirect Assessments

Indirect assessment tools must also be carefully designed to maximize the validity and reliability of your measures. They pose their own unique challenges. As educators, we are used to assessing student work—that is our area of expertise. What we are not used to doing is formulating survey questions and facilitating focus groups.

Learn More About It

For a comprehensive dis-
cussion of the various
types of indirect assess-
ment methods, we
highly recommend the
following guide:

Mary J. Allen, *Assessing
Academic Programs in
Higher Education* (2004).

Our most important piece of advice on the use of indirect tools is to seek help from your institutional research office and other experts at your university. Given the small scale of most of your projects, it will likely be available for free, and it will be invaluable to you. (There may even be a graduate school class looking for this type of real-world project with which to assist.) If you happen to be at a freestanding law school, which does not have an institutional research office, look for consultants at neighboring schools.

With the exception of surveys, most of the indirect assessment tools that you are likely to use (interviews, focus groups, etc.) will provide qualitative rather than quantitative data. **Quantitative data** is *data that can be measured (i.e., assigned a number)*. **Qualitative data** is *data that can be observed and described but not measured*. You will need the assistance of experts in both gathering and interpreting this qualitative data.

Further, bringing in a trained neutral is a best practice. Those participating in focus groups, etc. are more likely to be open and honest with a neutral than with another member of the law school community.

Your assessment task force can certainly take a stab at formulating survey questions, but consulting with an expert as to his form is never a bad idea, and he can assist you in determining how to get a representative sample, etc. Experts know how to get to the information you really want. There are a multitude of tricks to the trade, such as seeking the same information in two different questions framed in two different ways. And, even with quantitative data, you will likely require assistance in interpreting its true meaning.

When possible, you should also consider "test driving" the questions you plan to pose in a survey, focus group, etc. Run a pilot program with a small number of participants to determine if the questions are clear (to help ensure reliability) and provide the information you desire (to help ensure validity).

Finally, we advise that you consider holding off on designing and using your indirect assessment tools until you have at least begun to gather data from your direct assessment tools. The indirect tools are best used to complement the direct tools. Even preliminary results from direct tools can assist you in determining the areas about which you would like more information. Indirect tools can help answer questions like why students are struggling with a particular skill and whether employers agree with the faculty's assessment that students are by and large competent at a particular skill. Use indirect tools to dig just a bit deeper.

Practical Example A (Analytical Skills): **Scenario A-3:**

Assume that your school has adopted the following learning outcome, "Graduates will demonstrate competency in analytical and problem-solving skills," and performance criterion, "When appropriate, graduates will demonstrate achievement of this learning outcome by analogizing the facts to and distinguishing the facts from those of precedent cases in specific and helpful ways to determine the likely outcome of the case." How might you "triangulate" your assessment using both direct and indirect assessment tools?

One direct tool could be a practice Multistate Performance Test (MPT). Much like a closed memo assignment, the MPT provides students with a case file, a library of relevant authorities, and a task to be accomplished. The task can be anything from drafting a memorandum or brief to designing a discovery plan.

Faculty in some of our doctrinal and skills courses have embedded this instrument in their courses and found it to be useful as a teaching tool as well as an assessment tool. It can be used in courses from the first to the third year.

The MPT provides a *subjective* direct assessment. You can use a released MPT from the NCBE or craft your own. For example, Vicki created an MPT for her first-year legal research and writing course that involved the statutory interpretation of the term "deadly weapon" as used in a felonious assault statute in the fictional jurisdiction of Franklin. The students were asked to write an objective memorandum analyzing whether a putty knife used by a defendant constituted a deadly weapon for the purposes of the felonious assault charge. She provided the students with a client interview, the felonious assault statute, the statutory definition of "deadly weapon," and excerpts from two fictional cases.

This assignment assessed many of the learning outcomes for the legal research and writing course. However, the assignment could also be used as an institutional assessment tool. A cold rubric for the institutional tool, focusing solely on the skill of analogical reasoning might look like this. Remember the cold rubric merely sets forth the dimensions (the relevant components) of the task of analogical reasoning. You'll create the hot rubric once you have some student samples to evaluate.

Task Description: *Analogizing the facts of a case to and distinguishing the facts of a case from applicable precedent to determine the likely outcome of the case.*

Dimensions	Scale Level 1 Sophisticated	Scale Level 2 Competent	Scale Level 3 Not Yet Competent
Draws analogies and distinctions when appropriate			
Articulates that the issue in the precedent case is the same as the present case			
Identifies each precedent case's determinative facts			
Compares each precedent case's determinative facts to the facts of the present case			
Explains the relevance of the comparisons			

A second direct tool could be a series of multiple-choice questions embedded in a course or courses. A classroom response system (*i.e.*, "clickers") could be used to track and tabulate responses. This tool would provide an *objective* direct assessment.

Here is how it might work. A professor agrees to embed multiple-choice and/or true/false questions into her course. Let's assume she teaches criminal law. During class, a question is displayed on a screen, and students use clickers similar to TV remote controls to select their answers. Once everyone has selected an answer, the results of the "vote" are displayed, and the professor uses the results as part of a discussion of what the correct answer is.

Clicker systems are very easy to use. It's the equivalent of setting up a PowerPoint slide. Some schools assign a clicker to each student, which allows that student's responses to be tracked by the professor. Some professors then use these responses as a kind of early warning system to make them aware if a student might benefit from intervention. Some professors also count a student's performance on each question towards that student's final grade. You would not have to do so for institutional assessment purposes, but as discussed above, making an assessment part of a grade would increase the reliability of the measure.

So how many questions might there be? Even one question per class would yield anywhere from 26 to 56, depending on the number of class meetings per week, and you could learn a great deal about your students' ability to analogize with even 12–15 questions. (You could even spread the burden across second-semester courses, having each professor ask three or four questions over the course of the semester.)

And what might a question look like? It would be based on whatever case or cases students read the night before. For example, assume that students had read *United States v. Conento-Pachon*, 723 F.2d 691 (9th Cir. 1984), which relates to the defense of duress, for class. During class, the following hypothetical would be distributed.

> *Defendant is charged with transportation of stolen property. For the past two years, he has been a member of the DSB, a local street gang. On the evening of May 15 at around 11:30 p.m. EST, members of the DSB allegedly broke into an Apple Store in Dayton, stealing over $95,000 in computers, phones, etc. At 8:05 p.m. EST on the evening of May 16, Defendant, who was driving a truck, was pulled over by police in Chicago for driving erratically. When police discovered marijuana in the cab, they searched the back of the truck and found the items that had been stolen from the Apple Store.*

> *Defendant confessed to prosecutors that he knew the items were stolen, but said that he had only transported them under duress. He said that at around 3:00 a.m., he had been awakened by a call from one of the DSB's leaders ordering him to come get the items and deliver them to a Chicago address. Defendant told the prosecutor he had been trying to straighten out his life and didn't want to do it, so he told the leader, "I'm sick, man. I can't do it." The leader hung up but called him back in half an hour and said, "I don't want to hear your excuses. If you know what's good for you, you will do it. Come get the stuff."*

> *Defendant said he was afraid of what might happen if he refused. He knew that the DSB had severely beaten gang members who had cooperated with police. His cousin, who was at the house when the calls were made told him, "Do it. Those guys are dangerous, and I don't want you hurt."*

So, he picked up the items, loaded up his truck, and drove off to Chicago. Another member of the DSB rode along with him to help unload the truck.

After students have been given a few moments to read the hypothetical and review their notes, the following would appear on the screen:

In *Conento-Pachon*, the court held that the facts were sufficient to support the existence of an immediate threat. Is the same outcome on this element likely in the hypothetical case?

    A. Yes, because like the defendant in *C-P*, Defendant believed he was threatened with death or serious bodily harm.

    B. Yes, because as in *C-P*, the large sums of money involved gave Defendant good reason to believe that the threat would be carried out.

    C. No, because unlike the specific threat to the defendant in *C-P*, the threat to the Defendant was a vague threat of some possible future harm.

    D. No, because unlike the threat to the defendant in *C-P*, the threat to the Defendant did not involve death.

The question focuses students on the key issue of what type of threat is needed to establish duress, which is a point the professor would be addressing in the normal course of business anyway. (The correct answer is "C.")

An indirect tool could be one or more survey questions embedded in the evaluations of a course or courses or included in a graduating student survey. They might look something like the following:

Checklist Style:

Which of the following activities do you feel competent to perform?

_____ Selecting cases that are factually useful for drawing analogies and distinctions.

_____ Making analogies and distinctions that compare and contrast the relevant facts in specific and helpful ways.

or

Frequency/Behavioral Style:

In drafting a legal memorandum or brief, I provide the reader with explicit analogies and distinctions:

_____ Never _____ Seldom _____ Sometimes _____ Often

or

Rating Scale Style:

Rate your ability to do the following on a scale of 1 to 3:

A. Select cases that are factually useful for drawing analogies and distinctions

   1. Nonexistent/Poor

   2. Functionally Adequate/Competent

   3. Advanced/Exemplary

B. Make analogies and distinctions that compare and contrast the relevant facts in specific and helpful ways.

   1. Nonexistent/Poor

   2. Functionally Adequate/Competent

   3. Advanced/Exemplary

None of the three tools provides a perfect picture of our students' learning, but together they provide us with a decent picture, and that is really all we are seeking.

Developing Performance Thresholds

The final task in designing direct tools and indirect quantifiable tools is to set **performance thresholds,** *minimum expectation levels,* for the group as a whole. Performance thresholds for direct tools describe your expectations for students' collective performance in a quantifiable way. Performance thresholds for indirect quantifiable tools describe your expectations as to what students, alumni, employers, and/or other constituencies should perceive students have learned and do so in a quantifiable way. Failure to achieve a threshold should trigger action of some kind on the part of your school.

Performance thresholds are most typically expressed as percentages. So, for instance, in the practical example above, the assessment task force might set a threshold that 80% of participating students receive a score of "competent" or higher on the MPT tool; 80% of participating students receive a score of "competent" or higher on the multiple-choice tool; and 90% of participating students rate themselves as at least "competent" at selecting cases and making analogies on the grad-

Distinguishing Performance Thresholds from Performance Targets

You may sometimes hear a performance threshold called a "performance target" or "target." However, as used in this Guide, the terms "threshold" and "target" are not synonymous.

A **target** is an *aspirational goal of what you would like your students to achieve*, whereas, a threshold sets the minimum standard. For example, your faculty may be pleased that a performance threshold of 80% was satisfied by your students (*e.g.*, 80% were competent at oral advocacy), but set a performance target of improving that number to 85% within five years.

uating student survey. If these measures are met, it serves as evidence that the criterion at issue is being satisfied.

The phrase that we have heard over and over is that thresholds should be "aggressive but attainable." Yes, you want every single student to walk out of your school having achieved the learning outcomes, but a threshold of 100% may not always be realistic.

As a rule of thumb, some experts argue for an 80% standard for thresholds. This threshold is based in large part on Bloom's mastery learning standard.

To date, the ABA has not set a threshold other than to state that students should be "competent" in the learning outcomes. So, it will be up to you and your faculty to define "competency" for your students.

The question you need to ask is what level of achievement the faculty would find to be acceptable. You want a threshold that is not so easy to achieve that it is meaningless. It should be something that pushes or stretches both the students and the school a bit, but it should not be impossible to achieve.

The faculty need not vote on every threshold, but the topic of what the faculty would find acceptable in general is worthy of discussion (and possibly a vote) at a faculty meeting. What could be more important than reaching a consensus on our expectations for our graduates' levels of achievement?

Since institutional outcomes assessment is such a new concept to law schools, we suspect that it will take some time for most law schools to find their feet in terms of setting thresholds. We are going to have to go through a few cycles to see how realistic our thresholds really are. And that's okay. We are striving for continuous improvement in our assessment processes, not perfection.

Settling on the "Who"

Having selected the proper tools, you are almost ready to begin collecting data. However, before you do, you need to consider one more thing: the "who." Who is going to actually make the assessment? The "who" here refers to two different sets of people: the scorers and the evaluators. We will spend more time in Chapter 6 discussing the role of both the scorers and the evaluators; however, when implementing your assessment activity, you want to give more than a passing thought as to who those people might be.

The **scorer** will be *the person or persons who actually score the data collected from subjective direct assessments using rubrics.* (You won't need a scorer for objective direct or indirect assessments because there is no "scoring" to be done!) The **evaluator** will be *the person or persons who evaluate the data collected from an assessment activity and draw conclusions about the data.* Evaluators are needed for all types of assessment tools.

While the scorers and evaluators will not begin their work until the Evaluation Stage, you need to nail down exactly who will be playing these important roles now. You do not want to go through the whole data collection process only to discover that you have no one to score or evaluate the data.

Selecting Scorers

Assessment would be exponentially easier if every criterion could be measured using a multiple-choice test. But the simple fact is that many things, such as oral advocacy skills, can only be measured using a direct subjective assessment tool. When such tools are used, your assessment is only as good as your scorer.

In selecting the appropriate scorer, take a long hard look at the activity itself—should someone familiar with this type of activity be scoring it? For example, will scoring this particular assessment tool take someone with a specialized knowledge or expertise? Will you want to hire someone to score the activity, and if so, will you have the funds to do so? Or, will you use faculty members to score or evaluate the activity? If so, will it be someone on the task force or a faculty member completely removed from the activity (potentially to lessen any possible bias)? If you choose to use a faculty member, how will they be "compensated" for their work—as part of their service to the law school or through a stipend? And again, is that in the budget? Additionally, how many scorers or evaluators do you need? We can't answer these questions for you, but we can pass along some advice.

Good scorers can come from the ranks of the faculty or from outside your law school.

The benefit of using faculty members is several fold. First, they understand law school pedagogy and have a familiarity with student work product. Second, their involvement in assessment is a positive step in creating a culture of assessment at your institution. Assessment is not merely busy work for a committee or an accreditation task to be checked off and forgotten. It is a responsibility of the whole institution for the common good of improving student learning. Third, involving faculty in assessment projects provides for professional development opportunities. We call this the "light bulb effect," where faculty members who have yet to experiment with multiple formative assessments and rubrics can be "enlightened" by seeing how to break down components in an assignment and learn how to isolate components. We have heard this story over and over: "I teach close case reading, but I am not sure how to assess it."

But using faculty as scorers can have some drawbacks. The most significant drawback is the bias towards a curve. Carefully crafted rubrics, created with scorer involvement, can help overcome this tendency. Scorer involvement in the creation of rubrics will be discussed in Chapter 6.

You will also need to find a way to deal with the fact that you will be asking someone to do extra work. If you chose to use a faculty member, the law school in the form of the dean must determine how will they be "compensated" for that work.

If the assessment tool is an embedded tool that a particular faculty member created and actually graded as part of his or her course work, then that faculty member should not be used as the scorer. The grading process demands a holistic approach, and having applied such an approach to paper after paper, it is difficult to switch gears and isolate one learning outcome.

Outside scorers can bring their own strengths to the table. Their assessment may be more credible to the public because it comes from "outside" the institution, and they lack the bias possessed by faculty members, who are accustomed to curving. They may also have expertise in exactly the skill set you seek to measure. For example, who better than judges and litigators to assess oral advocacy skills?

But outside scorers have their downside as well. Legal professionals may be overly critical. They may not remember their own struggles to learn their profession. As is the case with law faculty, a good rubric can help keep them on track. Another downside is that there may be a cost. You will want to compensate or otherwise recognize the outside evaluators in some manner. Again the question arises, is some form of compensation in the budget?

Outside scorers need not be "professional assessors." Think who your resources are: adjuncts, field supervisors, alumni, bar examiners, judges, members of the advisory board, etc. The best outside scorers have the following qualifications:

1. Substantial experience and reputation for competency in the law.
2. Experience with student work product or a genuine willingness to get up to speed on student performance levels.
3. An understanding of learning outcomes and performance criteria.
4. Training in using rubrics.

It will be up to you to provide numbers three and four.

Finally, we have one last piece of advice on the subject of scorers. Use multiple scorers. Even when armed with a great rubric, scorers bring their own views to the table with them. Using multiple scorers takes out individual biases and improves the reliability of the measure. This is called "**scorer triangulation**," *which involves using multiple scorers to assess performance on a tool.* We recommend that you use at least three people as scorers—you always need that "tie-breaker" if there is an issue in scoring the results. You can use all faculty members, all outside evaluators, or a mix.

Selecting Evaluators

Evaluators are charged with the challenging task of interpreting the data that has been gathered. As will be discussed in greater detail in Chapter 6, they are tasked with determining whether students' performance is "good enough" to establish the learning outcome has been met. If students' performance fails to reach the desired thresholds, they will be charged with identifying the possible root causes for the failure and developing and implementing an action plan to address the failure.

The members of the task force in charge of this outcome are the chief evaluators. As discussed in Chapter 4, the task force for each outcome should be carefully chosen with a focus on appointing faculty members with particular expertise in the area being assessed. The task force will be digesting the data and reporting it — so, its familiarity at the Evaluation Stage cannot be downplayed.

The task force should seek out assistance where there are gaps in its collective expertise. As noted above, institutional researchers, statisticians, and others can be of invaluable assistance when it comes to interpreting results. Ideally, they will be involved in every aspect of the project from its creation, to its evaluation, to the final report to the faculty as a whole.

Documenting Your Progress

As discussed above, using an Assessment Blueprint Form (*See* Table 5.3) is a great way to keep you on task and to document the progress of the task force. Now that you understand the various activities in which you will be engaged, let's look at exactly how you might memorialize them.

Although we are discussing this form near the end of the chapter, please be aware that the wisest course is to document your work as you go along. For instance, you should not wait until all three tools are fully developed to start adding items to the form.

The requirements of the first row are for the most part self-explanatory. One point we want to emphasize is that it really is important to list the names of those serving on the task force and update that list as membership changes. This criterion will be assessed again at some point in the future, and the members of that task force might have some questions about the work of this task force. Make it easy for your successors to track you down.

A second important point is that if your task force has developed an agreed upon interpretation of the criterion, you should attach it as an appendix to the form. Referring back to this interpretation throughout the process will help keep the task force on track. The interpretation will also be of interest to faculty and others reviewing the work of the task force now and in the future.

The purpose of Column A is to identify and describe the assessment tools you have selected. As you can see from Table 5.3, the description provided on the form can be quite brief. You simply need to describe the nature of the tool (*e.g.,* oral argument, memo, focus group, etc.).

Along with the description, you should provide an appendix that contains a clean copy of the tool. Files get cleaned out, and hard drives get erased. You should never depend on being able to retrieve a file from anyone's personal "archive." Add key files in your Assessment Blueprint as soon as practicable.

For some tools, you may also need to attach an appendix with a brief description of how the tool works. For instance, while readers will readily understand what a final exam is and how it works as an assessment tool, they may not have a clue as to how embedded multiple-choice questions work as an assessment tool. The necessary explanations will typically be brief, a paragraph or two will often do.

Column B requires you to identify the tool type: direct or indirect; objective or subjective; and quantitative or qualitative. The purpose of this column is to compel the task force to review its choice of tools to ensure they are of different types. As discussed above, the purpose of triangulation is to allow an issue to be viewed from multiple perspectives. If all of the tools are direct objective tools or all of the tools are indirect qualitative tools, the task force may be limiting its perspective.

The next few columns are easy to fill out. Column C requires you to identify where and when the data will be collected. You are essentially providing the reader with a timeline. Column D requires you to set forth the desired performance threshold, if any, for each tool. Column E requires you to identify the scorers/tabulators. Finally, Column F requires you to identify who will be responsible for evaluating the data.

When completed, this simple form, along with its appendices, provides everything your primary stakeholders—faculty, administrators, and accreditors—might wish to know about your implementation process. If someone simply wants a quick summary, the form itself provides the most critical information. If someone wants to dive into the details, the appendices provide them.

Table 5.3. Assessment Blueprint Form

Assessment Blueprint Form

Outcome: *E.g.,* Graduates will demonstrate competency in analytical and problem-solving skills.

Criterion: *E.g.,* When appropriate, graduates will demonstrate achievement of this learning outcome by analogizing the facts to and distinguishing the facts from those of precedent cases in specific and helpful ways to determine the likely outcome of the case. An explanation of the task force's interpretation is attached as Appendix ____.

Assessment Cycle: *E.g.,* 2015–2022

Assessment Task Force Members: (List the names and years of service on the task force.) *E.g.,* Professor Bella Cattus (2015–Present) (Recorder); Professor Richard Thomas (2015–Present); Professor Mel Victorias (2015–Present)

Column A	Column B	Column C	Column D	Column E	Column F
Tools/Measures	Tool Type (Direct or Indirect; Objective or Subjective; Quantitative or Qualitative)	Where and when will data be collected (*i.e.*, in what class or other setting)?	What is the performance threshold?	Who will score/tabulate the data?	Who will evaluate the data?
Tool 1 *E.g.,* MPT Problem A copy of this assignment is attached as Appendix ____.	Direct Subjective	Legal Writing II (Section 03) Professor VanZandt Spring 2018	80% or more students achieve at least competency	1) Professor Zink 2) Professor Rucker 3) Professor Platfoot-Lacey	Assessment Task Force
Tool 2 *E.g.,* Embedded Multiple-Choice Questions A copy of this assignment, including a description of the process, is attached as Appendix ____.	Direct Objective	Criminal Law (Section 01) Professor Shaw Fall 2017	80% or more students achieve at least competency	Computer Scoring	Assessment Task Force
Tool 3 *E.g.,* Graduating Student Survey A copy of this survey is attached as Appendix ____.	Indirect Quantitative	Dean of Students' Office Spring 2018	90% or more graduates report they feel competent at each listed task.	Computer Scoring	Assessment Task Force with assistance of office of institutional research

* Adapted from http://www.apta.org/outcomesassessment/, with permission of the American Physical Therapy Association. Copyright © 2006 American Physical Therapy Association.

Activity 5: Collect Data

Once you have your tools and your people in place, you are ready to move full speed ahead with data collection. We have only two words of advice on this activity. First, make someone personally accountable for the data gathering for each project. When you have a task force or committee, it is all too easy to assume that *someone* will make certain that what needs to take place is taking place. Assign a different task force member to head each project, working directly with the professor or other data collector to make certain that everything is on schedule.

Second, make sure that you actually have a schedule for each tool with deadlines for completing a first draft, task force review, data collection, etc. The head of each project should provide monthly updates to the task force on the progress achieved.

Once the data has been collected, it is time to move on to the Evaluation Stage!

Action List

Create an Assessment Blueprint for the performance criterion that you are assessing this cycle.

Activity 1: Review performance criteria that defined the outcome.

- Choose the order in which you assess the criteria.
- Select which performance criterion or criteria will be the focus of the assessment cycle.
- Suggest formal amendments to criterion, if needed.

Activity 2: Map (or review map of) where your school addresses and assesses the criteria.

Activity 3: Use the map to determine where data will/can be collected.

Activity 4: Develop and/or review assessment tools used to assess performance criteria.

- Choose three tools—two direct and one indirect (Fill out Columns A, B, and C in the Assessment Blueprint).
- Test the tools for validity and reliability.
- Create cold rubrics for the subjective direct tools, if any.
- Set performance thresholds for all three tools (Fill out Column D in the Assessment Blueprint).

- Set sample size and sampling method for each tool.
- Select scorers and evaluators (Fill out Column E in the Assessment Blueprint).

Activity 5: Collect the data.

- Assign responsibility to one person for collection of data.
- Create and adhere to schedule for assessment cycle.

Chapter 6

How?
Outcomes Assessment:
The Evaluation Stage

Learning Outcome: Readers will thoroughly evaluate the data they collect, effectively communicate key findings to their stakeholders, and, if the findings warrant change, close the loop by developing and implementing an action plan and making any needed permanent improvements to their educational programs.

Readers will demonstrate achievement of this learning outcome by

✓ Systematically gathering and accurately scoring and/or tallying the data collected.

✓ Using performance thresholds and other appropriate means to interpret the results of the individual assessment measures to determine if they suggest the performance criterion at issue has been achieved.

✓ Conducting a triangulated analysis (*i.e.,* comparing the results of all the individual measures) to determine whether the performance criterion at issue has been achieved or a need exists for change or further analysis.

✓ Developing reasonable hypotheses as to the possible root causes of both favorable and unfavorable results.

✓ Developing and implementing a specific action plan to address any failures, accurately assessing the efficacy of actions taken under the plan, and taking a leadership role in making any needed institutional changes.

✓ Creating and implementing a communication plan appropriate for each group of stakeholders.

✓ Meticulously documenting their work in a Triangulated Analysis Form and, if needed, a Specific Action Plan.

You are now entering the home stretch. Having implemented your outcome measures projects and collected the necessary data, you are set to begin the Evaluation Stage. You have come a long way since you first began thinking about outcomes assessment, but the race is not over. Historically, law schools have been good at collecting data but mediocre when it comes to putting it to good use. We start the race well but never make it to the finish line.

Figure 6.A

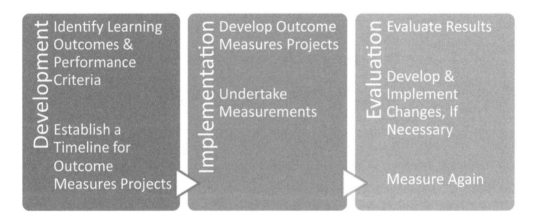

To illustrate, here is a small challenge for you. Think about the last time your school administered the Law School Survey of Student Engagement (LSSSE), most schools' most significant effort to collect data about students. Can you name the most significant findings of this instrument? Were the findings compared to other data collected by the school? Did any negative findings generate discussion of possible improvements to your programming by faculty? Was there follow-up on this discussion? Was the need for change further explored and/or were any changes actually made? Our guess is that most of you answered "No" to one or more of these questions.

As described in Chapters 4 and 5 and shown in Figure 6.B, the assessment of each outcome has a natural cycle that must be *completed* for assessment to be meaningful. Law schools are quite simply not completing the cycle.

Figure 6.B

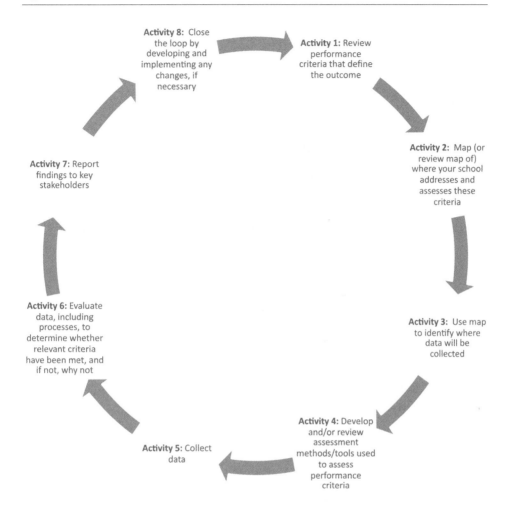

For institutional assessment to have any value, the traditional law school pattern of merely collecting data must be broken. We need to learn to effectively evaluate the data we collect, including finding the root cause or causes of any failure to meet a criterion or criteria (Activity 6); communicate key findings to our stakeholders (Activity 7); and, if the findings warrant change, close the loop by developing and implementing an action plan and making any needed permanent improvements to our educational programs (Activity 8). This Chapter describes how to effectively undertake each of these activities.

But before you move on to the nuts and bolts of closing the loop, we ask that you take a moment and think about what a change for the better this process will bring to legal education. Law faculty members do care about their students' education, and they have made individual efforts to address perceived weaknesses. But properly done, outcomes assessment will create thoughtful, systematic, evidence-based opportunities for change and improvement at the institutional level.

It will also create accountability. When a problem is identified, the assessment task force members cannot simply shrug their shoulders and voice their concerns. They are required to do something. That something may or may not work, but at least we are trying, and some efforts will succeed.

Turning Raw Data into Useable Information — Activity 6: Evaluate Assessment Data, Including Processes

You will begin the Evaluation Stage with lots of raw data in hand. Your first mission, should you choose to accept it, is to turn that raw data into *meaningful* measures, measures that answer the fundamental question "Are our students achieving competency in the learning outcome or performance criterion?" But simply generating numbers is not enough. True evaluation requires that you also make some attempt to interpret these measures, to explain why they are what they are.

Table 6.1. Triangulated Analysis Form

Outcome: Criterion: Assessment Cycle: 20__–20__ Assessment Task Force Members:					
	Column G	Column H	Column I	Column J	Column K
◄——— Link with Assessment Blueprint	Record your findings and indicate if there is a trigger for change or further analysis.	Analysis of data collected for relevant criterion. What does your triangulated analysis indicate?	Hypothesis? What are the possible causes of the findings (favorable or unfavorable)? List as many as may apply.	Report findings to appropriate stakeholders.	———► Link with Specific Action Plan, if necessary
Tool 1					
Tool 2					
Tool 3					

* Adapted from http://www.apta.org/outcomesassessment/, with permission of the American Physical Therapy Association. Copyright © 2006 American Physical Therapy Association.

So, where you do begin? As discussed in Chapter 5, ideally you are triangulating your measurement (*i.e.*, employing three different tools to measure achievement of the outcome/criterion). Your first task in completing your evaluation mission will be to analyze the individual measures. Your second task will be to analyze what the results mean when considered in combination.

As discussed in Chapter 5, documenting the work of the assessment task force is vital. You will begin the Evaluation Stage with your Assessment Blueprint in hand. As you progress through Activity 6, you can use the Triangulated Analysis Form in Table 6.1 to document your findings. (The last column of this form, which requires you to report your findings, will be addressed under Activity 7.)

When completed, this form and its appendices will be placed in the Institutional Assessment Plan binder with the other materials relating to the outcome being measured.

Analyzing the Individual Measures

Your analysis of *each* individual measure will require a stepped process. You must gather, score/tabulate, and analyze the data collected.

Step 1: Gather the Data Collected

Step 1 is easy. You simply need to make certain that the outputs, etc. to be measured are actually in the possession of the task force and/or any needed scorers/tabulators. Ideally, a different member of the task force should be responsible for supervising each assessment project and making sure everything that is supposed to be happening is happening.

Someone who is not on the assessment task force may well be the person in possession of your raw data. For example, your dean of students may be the person to whom graduating student surveys are submitted. If someone else is in control, try to retrieve the data as soon as possible. It's all too easy for something to be inadvertently misplaced, altered, or destroyed.

As discussed at length in Chapter 5, if you are using a sample, you will have made decisions as to its size and content before undertaking the project. Now, you need to pull that sample, which will often require help from the registrar or another data collector. Always provide a written explanation as to how the sample is to be drawn.

If your school has an assessment coordinator, she should receive copies of all materials gathered and produced by the individual assessment task forces. Having a central repository will be an incredibly helpful thing come site visit time. A site visit team could ask to see the work product on which an assessment was based. We are not saying it will, but you never know. So, you should at least retain the relevant outputs until your next site visit has been completed. As discussed in Chapter 5, it's all about documentation!

Practical Example A (Analytical Skills): Scenario A-4:

Once again, assume that your school has adopted the learning outcome "Graduates will demonstrate competency in analytical and problem-solving skills" and performance criterion "When appropriate, graduates will demonstrate achievement of this learning outcome by analogizing the facts to and distinguishing the facts from those of precedent cases in specific and helpful ways to determine the likely outcome of the case." You have opted to triangulate your assessment of the achievement of this criterion by using three tools:

1. a practice Multistate Performance Test (MPT)—a direct subjective tool.

2. a series of multiple-choice questions embedded in a course and answered using a classroom response system ("clickers")—a direct objective tool.

3. a series of survey questions embedded in a course evaluation—an indirect quantitative tool.

Since the **MPT** is a subjective tool, which required some effort to score, the assessment task force opted to measure only a sample of the student performances. Assume that 120 students took the practice MPT. Under the rule of thumb provided in Chapter 5, that means that a minimum of 12 MPT performances should be measured. To enhance the reliability of the measure, the assessment task force opted to measure 20 performances. (Assume it had the scoring resources needed to score this larger number.) It opted for a simple random sampling. The registrar used a random number generator to select the answers to be assessed. (It could just as easily have opted to conduct a cluster random sampling. For instance, if the MPT were administered to 6 small sections consisting of 20 students, it could have opted to score one of those sections.)

Since the **multiple-choice question project** is an objective tool, no effort was required to score it. Thus, the task force opted to conduct a census, an assessment of the performances of the entire group. The task force member responsible for this project simply needed to obtain the spreadsheet of the scores, which had been automatically generated by the classroom response system, from the faculty member involved.

Since the **survey questions** provided a quantitative tool, again, no effort was required to score this measure. So again, the task force opted to conduct a census, considering every response to the questions. The task force member responsible for this project simply needed to obtain the spreadsheet of the responses from the registrar.

Step 2: Score/Tally the Data Collected

The goal for Step 2, scoring and/or tallying the data collected, is simple. You want to take all of that meaningless raw data you have collected and turn it into something your school can actually use. The amount of time, effort, and skill required for Step 2 depends entirely on the type of assessment tool being used, direct subjective, direct objective, indirect quantitative, or indirect qualitative.

Direct Subjective Tools

As you may recall from Chapter 5, direct assessment tools allow the assessor to examine or observe student work product to determine what specific learning has taken place. Direct *subjective* assessment tools, such as essay exams, memoranda, and oral arguments, require specialized expertise to score correctly. To score student performances using a subjective tool, you must finalize your rubric (*i.e.,* make your "cold" rubric "hot" by drafting descriptions that set your benchmark for competency); norm your scorers; and use the rubric to score the individual assignments.

Finalizing Your Rubric

During the Implementation Stage, the author of each subjective tool, working with the assessment task force, developed its cold rubric. The cold rubric provides a list of the dimensions of the assignment, the components you must be able to observe in a student's performance for you to consider it to be successful in relation to the criterion or criteria being assessed. For example, the cold rubric in Table 6.2 lists the dimensions of the successful use of case analogies in an objective memorandum of law.

Table 6.2. Cold Rubric Sample

Task Description: Analogizing the facts of a case to and distinguishing the facts of a case from applicable precedent to determine the likely outcome of the case.

Dimensions	Scale Level 1 Sophisticated	Scale Level 2 Competent	Scale Level 3 Not Yet Competent
Draws analogies and distinctions when appropriate			
Articulates that the issue in the precedent case is the same as the present case			
Identifies each precedent case's determinative facts			
Compares each precedent case's determinative facts to the facts of the present case			
Explains the relevance of the comparisons			

Now, the time has come to complete the rubric (to make it "hot") by filling in the blanks (*i.e.*, the descriptions for each scale level of each dimension). The descriptions set forth the observable evidence that would establish each quality level for each dimension. (*See* Table 6.3.)

Table 6.3. Hot Rubric Format

Task Description:

_____.

What task is the student expected to complete?

Dimensions (What components are needed to successfully complete the task?)	Scale Level 1 *What is the quality level of the task?* Sophisticated	Scale Level 2 *What is the quality level of the work?* Competent	Scale Level 3 *What is the quality level of the work?* Not Yet Competent
Dimension 1	Description—*Sets forth the observable evidence that would establish this quality level for this dimension.*	Description	Description
Dimension 2	Description	Description	Description
Dimension 3	Description	Description	Description
Dimension 4	Description	Description	Description
Dimension 5	Description	Description	Description

The author of the tool in question could provide the descriptions, but we recommend that others be involved in this process as well. Specifically, we believe that collaboration among the author, the assessment task force, and the scorers will ultimately provide the most valid and reliable data. The author knows the ins and outs of the assignment, and the assessment task force probably understands the criterion or criteria being examined better than anyone. Involving the scorers in drafting the descriptions helps ensure that they fully understand what it is they are being asked to measure. Having everyone on the same page is invaluable.

You may be wondering why the descriptions could not simply have been included when the rubric was created (*i.e.,* during the Implementation Stage). The answer is that they could have been drafted at that point, but there is a benefit to allowing everyone to read a few outputs before attempting to draft the descriptions. It is extraordinarily helpful to see what a good paper looks like before you attempt to describe its characteristics.

The one danger you need to avoid is turning this process into an exercise in curving the results. Your goal is to determine what a competently completed paper looks like, *not* what an average paper looks like. The standard for competency is an objective one.

Adding the descriptions is honestly not that difficult. For each dimension, you simply need to ask yourself the following questions: "What would I see (or not see) in a sophisticated performance?" "What would I see (or not see) in a competent performance?" "What would I see (or not see) in a not yet competent performance?"

It is usually easiest for the group to begin its creation of descriptions by looking at what it believes to be one or two excellent/"sophisticated" outputs. Discuss what qualities make them stand out, and list those qualities in the appropriate row and column.

In drafting the descriptions, be as specific as you can about what the scorer should see. Notice that in the sample hot rubric set forth in Practical Example A, Scenario A-5, we referenced the specific cases and facts that could be used to demonstrate a dimension is satisfied. Also, try to avoid using terms like "good" and "poor" that call for subjective judgments. The goal is to keep the scorers on the same page.

Next, repeat the process by reviewing one or two outputs that the group agrees are less than excellent but at least minimally acceptable/ "competent." Use the descriptions you drafted for the sophisticated outputs as a starting point for drafting this column. How are these outputs flawed? What is missing? Perhaps more important, how are these outputs like those deemed sophisticated? What qualities make them acceptable? What is the minimum the student must do to demonstrate competency?

The last question is really at the heart of the matter. As a group, you need to decide what skill level is required of an entry-level lawyer. That issue is deserving of serious thought and discussion. The more perspectives you have at the table, the better. For example, an outside scorer who is a practitioner may help remind the group that you can be a fine attorney without having the sophisticated skills needed to write a stellar law review article. (Law professors occasionally forget not everyone is like them, and (gasp!) not everyone has to be like them.) In considering competence, ask yourself if you would feel comfortable having this student serve as counsel for a friend or family member.

Finally, repeat the process one last time by reviewing one or two outputs that the group agrees are not even minimally acceptable. Use the descriptions you drafted for the competent outputs as a starting point for drafting this column. How are these outputs different? What additional flaws are present? What is missing?

Practical Example A (Analytical Skills): Scenario A-5:
Multistate Performance Test (MPT) Hot Rubric
Task Description: Analogizing the facts of a case to and distinguishing the facts of a case from applicable precedent to determine the likely outcome of the case.

Dimensions *What components are needed to successfully complete the task?*	Scale Level 1 *What is the quality level of the task?* Sophisticated	Scale Level 2 *What is the quality level of the work?* Competent	Scale Level 3 *What is the quality level of the work?* Not Yet Competent
Draws analogies and distinctions when appropriate	Makes *continual*, *useful* analogies and distinctions to *key cases* (*Covington* and *Cathel*) that are jurisdictionally appropriate and factually useful for drawing comparisons. In sum, the student's case selection demonstrates her ability to discern the legally significant facts, and her case use shows her *highly developed ability* to recognize points of law that can and should be clarified through the use of analogies.	Makes *sporadic*, but *useful* analogies and distinctions to *key cases*, but could have drawn more comparisons. In sum, while the student missed some opportunities to provide clarifying analogies and distinctions, her case selection demonstrates her ability to discern the legally significant facts, and her case use shows her *basic ability* to recognize points of law that can be clarified.	Makes no useful analogies and distinctions to *key cases*. In sum, either the student is not attempting to analogize at all or lacks the ability to discern which cases are jurisdictionally appropriate and factually useful.
Articulates that the issue in each precedent case is the same as the present case	Articulates that both cases involve the interpretation of the element "deadly weapon."	Articulates that both cases involve the interpretation of the element "deadly weapon."	Fails to articulate that both cases involve the interpretation of the element "deadly weapon."
Identifies each precedent case's determinative facts	Fact sensitivity is apparent through the rich explanation of the relevant details of precedent case, including the length of the blade of the carpet knife, the fact the blade was out, the fact the defendant was "brandishing the knife," and the fact defendant was not using it to cut carpet or for any normal use.	Could be more fact sensitive, but explains enough of the relevant details of precedent case to allow the reader to understand the basis for the court's decision.	Factually weak and fails to explain enough of the relevant details of precedent case to allow the reader to understand the basis for the court's decision.
Compares each precedent case's determinative facts to the facts of the present case	Analogies and distinctions are made explicit. The facts of the precedent case are expressly compared and contrasted to the facts of the case in specific and helpful ways and are used to support legal arguments and conclusions. The student's analysis expressly compares all or almost all of the relevant details of the carpet knife to the putty knife and defendants' uses of the knives.	Analogies and distinctions are made but they could be made more explicit by making fact-to-fact comparisons and by tying facts directly to conclusions. Comparisons are overly conclusive versus being analytical and nuanced. The student's analysis compares many of the details of the carpet knife to the putty knife and defendants' uses of the knives.	Analogies and distinctions are not explicit, non-existent, or uniformly weak. The student's analysis does not compare *the details* of the carpet knife to the putty knife and defendants' uses of the knives.
Explains the relevance of the comparison	Always explains the relevance of the comparison (*i.e.*, why the comparison matters) and states the likely outcome.	Usually explains the relevance of the comparison and states the likely outcome.	Rarely or never explains the relevance of the comparison and/or the likely outcome.

Developing a Rating Scale — Setting Your Benchmark for Competency

There is one more very important question that must be answered before the scorers can get to work. What happens if a student is found to be competent on some, but not all, of the dimensions?

For example, using the rubric shown in Scenario A-5, let's assume that a student named Claudia scored "sophisticated" on one, drawing analogies and distinctions when appropriate; two, articulating that the issue in the precedent case is the same as the present case; three identifying the precedent's determinative facts; and, four, comparing the precedent case's determinative facts to the facts of the present case. Unfortunately, she simply did not understand the need to explain the relevance of the comparison, so she received a score of "not yet competent" on that dimension. What should her overall score be, sophisticated, competent, or not yet competent?

The task force could decide to look at the **average of the scores** for the various dimensions. Assume that the score for a sophisticated performance is 1; the score for a competent performance is 2; and the score for a not yet competent performance is 3. The task force could decide that any average score of 2 or lower rates an overall score of "competent." Claudia's average score is 1.4, so she would receive a score of competent under this scheme.

While using this type of averaging system is one possibility, we believe that the better practice is to **require a score of at least "competent" on every dimension to receive an overall score of "competent."** These dimensions were chosen because each was deemed essential to satisfying the criterion of demonstrating the ability to analogize the facts of a case to applicable precedent to determine the likely outcome of the case. Either Claudia can make proper use of analogies, or she cannot do so. If one of these dimensions is lacking, Claudia is not yet competent. Our educational programs are only going to improve if we recognize our weaknesses and seek to correct them.

Whatever scheme you choose to use, you must make it clear to the scorers, so that they can provide the task force with an overall score for each student.

Norming the Scorers

A final step you can use to increase the reliability of the scoring is to **"norm"** the scorers. **"Norming"** *is an effort to calibrate the scoring of individual scorers.* Inter-rater reliability is required for accurate assessment data. Ideally, every dimension on every paper would receive the same score from every scorer. Since we do not live in an ideal world, that is not likely to happen, but there is one simple step that you can take to make it more likely.

Having involved the scorers in the creation of the hot rubric, they should already share a common understanding of the descriptions. You can test that understanding by asking each of the three to score a sample assignment or two using the rubric and then sit down together and compare their scores. If discrepancies exist, they should talk them through and seek to come to a consensus as to exactly what each description requires. The idea is to reconcile any major differences in interpretation.

If they cannot reach a consensus, you should consider reconvening the group that created the rubric (*i.e.,* the tool's author, the assessment task force, and the scorers) and revising the descriptions to improve their clarity.

Scoring the Samples

Finally, the time has come to put the scorers to work. If they have a carefully crafted rubric in hand and have been normed, the scoring process itself should take very little time. Ideally, each will score the samples in one sitting (or at most, in one day). Each scorer should provide the assessment task force with a completed rubric that provides the score for each dimension as well as an overall score.

The task force member charged with overseeing the completion of the project should compile the scores for each student and determine what level of competency he achieved. If at least two scorers out of three scored his overall performance "competent" or "sophisticated," it is viewed as having satisfied the criterion at issue. If at least two scorers out of three scored his overall performance "not yet competent," it is viewed as not having satisfied the criterion at issue.

Direct Objective Tools

The scoring process for direct *objective* tools is quite simple. As discussed in Chapter 5, objective tools, such as multiple-choice and true/false questions, require no specialized expertise to score correctly. You need not worry about developing rubrics, undertaking norming, etc., and the scoring has likely already been done by a computer.

The one task on which the assessment task force does need to focus is developing a rating scale (*i.e.,* setting the benchmark for competency). You need to determine what percentage of questions must have been answered correctly for a student to be deemed "competent" and the number required for him to be deemed "sophisticated." Then, you need to tally how many students achieved those scores. It's that easy.

Indirect Quantitative Tools

As discussed in Chapter 5, indirect measures are based upon opinion, either the student's opinion or any other observer's opinion.

Quantitative data is data that can be measured (*i.e.*, assigned a number). The real work with this type of tool is front-loaded. The questions must be drafted with extreme care and efforts must be made to maximize the response rate.

Quantitative indirect tools, such as surveys using closed-ended questions, typically take little to no effort to score/tabulate. For example, it would be easy to tabulate the results of a survey that asked students to complete the following sentence: "In drafting a legal memorandum or brief, I provide the reader with explicit analogies and distinctions: never, seldom, sometimes, or often." The results are usually tabulated using a computer.

Indirect Qualitative Tools

In contrast, tabulating the results of qualitative tools requires both time and expertise. As explained in Chapter 5, qualitative data is data that can be observed and described but not measured. Examples include data gathered from focus groups, structured interviews, and open-ended survey questions. You will need the assistance of experts in tabulating this qualitative data in a way that is meaningful and easily understandable.

For example, if the tool involved is a focus group, the facilitator is usually charged with indexing and managing the data collected. When, as is often the case, multiple focus groups are employed, the task becomes even more challenging. **Indexing** *requires the facilitator to read through the transcripts or summaries and assign a code/label to each piece of information that reflects the question to which it relates and the perspective expressed.* **Managing** *requires the facilitator to bring together (collate) all of the pieces of information assigned the same code/label.* Indexing and managing can be done manually or through the use of sophisticated computer software.

So, if the first question addressed by a focus group of externship supervisors is whether your students are able to devise and implement an effective research strategy, positive responses might be coded "1A" and negative responses might be coded "1B." And if the second question is whether your students research in an efficient and cost-effective manner, positive responses might be coded "2A" and negative responses might be coded "2B." (It could even be broken down further to "1A1," "1A2," etc. if sub-themes emerge.)

Step 3: Analyze the Data Collected

The goal for Step 3, analyzing the data collected, is to begin to make meaning of the data, to use the individual tools to begin to answer the question "Are our students achieving competency in the learning outcome or performance criterion?" As was the case with Step 2, the amount of time, effort, and skill required for Step 3 depends entirely on the type of assessment tool being used, direct subjective, direct objective, indirect quantitative, or indirect qualitative.

Direct Tools & Indirect Quantitative Tools

The final task in evaluating performance on the individual direct subjective tools, direct objective tools, and indirect quantifiable tools is to apply the performance thresholds set during the Implementation Stage. As discussed in Chapter 5, performance thresholds describe your expectations for students' collective performance in a quantifiable way.

The question is simple. Has your students' collective performance met the threshold set by your faculty for each tool?

Practical Example A (Analytical Skills): Scenario A-6:

If your faculty set a performance threshold that 80% of participating students receive a score of "competent" or higher on the MPT tool and 87% received such a score, you have evidence in hand that your students are able to analogize the facts of a case to applicable precedent to determine the likely outcome of the case.

Indirect Qualitative Tools

The final task in evaluating performance on the individual indirect qualitative tools, such as focus groups, is more challenging. The facilitator must **interpret** the results. There is no "bright line" performance threshold. **Interpretation** *involves developing summary statements that reflect the common themes that emerged with regard to each question.* Accurately summarizing the results takes time and expertise.

The facilitator's report of her analysis can take many different forms from narratives to bullet-pointed lists. It is typically organized around the major questions being explored. In terms of content, for each question, it summarizes the major and minor themes identified. It should describe the strength of the views expressed by participants on various issues (*e.g.,* were participants mildly or deeply concerned), and if there is disagreement on an issue, identify the different perspectives held. Along with the summaries, direct quotes may be used to depict the tone of the participants. *See* Scenario B-1 for an example.

Practical Example B (Research Skills): Scenario B-1:

For purposes of this example, assume that your school has adopted the following learning outcome: "Graduates will research effectively and efficiently." Among the tools being used to measure achievement of this outcome is a focus group consisting of externship field supervisors. The facilitator's report on a question to the focus group might look something like this:

Do the students research in an efficient and cost-effective manner?

Although there was a general consensus that students knew how to engage in research on-line and were often seen as better online researchers than the externship field supervisors, there was some skepticism as to the accuracy of the research and whether it was being done in the most cost-effective manner.

First, the field supervisors noted the tension between effective research and accurate research, generally noting that students are able to do research quickly but sacrifice some of the accuracy of the results.

- "Sometimes students are more focused on getting the answer quickly, instead of getting the right answer."

- "Students don't seem to realize that although I need the answer now, I need it to be the right answer. So, if you can't find the right answer, don't give me anything at all."

Second, a number of field supervisors opined that students were not comfortable using free online research sources, like Casemaker.

- "They are so used to using LEXIS and Westlaw in school that they don't even want to think about using something different. They don't understand the business side of practice at all."

Documenting Your Progress

Having completed your individual measures, you are ready to fill in Column G of the Triangulated Analysis Form. (*See* Table 6.4.) The purpose of this section is simply to memorialize your findings and indicate if the desired performance threshold for each direct tool and each indirect quantifiable tool has been met. This brief description is all that you absolutely must provide, but if your assessment task force has prepared a more detailed report or memorandum on the results, you may attach it as an appendix to the form.

You should also attach a clean copy of any rubrics employed. By the time this criterion is examined again, the assessment task force may have an entirely different composition. The new task force members will not want to reinvent the wheel, and they will not want to have to track you down and ask you to find the rubric that you know is "somewhere on an old flash drive."

For indirect qualitative tools, provide a very brief summary of whether the findings were favorable or unfavorable overall and whether they indicate some need for action (*i.e.,* trigger any action). Attach the full report for any qualitative tool as an appendix to the form.

Provide the assessment coordinator with copies of any scored rubrics and any other assessment task force work product produced as part of this activity. As noted above, you want to keep all of your assessment materials on file at least until your next accreditation site visit.

Triangulating Your Analysis

After months of planning and implementation, you finally have all of the pieces in hand needed to answer a very fundamental question: Does the evidence supplied by our assessment tools indicate our students are achieving the learning outcome or performance criterion at issue? Are our students learning what we want them to learn?

As attorneys, we are trained to weigh all of the evidence before reaching a conclusion. It is ingrained in us that different witnesses can tell different stories, not because anyone is lying, but because each brings a different perspective of the events to the witness stand. Witness A saw the defendant shoot and kill the victim and is convinced she witnessed a murder. Witness B, who viewed the events from a different angle, saw the victim draw a weapon first. His testimony establishes the defendant acted in self defense. The jury needed to hear what happened from both perspectives to obtain a clear picture of what happened.

As we discussed in Chapter 5, **triangulation**, *using multiple tools of different types to measure the same criterion,* serves the same clarifying role for the assessment task force. The assessment task force should begin by comparing the results of the three tools. The more consistent the results are, the stronger the evidence they are reliable. *If the performance threshold for any one tool is not achieved, some action on the part of the law school should be triggered. However, what action is triggered will depend on the evidence provided by the other two tools.*

It is important to understand the appropriate actions fall across an extremely broad spectrum. Sometimes, there is no cause for any change at all, and other times, there may be a need for significant curricular reform. Let's take a few moments to look at the possible combinations.

Table 6.4. Triangulated Analysis Form

Outcome:
Criterion:
Assessment Cycle: 20___–20___
Assessment Task Force Members:

	Column G	Column H	Column I	Column J	Column K
← Link with Assessment Blueprint	Record your findings and indicate if there is a trigger for change or further analysis.	Analysis of data collected for relevant criterion. What does your triangulated analysis indicate?	Hypothesis? What are the possible causes of the findings (favorable or unfavorable)? List as many as may apply.	Report findings to appropriate stakeholders.	Link with Specific Action Plan, if necessary
Tool 1	___ of ___ (__%) of students demonstrated competency. Action is/is not triggered.				
Tool 2	___ of ___ (__%) of students demonstrated competency. Action is/is not triggered.				
Tool 3	Survey results did/did not satisfy threshold requirements. Action is/is not triggered. *See* Appendix ___ for the complete survey results.				

* Adapted from http://www.apta.org/outcomesassessment/, with permission of the American Physical Therapy Association. Copyright © 2006 American Physical Therapy Association.

All Three Results Are Favorable

If all three results support the idea that the criterion has been satisfied, you are probably safe in assuming it has been satisfied. The

Indirect Measures as "Outliers"

What We Have Here Is a Failure to Communicate

If the tool that appears to be the "outlier" provides an indirect measure, it may be that the problem relates not to what students have learned, but what they perceive themselves as having learned. The law school may need to focus on improving communication about learning. So, for example, students might benefit from having learning outcomes set forth in syllabi and discussed in class and from receiving feedback as to whether they are achieving the outcomes via a rubric or other device.

appropriate action is no action. During the next assessment cycle, you can move on to a different criterion.

Two of Three Results Are Favorable

If your results are mixed, with two tools suggesting the criterion has been satisfied and one suggesting it has not been satisfied, you need to review your assessment processes. One or more of the measures/tools may be flawed (*i.e.*, unreliable for some reason). In the alternative, the tools may actually be measuring different things, which brings the validity of the assessment into question.

It is the job of the assessment task force to attempt to determine why the results are mixed and to take steps (action) to clarify the picture. That action might be revamping a tool, trying a different tool, enlarging a sample size, or something else. This would be a good time to call upon your university's office of institutional research for assistance. Let the experts lend a hand!

If the assessment task force concludes that there was a flaw in the tool that seemed to be the outlier, it will need to consider when and how to address that error. If the solution is something simple like rewording a survey question, it may be possible to quickly take another measure using the corrected tool before reporting your findings to the faculty as a whole.

However, you must be very careful to respect the data collection cycle set forth in your institutional assessment plan. As discussed in Chapter 4, your school should *not* be gathering evidence on every outcome every year. It is vital to be cognizant of the possibility of creating survey fatigue, data overload, etc. Collecting data out of sequence may negatively impact data collection being conducted by a different task force. If you can easily do some retesting in the year assigned to your outcome for data collection, doing so is fine.

But if that year has passed, you should wait until the next cycle at the earliest to retest. You may wish to delay retesting until the next cycle in which this particular criterion is scheduled to be evaluated to avoid falling behind on measuring other criteria. There is no great rush. After all, two of the three measures indicated all is well as to this criterion. Assessment is a marathon, not a sprint. It is entirely proper to conclude that the appropriate action is to revamp the measures and retest at a later date.

And we feel compelled to add one last point. As discussed above, typically, if two of the three measures are favorable, you will not and should not feel the need to create a full-blown action plan that involves changes to your educational program. However, if the assessment task force is considering a criterion that it believes is foundational (*e.g.*, a demonstrated ability to critically read legal authority) and if it finds the sole unfavorable result to be deeply troubling for some reason (*e.g.*, the scores were off-the-charts bad), it may elect to move forward with the creation of the action plan described in Activity 7.

Do not be afraid to follow your gut in such situations. But before doing so, undertake a cost/benefit analysis. Every project has a cost. Think about whether the resources of the task force (and the law school) could be better utilized on this project or other assessment projects. Again, you will be measuring achievement of this criterion again at some point. The only question is when.

Two or More of Three Results Are Unfavorable

If all three results support the idea that the criterion has not been satisfied, you are probably safe in assuming it has not been satisfied. For that matter, even if two of the three are unfavorable, there is sufficient evidence to warrant serious concern. The burning question then becomes "Why?"

Documenting Your Progress

Having triangulated your analysis of the results of the individual measures, you are ready to fill in Column H of the Triangulated Analysis Form. The purpose of this section is to memorialize your findings and indicate if action of some type, including, but not limited to, further analysis, is warranted.

As you can see from Table 6.5, the explanation can be very bare bones. Again, if your assessment task force wishes to provide a more comprehensive explanation of its findings, it may do so in an appendix.

Why? Seeking the Root Cause

In cases in which the triangulated analysis is unfavorable/negative (*i.e.*, further action is required), the assessment task force **must** consider causation. What does the assessment task force believe might be the root/underlying cause of any negative findings? You cannot fix a problem that you have not identified.

In cases in which the triangulated analysis is favorable/positive (*i.e.*, no further analysis or action is required), the assessment task force **should** consider causation. What were the keys to success? If you can identify what is working, you may be able to replicate the success in other areas. Your analysis of a success need not be quite as in depth as your analysis of a failure, but it should exist.

As discussed in Chapter 4, the members appointed to the task force for each outcome should have expertise relating to that outcome. Hypothesizing as to why a particular outcome or criterion is or is not being achieved is far from a perfect science, but this group of

Table 6.5. Triangulated Analysis Form

Outcome: Criterion: Assessment Cycle: 20__–20__ Assessment Task Force Members:					
	Column G	Column H	Column I	Column J	Column K
← Link with Assessment Blueprint	Record your findings and indicate if there is a trigger for change or further analysis.	Analysis of data collected for relevant criterion. What does your triangulated analysis indicate?	Hypothesis? What are the possible causes of the findings (favorable or unfavorable)? List as many as may apply.	Report findings to appropriate stakeholders.	Link with Specific Action Plan, if necessary
Tool 1	___ of ___ (__%) of students demonstrated competency. Action is/is not triggered.	*E.g.,* All measures support the conclusion that the criterion is being achieved. Thus, the task force recommends no further action be taken.			
Tool 2	___ of ___ (__%) of students demonstrated competency. Action is/is not triggered.	*or* All measures support the conclusion that the criterion is not being achieved. Thus, the task force recommends action be taken to address the problem.			
Tool 3	Survey results did/did not satisfy threshold requirements. Action is/is not triggered. *See* Appendix ___ for the complete survey results.	*or* ___ of ___ measures support the conclusion that the criterion is not being achieved. The task force recommends further _____ (analysis or action). **Note:** If further analysis is necessary, such as retooling one of the instruments and assessing again at a future date, briefly describe the process to be undertaken, including the timeline, here. Attach an appendix, if necessary.			

* Adapted from http://www.apta.org/outcomesassessment/, with permission of the American Physical Therapy Association. Copyright © 2006 American Physical Therapy Association.

individuals is as well qualified as anyone at the law school to take on the task. It's okay if the task force develops multiple hypotheses. There may be multiple reasons for a success or failure. And it's okay if a hypothesis turns out to be incorrect. The law school is not going to make any permanent changes based on any hypothesis until it has been tested.

To this point, the entire assessment process has been approached in a thoughtful, methodical way. Now is not the time to abandon that thoughtful process. The task force should approach developing its hypotheses in a systematic way, particularly when further action is required.

The following questions may be used as a guide in identifying the root cause of any failure.

1. **Does our curriculum provide sufficient opportunities to learn X?**

    When looking for the root cause for a failure to learn, an excellent place to begin is with your school's curriculum map. What courses/professors purport to teach this knowledge, skill, or value? Do they purport to introduce it, produce students who are competent, or produce students who are proficient?

    There could be a multitude of explanations found within the structure of your curriculum. If almost no courses are touching on this knowledge, skill, or value, you may have found your answer. If the knowledge, skill, or value is taught in one first-year course, but never touched upon again, students may need more exposure. On the other hand, if the knowledge, skill, or value is supposedly being taught across a range of courses, but not emphasized in any one course, students may need a course that really focuses on it.

    Along with looking at the curriculum map, you should be talking to members of the faculty who purport to teach this knowledge, skill, or value. Dig a little deeper. Talk to them about how much time, etc. is devoted to it. And if little time is being devoted to the topic, listen to their explanation of why. For example, every professor who teaches a two hour class is convinced she could do a much better job with three hours, so it is all too easy to roll your eyes when a colleague bemoans the lack of time. But sometimes we really are asking that too much be covered in too few instructional minutes.

2. **Are *all* students provided with those opportunities?**

    Again, take a look at your curriculum map. It may be that your curriculum affords multiple learning opportunities relating to the knowledge, skill, or value at issue, but that none of them are in required courses. It may also be that in a given required course, such as Contracts, one section is being provided a learning opportunity that the other is not. For example, one professor uses the Socratic Method exclusively while the other has students drafting contract clauses.

3. **Could our teaching of X be improved? Are we making the best pedagogical choices?**

    Talk to the faculty who purport to teach this skill about how it is being taught. The idea is not to attack or place blame on anyone. Rather it is to find out the teaching methods currently being employed.

    One key question is whether and how the knowledge, skill, or value is being assessed. If it is not being assessed (or if students do not know it is being assessed), that could explain why they are not learning as well as you might like. A second possible question is how much practice students are getting at using the knowledge, skill, etc.? Another question is what feedback is being provided. If students are not being provided with formative assessment, that could explain the deficiency in their performance.

    Again, it is vital to listen when a colleague attempts to explain why the course is being taught as it is. For instance, class size can be an issue. It is much easier to provide formative assessment to a class of 40 than 80. (That does not mean it cannot be done, but the faculty involved might need a teaching assistant or faculty development on some of the methods of formative assessment, that are less time consuming for the professor.)

    While more fully exploring what is happening at your own school is key, do not forget to look to the outside for guidance and new ideas. More and more law faculty members are producing scholarship on pedagogical issues. Do some research to see if others in the academy are having success with methods you have not yet attempted.

4. **Do we emphasize the importance of X to students?**

    Students take their cues from faculty. If we want them to take something seriously, we need to expressly state we believe this knowledge, skill, or value is important. Are members of your faculty doing that? Are they identifying this outcome in their syllabi? Are they mentioning it in class? And are they putting their money where their mouth is by making it part of the grade?

Again, the idea is not to put down any faculty member who answers one of these questions in the negative. (Who knows if including course outcomes in a syllabus will make any real difference?) But you need to know what is currently being done to evaluate what changes *might* make a difference.

And don't forget to talk to students themselves. A focus group or two could give you invaluable information on the student viewpoint on this question.

5. **Are we providing sufficient support to students who are struggling with X?**

In looking at the numbers, you may see that while the desired thresholds were not met, they were not that far off. That could mean that a certain segment of the student population needs more assistance.

Talk with your academic support team and find out if this knowledge, skill, or value is being addressed, and if so, how. Talk to students about whether they think their needs are being met.

All of the questions listed above involve our input to the learning process, but as discussed in Chapter 1, the raw materials used affect outcomes as well. If students are struggling with learning outcomes across the board, the law school may need to ask some more difficult questions. Are we admitting adequately credentialed students? Do we need to look at our admissions process? While those questions are sometimes appropriate, they do not abrogate the need to carefully examine our educational program.

Documenting Your Progress

Having identified the possible root causes, you are ready to fill in Column I of the Triangulated Analysis Form. (*See* Table 6.6.) The purpose of this section is to set forth your hypotheses as to why the success or failure occurred.

If you do need to set forth a hypothesis as to a failure, word it with care. There is no need to state things in a negative way. You will only raise the hackles of your colleagues. So, instead of saying, "Faculty members teaching in this area are not providing sufficient formative assessment," you might say, "While students are being assessed on this skill on final exams, they might benefit from additional practice and feedback over the course of the semester."

Table 6.6. Triangulated Analysis Form

Outcome: Criterion: Assessment Cycle: 20__–20__ Assessment Task Force Members:				
	Column G	Column H	Column I	Column J	Column K
← _____ Link with Assessment Blueprint	Record your findings and indicate if there is a trigger for change or further analysis.	Analysis of data collected for relevant criterion. What does your triangulated analysis indicate?	Hypothesis? What are the possible causes of the findings (favorable or unfavorable)? List as many as may apply.	Report findings to appropriate stakeholders.	Link with Specific Action Plan, if necessary
Tool 1	___ of ___ (__%) of students demonstrated competency. Action is/is not triggered.	*E.g.,* All measures support the conclusion that the criterion is being achieved. Thus, the task force recommends no further action be taken. *or* All measures support the conclusion that the criterion is not being achieved. Thus, the task force recommends action be taken to address the problem. *or* ___ of ___ measures support the conclusion that the criterion is not being achieved. The task force recommends further _____ (analysis or action). **Note:** If further analysis is necessary, such as retooling one of the instruments and assessing again at a future date, briefly describe the process to be undertaken, including the timeline, here. Attach an appendix, if necessary.	*E.g. . .* **Unfavorable** 1. X is covered in only two courses, neither of which is required, so most students are never exposed to it. and/or 2. While students are being assessed on X on final exams, they might benefit from additional practice and feedback over the course of the semester. and/or **Favorable** 1. When surveyed, students noted how helpful ____ was in learning X.		
Tool 2	___ of ___ (__%) of students demonstrated competency. Action is/is not triggered.				
Tool 3	Survey results did/did not satisfy threshold requirements. Action is/is not triggered. *See* Appendix __ for the complete survey results.				

* Adapted from http://www.apta.org/outcomesassessment/, with permission of the American Physical Therapy Association. Copyright © 2006 American Physical Therapy Association.

Practical Example A (Analytical Skills): Scenario A-7:

The following examples illustrate the types of situations an assessment task force might face in conducting a triangulated analysis of students' ability to effectively use analogies. They demonstrate how viewing the totality of the findings influences the action, if any, taken.

- **Example 1**—The findings from the MPT, the multiple-choice tool, and the student survey all satisfy the performance threshold. The consistency among the findings provides strong evidence that competency in the criterion at issue is being achieved and no further analysis or action is necessary.

- **Example 2**—The findings from the MPT and the multiple-choice tool both satisfy the performance threshold, but the student survey does not. This mixed message indicates that further analysis is required, but further action is not yet necessary. It may be that students do not appreciate how much they have learned and/or feel inadequate for some other reason. These findings suggest the need to more fully explore this disconnect. For example, the assessment task force may wish to use student focus groups to help identify the basis for student concerns.

- **Example 3**—The findings from the student survey and MPT satisfy the performance threshold, but those from the multiple-choice tool do not. This mixed message indicates that further analysis is required, but further action is not yet necessary. It creates some question as to the validity or reliability of one of the direct tools. The assessment task force should review whether the assessment process was flawed in some way and correct these flaws in future assessments.

- **Example 4**—The findings from the student survey satisfy the performance threshold, but those from the MPT and the multiple-choice tool do not. This disconnect may indicate that students are so uninformed about the skill at issue that they cannot even recognize their own weaknesses. (On some levels this combination is more troubling than if all three tools had failed to meet the threshold.) The disconnect coupled with the evidence provided by the direct tools indicates significant action, such as the creation of a pilot project geared towards enhancing skills, may be needed.

- **Example 5**—For purposes of this scenario, assume that instead of surveying students about the criterion, you conducted a focus group with employers (*i.e.*, you used an indirect, qualitative tool). The findings from the MPT and the multiple-choice tool both satisfy the performance threshold, but you received a surprise when you read the focus group report. Employers complained that your students' office memoranda were too long and detailed. They did not provide the quick and dirty overview the employers wanted. Students were using too many analogies. This mixed message indicates that while students may be learning what you are trying to teach them, you may be teaching them the wrong thing or failing to teach them something important. It suggests that the assessment task force may need to engage in further analysis (*i.e.*, conduct more employer focus groups) to determine if there is a need to make a change in the curriculum.

Sharing What You Have Learned — Activity 7: Report Findings to Key Stakeholders

Once the assessment task force has the findings in hand, it needs to determine how best to communicate those findings to the law school's key stakeholders. Realize that there are different audiences with different needs, including faculty, administrators, and senior staff; accreditors; and other stakeholders, students, potential students, parents, and the general public. In creating a communication plan for each audience, consider why it needs the information, how it will use the information, exactly what information it needs, and when it needs to have the information in hand.

Faculty, Administrators, and Senior Staff

The obvious first audience will be full-time faculty, administrators, and senior staff. These groups will use the information in making essential decisions about your school's academic programs. It is imperative that you share the data with them, as they are the ones who must take action on the results.

And you need to do so in a timely fashion. Data loses value with each passing day. (Make certain that you follow the schedule set forth in the assessment cycle table described in Chapter 4.) The type of action taken (and information required) will depend on whether the findings are favorable or unfavorable.

Favorable Findings

Favorable findings (*i.e.*, findings in which at least two of the three tools indicate competency in the relevant criterion is being achieved) can be shared by providing the group with the completed Assessment Blueprint Form and Triangulated Analysis Form and their appendices.

These documents provide a precise description of everything this audience needs to know about the work of the assessment task force:

- the criterion or criteria being measured
- the tools/measures used
- where the measures took place
- who scored and/or measured the data
- who evaluated the data
- what the performance threshold was
- the exact findings for each tool
- the triangulated analysis
- the assessment task force's strategy for addressing mixed results (*i.e.*, overhauling any flawed tool or process)

If someone simply wishes to get an overview, reading the forms themselves will provide it. If she wants to undertake a more in-depth analysis, the appendices allow her to do so. The work of the task force is made completely transparent by these documents. The task force could opt to attach a very brief (one-page) executive summary to the forms to make things even more reader friendly.

One benefit of having every task force use the same forms and every member of the faculty serve on at least one task force is that over time, a common language and understanding can be developed. The completed forms should make sense to everyone.

Task force members could also briefly present their findings at a faculty meeting. Favorable findings provide both a reason for celebration and a learning opportunity. Perhaps it is human nature, but it is so easy to jump right to the negative. (Both authors of this Guide readily admit that if they get thirty-nine glowing student evaluations and one negative student evaluation, it's the negative that seems seared onto their brains!)

But when we are doing something well, it's not a bad thing to take ten minutes to encourage faculty members to ponder why. (Time at faculty meetings has certainly been devoted to less important topics!) There may be takeaways that can be useful in addressing problem areas in the achievement of other outcomes.

If one of the three tools provided an unfavorable result, and the task force is undertaking further analysis of that tool, Column H will provide notice of that analysis and an opportunity for faculty members, etc. to comment on the steps being undertaken by the task force. Another task force may have experienced the same type of difficulty and have suggestions as to how to improve the tool/process.

Unfavorable Findings

Unfavorable findings (*i.e.*, findings in which at least two of the three tools indicate competency in the relevant criterion is not being achieved) can also be shared by providing this group with the completed Assessment Blueprint Form and Triangulated Analysis Form and their appendices. This will be the first of several necessary communications with the faculty.

As discussed above, these documents provide a precise description of the criterion or criteria being measured, the tools/measures used, the exact findings for each tool, the triangulated analysis, etc. Column I also provides the assessment task force's hypothesis as to the root cause of the failure.

Before moving on to Activity 8, which involves the creation of an action plan to address the failure, the task force should have the opportunity to present its hypothesis or hypotheses to the faculty at a faculty meeting. This presentation will allow the faculty as a whole to weigh in on whether the task force appears to be on the right track in

A Word about Confidentiality

Dealing with Sensitive Materials

We strongly advise that all forms and other materials provided to faculty, administrators, and senior staff be clearly and properly marked as confidential, privileged, and proprietary. As discussed below, some of the information contained in the forms will be released to students, prospective students, and members of the general public, but such communications must be part of a carefully planned communication strategy. Individuals should not have the ability to share this information.

We also strongly advise that with regard to indirect measures, such as surveys, only statistical summaries and broad overviews of qualitative results be shared with faculty, etc. Responses to open-ended questions can include unfounded and defamatory attacks on individuals. Sharing this type of raw data from a survey is grossly unfair.

identifying the root cause of the problem. It also provides the faculty with the opportunity to suggest possible actions, which the task force can consider in developing an action plan.

As discussed in Activity 8, there will be at least two follow-up communications. The first will take place once the task force has developed an action plan, and the second will take place once the action plan has been completed.

Accrediting Bodies

A second key audience will be your school's accrediting bodies (the regional accrediting body, the ABA, and the American Association of Law Schools (AALS)). Although the AALS is not an accrediting body, most schools view membership in the AALS as essential, so we are including it here as a potential audience.

What kind of reports will accreditors expect? Don't rely on guesswork—contact them for required forms, samples of reports, etc. Your university's assessment and/or accreditation committees will provide you with guidance on the regional accreditor's process. Make sure that you work closely with the university from the beginning so that you are not suddenly faced with creating an unexpected report.

It may take several years for the ABA to fully develop any standard required forms. In the meantime, we believe that providing the following items described in this Guide will stand you in very good stead:

- Your school's learning outcomes and related performance criteria (*See* Chapter 4)
- Your school's most recent curriculum map (*See* Chapter 4)
- The Data Collection Cycle Table for your school's learning outcomes (*See* Chapter 4)
- The Three Year Cycle Table of implementation and evaluation activities for your school's learning outcomes (*See* Chapter 4)
- The Assessment Cycle Table for *each* learning outcome (*See* Chapter 4)
- The Parties Responsible for Implementation and Evaluation Table for *each* learning outcome (*See* Chapter 4)
- The Assessment Blueprint Form for *each* learning outcome for *each* assessment cycle and any appendices (*See* Chapter 5)
- The Triangulated Analysis Form for *each* learning outcome for *each* assessment cycle and any appendices (*See* Chapter 6)
- The Specific Action Plan Form(s) for each failed learning outcome for *each* assessment cycle and any appendices (*See* Chapter 6)

If you have been documenting your progress each step of the way and providing copies of this documentation to your institutional assessment coordinator, gathering materials for your accreditors will be a cinch. All you need to do is provide them with copies of your Institutional Assessment Plan binder.

And remember, accreditors are not expecting perfection. It's okay to have some failures. Accreditors just want to know that you are assessing your educational programs and using that assessment to create positive change.

Students, Potential Students, and Other Stakeholders

The third audience will be the other stakeholders in the success of the law school: students, alumni, potential students and their families, and the public generally. Each of these stakeholders has an interest in whether your institution's educational program is delivering on its promises.

Clearly, the interest of students and alumni is greatest. They are paying or have paid good money for a good education. They have a right to expect that you are making every effort to provide the best possible programs. Sharing assessment results is a sign of good faith. Also, these groups have been asked and are being asked to participate in various assessment activities. The best way to encourage participation in surveys and other assessment activities is to let people see that they are actually being used to improve programming.

Emails, newsletters, alumni magazines, etc., sent to these groups should routinely contain information about institutional assessment efforts. They should know that the law school is constantly striving to improve student learning and that they are helping by participating in assessment activities.

Potential students and their families and the general public also have an interest in what the law school is promising and whether it is living up to its promises. Particularly in this era in which law schools seem to be under attack from the media and others, transparency can only be viewed as a good thing. Law school and university websites provide a great forum for providing this crucial information.

What information do these groups need? That question is not without controversy. Some would argue that transparency requires detailed reports that describe all of the tools employed and the specific results of each tool.

The authors of this Guide respectfully disagree. We fear that the expectation that sensitive information will be released will create a chilling effect that will negatively impact the entire assessment process. We do not want schools to feel tempted to set performance expectations/thresholds low and avoid looking at problem areas to ensure that the

---

What the Experts Have to Say

The National Institute for Learning Outcomes Assessment has provided the following advice on the use of websites:

"To meet transparency obligations and responsibilities, institutions should make more information about student and institutional performance accessible via their websites. Care should also be taken to help multiple audiences interpret and understand the information posted. Toward this end, colleges and universities are recommended to take the following steps:

• Prominently post student learning outcomes statements and resources in multiple places on the institution's website and update those postings regularly....

• Explain the meaning and use of results of student learning outcomes assessments on the institution's website in layperson's language ...

• Minimize the need on the institution's website for password protection of student learning outcomes assessment resources, information, and results...."

Natasha Jankowski & Julia Panke Makela, *Exploring the Landscape: What Institutional Websites Reveal About Student Learning Outcomes Assessment Activities* (June 2010).

numbers look good to outsiders. Schools should be encouraged to self-audit and correct problems without having to fear public disclosure. So what information should be provided? We believe that the following items should be included in executive summaries available to all:

- **Your school's learning outcomes and related performance criteria (*See* Chapter 4)**

    Students have an absolute right to know what we expect of them, what we believe they should be learning. The general public, including and especially prospective students and employers, have a right to know what we are promising our students will learn.

- **A list of some of the tools your school is using to measure achievement of outcomes**

    Students and others have no need to know (and probably little interest in knowing) every single tool employed in the assessment process. But they should be provided with a list of examples that provides a sense of the depth and breadth of the law school's efforts to assess its programs.

- **A brief description of how the assessment process works and who is involved**

    Students and others should be made aware of the major steps in the assessment process. They may be particularly interested to know of the level of faculty involvement. Giving them a glimpse of the inner workings of the process will help them understand that your school takes assessment seriously.

- **Some examples of curricular and pedagogical changes that have been made based on assessment findings**

    This may be the most important piece of information provided. Let students and others see that the school is making positive changes based on its assessments. Assume, for example, a course is changed from two to three hours based on a need to provide further instruction on a skill that has been identified as a result of assessment. The executive summary might set forth the following in a bullet point: "After completing an assessment of students' oral advocacy skills, the faculty voted to add an hour to Appellate Advocacy to provide students with additional instruction and additional required arguments."

Finally, do not forget to use the experts in marketing and communications that are available at your institution. They can help you find the language, format, etc. that will make the most sense to a lay audience.

Table 6.7. Triangulated Analysis Form

Outcome: Criterion: Assessment Cycle: 20___–20___ Assessment Task Force Members:					
	Column G	Column H	Column I	Column J	Column K
← ——— Link with Assessment Blueprint	Record your findings and indicate if there is a trigger for change or further analysis.	Analysis of data collected for relevant criterion. What does your triangulated analysis indicate?	Hypothesis? What are the possible causes of the findings (favorable or unfavorable)? List as many as may apply.	Report findings to appropriate stakeholders.	Link with Specific Action Plan, if necessary
Tool 1	___ of ___ (__%) of students demonstrated competency. Action is/is not triggered.	*E.g.,* All measures support the conclusion that the criterion is being achieved. Thus, the task force recommends no further action be taken.	*E.g. . .* **Unfavorable** 1. X is covered in only two courses, neither of which is required, so most students are never exposed to it. and/or 2. While students are being assessed on X on final exams, they might benefit from additional practice and feedback over the course of the semester. and/or **Favorable** 1. When surveyed, students noted how helpful ____ was in learning X.	1. Provided faculty with Assessment Blueprint & Triangulated Evaluation/ Analysis via email on __/__/__ 2. Presented at faculty meeting on __/__/__. PowerPoint attached as Appendix ___. Minutes attached as Appendix ___. 3. Presented results to students and staff via law school newsletter article attached as Appendix ___.	
Tool 2	___ of ___ (__%) of students demonstrated competency. Action is/is not triggered.	*or* All measures support the conclusion that the criterion is not being achieved. Thus, the task force recommends action be taken to address the problem.			
Tool 3	Survey results did/did not satisfy threshold requirements. Action is/is not triggered. *See* Appendix __ for the complete survey results.	*or* ___ of ___ measures support the conclusion that the criterion is not being achieved. The task force recommends further _____ (analysis or action). **Note:** If further analysis is necessary, such as retooling one of the instruments and assessing again at a future date, briefly describe the process to be undertaken, including the timeline, here. Attach an appendix, if necessary.			

* Adapted from http://www.apta.org/outcomesassessment/, with permission of the American Physical Therapy Association. Copyright © 2006 American Physical Therapy Association.

Documenting Your Progress

Having communicated your findings to the relevant stakeholders, you are ready to fill in Column J of the Triangulated Analysis Form. (*See* Table 6.7.) The purpose of this column is to memorialize both your communications with stakeholders and their response, if any.

So, for example, you should record the date on which you provided the faculty with the Assessment Blueprint and other documents, and if you presented the results at a faculty meeting, the date of the meeting should be provided and a copy of the minutes attached as an appendix. If the minutes of the meeting lack relevant details, you should consider including the notes of one or more task force members, particularly if the faculty was providing feedback about an unfavorable result, a planned action, etc.

Hard or electronic copies of communications to other stakeholders should also be included. Since websites are constantly changing, make sure you retain any information presented via the web in a permanent form.

Your completed Triangulated Analysis Form should be submitted to your assessment coordinator, so it can be added to the Institutional Assessment Plan binder.

Improving Your Educational Program — Activity 8: Develop & Implement Changes, If Necessary

The authors of this Guide hope and believe that most of your findings will be favorable. Despite the recent spate of media criticism of legal education, we stand firm in the conviction that law schools by and large do an admirable job of educating lawyers and that institutional assessment will provide evidence to support the strength of our educational programs. That having been said, *every* law school has room for improvement.

Activity 8 focuses on closing the assessment loop by making that improvement a reality. Where triangulated analysis results in an unfavorable finding, the assessment task force is responsible for the following:

1. Developing and implementing an action plan aimed at improving student achievement of the outcome/criterion
2. Assessing the efficacy of the actions taken under the plan
3. Communicating findings with the faculty, administration, and other key stakeholders
4. Taking leadership in making any needed institutional changes

Table 6.8. Specific Action Plan Form (Required Only for Unfavorable Findings)

Outcome: Criterion: Assessment Cycle: 20__–20__ Assessment Task Force Members:						
Column K	Column L	Column M	Column N	Column O	Column P	Column Q
Specific action that constitutes the change (can be multiple actions).	Who are the change agents (*i.e.*, who will run the pilot)?	What is the time-frame for implementing and assessing of the specific action?	How will the effectiveness of this action be measured?	What does the analysis indicate?	When and how are the results shared with the faculty and others?	What was the final result? Institutionalize, revise, or discard the specific action? (Attach any documentation.)

* Adapted from http://www.apta.org/outcomesassessment/, with permission of the American Physical Therapy Association. Copyright © 2006 American Physical Therapy Association.

As you progress through Activity 8, you can use the Specific Action Plan Form in Table 6.8 to document your efforts.

Developing and Implementing an Action Plan

In completing Activity 6, the assessment task force was required to identify the root cause or causes of any failure to achieve the outcome. That was a challenge in and of itself. But now comes an even greater challenge—developing and implementing a plan of action to fix the problem.

It is important to understand that all you are being asked to do initially is develop and implement a pilot project. The idea is **not** to make change for the sake of making change. Instead, it is to develop a thoughtful, measured response to a problem. Undertaking a pilot program with a small group of students gives you the flexibility to experiment.

It also allows you to compare the results of any follow-up assessment with those of a control group (*i.e.*, students being taught within the traditional program). The idea is to assess the efficacy of any change before you consider making it a wholesale change.

Of course, some changes cannot be the subject of a pilot. It is relatively easy to create a pilot if the proposed change is a change in pedagogy. You simply need to convince a faculty member or group of faculty members (*e.g.*, everyone teaching in section one of the first year) to try a new teaching technique, incorporate a new formative assessment, etc.

If the proposed change is curricular in nature, creating a pilot may be difficult or even impossible. For example, requiring some, but not all, students to take a particular course to see if it boosts achievement poses a host of practical as well as ethical issues. There may also be times when your faculty is so concerned about an issue that it decides to forgo a small pilot and forge ahead with a curricular change.

That's fine, but even when conducting a pilot is impossible, change should be evidence based. So, for example, before recommending that a course be made mandatory, the task force should assess whether students who are currently taking that course as an elective are outperforming peers who are not taking this course. You may or may not be able to use the data you pulled as part of your initial assessment in making this determination. This is one of those situations where you should run, not walk, to your institution's office of institutional research for help!

Selecting an Action or Actions

So, how do you identify possible actions? The following rules of thumb may help you get started:

Rule 1: Think Small

This rule may surprise you. But unless your findings are absolutely horrific, huge changes to your educational programs could do more harm than good. Dr. Frederick Burrack, Director of the Office of Assessment at Kansas State University, puts it this way:

> Programs that show the strongest impact on program improvement consider assessment a continual process of curricular and instructional enhancement. Programs have found that the best way to modify the Learning Process is to consistently monitor student learning and address issues with small actions. Making an effective change is like hitting a golf ball. You can make a very small adjustment in the angle of the golf club and the result can be extreme. A little change, if selected wisely, can result in tremendous benefits. Then you have to be patient enough to wait to see what that result will be.

So, when considering your curriculum, maybe you don't need a new required course. Maybe you need to alter the sequence of existing courses or add an hour to an existing course or change a course description to ensure that a particular area is covered or add a topic to orientation. And maybe you don't even need to consider curricular change at all. Maybe simply adding an assignment or two in a class or making an ungraded assignment a graded assignment or providing more detailed critique on an assignment or all of the above would make a positive difference.

Rule 2: Engage Your Faculty and Administration

In completing Activity 7, the assessment task force presented its hypothesis about the reasons for the failure to the faculty and sought feedback on both whether the task force appeared to be on the right track in identifying the root cause of the problem and what possible remedies might exist.

As you consider what actions might improve student performance, take the advice of your colleagues seriously, and provide them with additional opportunities to brainstorm about possible solutions. Host workshops and brown bag lunches for faculty and other stakeholders you believe may have valuable suggestions. You need not adopt every suggestion, but you should at least explore it.

Here are a few questions you might find useful in facilitating conversation about possible actions:

- We are here today because at least some of our students seem to be struggling with "X." Has anyone dealt with a similar challenge in a course? Were you able to overcome it? If so, how? What worked for you?
- Is there any "low-hanging fruit" you think we could exploit? In other words, does anyone have a simple, low-cost solution in mind that might help at least some students improve their performance? It doesn't matter if it would not resolve the problem completely. We are simply looking for improvement.
- One idea that the assessment task force has bandied about is trying "Y." Do you think Y might make a difference? Why or why not?
- What do you see as the cost of Y? Education is often a zero sum game. If I add Y to my class (or if we add a course on Y to the curriculum), what would suffer? What must be cut? Would the benefit be worth the cost?
- If we try Y and it seems to work in the pilot, would the law school have the monetary and/or human resources needed to implement it on a wider scale?
- Would you be willing to be part of a pilot project in which you try Y in your class?
- If we try Y and it seems to have a favorable effect on student performance, do you think the faculty would be willing to support its implementation across the curriculum?

Once the assessment task force has developed its proposed pilot project, it should provide the faculty and administration with notice and the opportunity to comment. The idea is to be transparent throughout the process. Further information about the nature of this notice is provided below.

Rule 3: Look Beyond the Walls of Your Law School for Help

As you seek ideas for your action plan, remember that other law schools are struggling with exactly the same problems and they may have found solutions that will work for you, too. Go to conferences, look to the burgeoning scholarship on pedagogy within the academy, join a list serve, read a blog, call a colleague at another school, reach out for help.

One of the unexpected benefits of the advent of institutional assessment may well be an increased focus on fostering the professional development of law faculty. Both the authors of this Guide come from the ranks of legal research and writing professionals where scholarship on teaching is the norm and organizations like the Legal Writing Institute and the Association of Legal Writing Directors provide countless opportunities to share ideas with our peers. We look forward to the day when all law faculty members have similar resources and opportunities. If your school finds something that works, share it with the academy.

And don't forget to seek out resources from the greater university community. Consult with your teaching and learning center, and seek guidance from your colleagues in the school of education. You need not reinvent the wheel.

Fleshing Out Your Action Plan

Once you have decided what action or actions might enhance your students' learning, you need to set to work in earnest to develop a full-fledged action plan. That means fleshing out the specifics as to who will be responsible for the pilot project or projects (*i.e.,* who will be the "change agent or agents"), what the time frame for the project or projects will be, and how the results of the project or projects will be assessed.

Appointing the Change Agents

Every faculty member should give any request for assistance with a pilot from the task force thoughtful consideration, and the authors believe that most law faculty will do just that. Each of us has a vested interest in improving our students' learning.

Nonetheless, the reality is that the only way to ensure the needed faculty participation is for the administration to recognize and be fully supportive of the required faculty efforts. Developing a pilot takes work, and while the assessment task force will certainly assist, most of the heavy lifting must be done by the faculty member(s) responsible for the pilots.

Table 6.9. Assessment Cycle for Learning Outcome 1

Implementation & Evaluation Activity	2016–2017	2017–2018	2018–2019	2019–2020	2020–2021	2021–2022	2022–2023
Review performance criteria that define the outcome	•				•		
Map (or review map of) where your school addresses and assesses these criteria	•				•		
Use map to identify where data will be collected	•				•		
Develop a measurement strategy and the needed assessment tools for the performance criterion or criteria under review	•				•		
Collect data		•				•	
Evaluate assessment data, including processes			•				•
Report findings			•				•
Take action where necessary				•			

* Table adapted from *Assessment Planning Flow Chart* ©2004 Gloria M. Rogers, PH.D., ABET, Inc. (grogers@abet.org) Copyright 2005.

Some pilots will require relatively little effort. For instance, most of us could add a class or two on a topic to a course without overexerting ourselves. But some pilots will require significant effort. For example, if someone who has traditionally used the Socratic Method is asked to try a problem-based approach instead, it will require a reworking of the entire course.

Every effort, large or small, to assist with creating a pilot should be recognized and rewarded when salary, promotion, retention, and tenure decisions are made. Large efforts should also be rewarded with stipends, release time, etc.

Setting the Time Frame

In setting the time frame for your action plan, remember to refer to the Assessment Cycle Table for the outcome created by the assessment committee. *See* Chapter 4. Since the assessment task force will soon begin its assessment of another criterion, it needs to keep moving along. You may recall the example in Table 6.9 from Chapter 4.

It typically takes one or two semesters total to complete Activity 6 (evaluating the data) and Activity 7 (reporting to the faculty) and to develop a pilot project. So, for example, if you collect data in 2017/ 2018, you should expect to spend Fall 2018 evaluating it. Depending on the complexity of any proposed pilot project, it could take place as early as Spring 2019, but might be delayed until the 2019/2020 school year. Ideally, by the end of that school year, you will have determined what, if any, permanent action should be taken.

That having been said, as long as you are not allowing work on the failed criterion to interfere with the assessment schedule for other criteria, it is okay if you exceed the time limits discussed above. And that may happen. For instance, a pilot project may fail, and you may decide to start back at square one and create a new action plan.

Assessing the Results

As part of your action plan, you must develop a strategy for assessing the results of your pilot project. Ideally, you can reuse at least some of the tools you developed for the original assessment of the criterion. But you will not always be able to reuse a tool. For example, if one of the tools consisted of a focus group of employers, you will not be able to reuse that tool. It would take years for the results of a pilot project to trickle down to that level.

Because the pilot project will involve a relatively small number of students, your assessments will be smaller in scope as well. But that does not mean that you should forget all that you have learned about the keys to effective assessment. Your assessments must be valid and reliable, you should seek to triangulate your assessment, you should norm scoring, etc.

You can certainly look for improvement by comparing your findings from this triangulated assessment to those from the original assessment. However, if the tools used were not identical, the validity of the comparison may be questionable. A good way to address this issue is to create a **control group** of current students who are not part of the pilot and use the same tools to measure their learning. A **control group** *is a group of subjects/students who are not exposed to the change in question and serve as a benchmark.*

Practical Example C (Oral Advocacy Skills): Scenario C-1:

For purposes of this example, assume that your school has adopted the following learning outcome, "Graduates will communicate effectively and efficiently to individuals and groups" and performance criterion, "Graduates will demonstrate achievement of this learning outcome by speaking in a clear, concise, well-reasoned organized, and professional manner that is appropriate to the audience and the circumstances."

Unfortunately, when your assessment task force undertook its triangulated analysis of this criterion in 2017/2018, the result was unfavorable. The percentage of your students demonstrating competency on direct measures was below the identified threshold and in focus groups, students expressed a lack of confidence in their oral advocacy skills.

The assessment task force hypothesized that students lacked sufficient opportunities to develop their oral advocacy skills. All students were required to make a brief (10-minute), ungraded oral argument at the end of their second-semester Legal Research and Writing course. Taking either Legal Drafting, which involved no oral advocacy, or Appellate Advocacy satisfied the upper-level writing requirement, and students split about fifty-fifty between the two courses. Trial Practice was an elective course that about 60% of the students opted to take. A few other electives also offered the opportunity to hone oral advocacy skills. The bottom line was that the second-semester Legal Research and Writing course provided the only exposure to oral advocacy for 10%–20% of students.

In developing its action plan, the assessment task force made a point of seeking faculty input. A few faculty members were in favor of immediate **curricular change**. They believed that requiring every student to take Appellate Advocacy would resolve the issue. However, a larger number of faculty members expressed concern as to the cost of such a change. Many graduates went into transactional law, and the Legal Drafting course significantly increased their skills and marketability to employers. Requiring Appellate Advocacy would both reduce the faculty resources available to Legal Drafting and reduce enrollment. Faculty questioned the wisdom of requiring a student with no interest in appellate practice and a strong interest in transactional law to forgo Legal Drafting in favor of Appellate Advocacy.

A second option raised involved **pedagogical change**. It was suggested that placing greater emphasis on oral advocacy in the required second-semester Legal Research and Writing course might be sufficient to address the problem. One of the members of the Legal Research and Writing faculty agreed to pilot a project in her sections, which constituted one-third of the first-year class in Spring 2019.

The pilot involved increasing the number of classes devoted to oral advocacy from two to three, adding a mandatory full practice round, increasing the argument from 10 to 15 minutes, and making the argument worth 15% of the final grade. The administration pitched in by agreeing to fund teaching assistants culled from the ranks of the Moot Court Board to help judge and critique the mandatory practice round.

The assessment task force used three tools to measure whether the pilot project improved student performance. One, students' performance on the year-end argument was scored using a rubric. The performance of a sample group of students from the other sections was scored using the same rubric. (The sample group served as a control group.) The two scores were then compared. Two, students in both the pilot group and the control group were surveyed about their confidence in their oral advocacy skills as part of the course evaluation.

Three, the performance of members of both the pilot and control groups was measured yet again the following fall (Fall 2019) in Appellate Advocacy. (Of course, some members of both groups opted not to take this course.) The idea was to see if any positive effects of the enhanced training in the first-year were long term. Again, the performance of members of both groups was measured using the same rubric.

Documenting the Pilot Project

Having developed the pilot project, identified the persons responsible for running it, agreed upon its time frame, and determined how its results will be assessed, you are ready to fill out Columns K, L, M, and N of the Specific Action Plan. The purpose of these sections is to document your pilot project for interested stakeholders, including your faculty, administration, and accreditors.

As discussed above, if you are going to obtain the support of faculty and administrators for needed changes, it is important to be as transparent as possible. Once you have filled out Columns K through N, you should distribute the Action Plan to the faculty and administration to provide notice and the opportunity for comment. If someone sees a flaw in the plan, let him speak up now while there is still time to fix it.

In Column K, explain the basics of the pilot project—what course or courses it involves, what changes are being employed, etc. If you would like to expand on your description a bit—perhaps explaining why the task force selected this pilot—you can do so in an appendix. It is also a good idea to include any assignments used as appendices. Doing so not only gives interested faculty members a more complete view of what is happening, it provides a helpful archive for those who

Table 6.10. Specific Action Plan Form (Required Only for Unfavorable Findings)

Outcome:
Criterion:
Assessment Cycle: 20__–20__
Assessment Task Force Members:

Column K	Column L	Column M	Column N	Column O	Column P	Column Q
Specific action that constitutes the change (can be multiple actions).	Who are the change agents (*i.e.*, who will run the pilot)?	What is the time-frame for implementing and assessing the specific action?	How will the effectiveness of this action be measured?	What does the analysis indicate?	When and how are the results shared with the faculty and others?	What was the final result? Institutionalize, revise, or discard the specific action? (Attach any documentation)
E.g., Students in [course] will receive __ minutes additional instruction on X and will complete the following additional, graded assignments relating to X: _____. The assignments are attached as Appendix ___.	Professor Finn	The pilot will be run twice, once in Fall ____ and once in Spring ____. The results will be assessed during Fall ____.	*E.g.,* The assessment task force will undertake a triangulated assessment, featuring the following tools: _____. An Assessment Blueprint is attached as Appendix __.			

* Adapted from http://www.apta.org/outcomesassessment/, with permission of the American Physical Therapy Association. Copyright © 2006 American Physical Therapy Association.

may wish to review the project in the future. Institutional memory can be a short thing!

As you can see from the Specific Action Plan Form in Table 6.10, the information provided in Columns L and M is very bare bones. You are simply providing names and dates.

Column N is a different story. Your stakeholders will likely be very interested in how you plan to assess the results of the pilot project. You can provide an outline of your planned assessments on the form, but we suggest that you attach a completed Assessment Blueprint Form (*see* Chapter 5) as an appendix.

As always, remember to provide your school's assessment coordinator with copies of your report and any attachments. The Specific Action Plan should be placed in the Institutional Assessment Plan binder with the other materials relating to this outcome.

Executing the Pilot Project

The next step is simple — follow your action plan. The pilot program should move forward, the assessment tools be implemented, and the relevant data gathered and scored and/or tabulated. While the change agent or agents will be responsible for the pilot, the assessment task force will be responsible for staying on top of the assessment projects.

Closing the Loop — Using What You Have Learned

With the data from the pilot project in hand, the time has come to evaluate it, share your findings, and work with the faculty and administration to make some key decisions.

The evaluation process will largely mimic the process used for your initial assessment. The assessment task force will analyze whether the performance thresholds, if any, for the individual instruments have been satisfied and engage in a triangulated analysis of the results. The difference in the process is that you now have a baseline performance to which you can compare your results. Ideally, you will compare the results of the pilot to both the results of the original assessment and the current control group to gauge the impact of the specific action/changes instituted in the pilot.

Several key questions must be answered:

1. Did the changes improve student performance?
2. If so, by how much? Were the changes sufficient to bring student competency levels up to the desired performance threshold?
3. Were there any unexpected costs/issues involved in the pilot?
4. Should the changes be institutionalized, revised, or discarded? What is the recommendation of the assessment task force?

In determining whether to recommend that the changes should be institutionalized, revised, or discarded, the assessment task force should undertake a cost/benefit analysis. A pilot that produces positive change should normally be institutionalized — even if it does not entirely solve the problem (*i.e.*, even if the desired performance thresholds have yet to be satisfied). Continuous improvement should be your goal. Rome wasn't built in day.

However, any benefit of the proposed change must be weighed against its cost. It is important to talk to the change agent(s) (the person or persons who ran the pilot) to see if there were any unexpected costs. For instance, did the increased time and emphasis on X seem to detract from students' performance on Y? Did it take up an inordinate amount of the professor's time? If a change helps only a little and its cost is great, discarding it may be the best course of action.

The change agent(s) may also have suggestions on ways the action undertaken as part of the pilot might be improved. It is possible to institutionalize a revised version of the pilot project. You may or may not wish to run a pilot of the revised actions before institutionalizing them. If the changes are small, such as the addition of one assignment, a second pilot is probably unnecessary.

If the pilot failed to generate improvement (or, horrors, caused a decline) in performance, the action plan should be discarded. The question before the assessment task force at that point is what the next steps should be.

If great concern exists about the failure to satisfy this criterion — either because of its importance or the large percentage of students who failed to satisfy it — the task force should develop and implement another pilot. In extreme cases, the faculty as a whole may even opt to move forward with a curricular change aimed at addressing the problem.

On the other hand, if there is no great concern, the task force and faculty as a whole may be content to encourage individual experimentation by the faculty and wait until this criterion's next appearance on the assessment cycle to take another look at it.

Practical Example C (Oral Advocacy Skills): Scenario C-2:

For purposes of this example, again assume that your school has adopted the following learning outcome, "Graduates will communicate effectively and efficiently to individuals and groups" and performance criterion, "Graduates will demonstrate achievement of this learning outcome by speaking in a clear, concise, well-reasoned, organized, and professional manner that is appropriate to the audience and the circumstances."

Unfortunately, when your assessment task force undertook its triangulated analysis of this criterion in 2017/2018, the result was unfavorable. The assessment task force hypothesized that students lacked sufficient opportunities to develop their oral advocacy skills. A member of the Legal Research and Writing faculty agreed to pilot a project in her sections, which constituted one-third of the first-year class in Spring 2019. The pilot involved increasing the number of classes devoted to oral advocacy from two to three, adding a mandatory full practice round, increasing the argument from 10 to 15 minutes, and making the argument worth 15% of the final grade.

The assessment task force engaged in a triangulated analysis of the pilot in Spring 2020, using three tools to measure whether the pilot project improved student performance. One, students' performance on the year-end argument was scored using a rubric. The performance of a sample group of students from the other sections was scored using the same rubric. Two, students in both the pilot group and the control group were surveyed about their confidence in their oral advocacy skills as part of the course evaluation. Three, the performance of members of both the pilot and control groups was measured yet again the following fall (Fall 2019) in Appellate Advocacy.

The triangulated analysis showed that students taking part in the pilot project outperformed both the students in the control group and the students involved in the initial assessment on the year-end argument. Participants also outperformed the control group in Appellate Advocacy. Finally, when surveyed, participants in the pilot voiced a greater confidence in their oral advocacy skills than did members of the control group. Nonetheless, despite improvement in the numbers, the percentage of students reaching the competent level was slightly below the desired performance threshold.

When the task force shared the results with Legal Research and Writing faculty members, they recognized the benefit of the change, and as a group, agreed to institutionalize it. The task force provided the remainder of the faculty with a completed Triangulated Analysis Form and presented on the pilot at a faculty meeting.

Although pleased with the results of the pilot and supportive of the institutionalization of the changes to the second-semester Legal Research and Writing course, the faculty remained concerned about students' failure to meet the performance threshold. It has asked the Academic Affairs Committee to look into adding an upper-level oral advocacy graduation requirement that could be satisfied by a number of electives, including electives geared towards students planning a career in transactional law. If things go as planned, the new initiative should be well underway by the next scheduled assessment of this criterion.

So, as of today, your school has taken action, the efficacy of which is supported by evidence, not guesswork, to improve an area of weakness in your educational program, and has plans in place for further improvements. Your work on this criterion is complete— at least for the time being. On to the next criterion!

As the above discussion indicates, it is critical at this juncture to bring the faculty and administration into the loop. Whether the pilot project proved to be a hit or a miss, they need to be informed of its results and consulted as to next steps.

If a curricular change is sought, faculty will have to approve that change. If the change is pedagogical in nature, faculty and administrators will need to support it with their actions. For example, if the change requires additional assessments in some classes, the faculty members teaching those classes will have to agree to participate and follow through on that agreement, and if additional resources are needed, the administration must make those resources available.

An easy way to provide the needed information is to complete a Triangulated Analysis Form for the pilot project and distribute it to faculty, administrators, and senior staff. You may also need to report your findings and recommendations at a faculty meeting, and, if necessary, seek faculty approval of any recommended curricular change.

Documenting the Final Resolution

All that's left to do now is to document your good work by filling out Columns O, P, and Q of the Specific Action Plan. (*See* Table 6.11.)

The function of Column O is to document the findings of the task force. You should provide a very brief summary of the findings of the task force on the form itself and attach a completed Triangulated Analysis Form as an appendix.

In Column P, you should document your communications with the faculty, the administration, and other stakeholders. Attach any relevant meeting minutes, emails, etc. as appendices.

Finally, in Column Q, you describe the final action taken by the law school. What is the end of the story? You may wish to attach a brief (one- or two-page) memo that describes not only what the final result was, but any follow-up that is required for the future. This memo will provide a jumpstart to the process the next time this criterion comes under review.

Table 6.11. Specific Action Plan Form (Required Only for Unfavorable Findings)

Outcome:
Criterion:
Assessment Cycle: 20___–20___
Assessment Task Force Members:

Column K	Column L	Column M	Column N	Column O	Column P	Column Q
Specific action that constitutes the change (can be multiple actions).	Who are the change agents (*i.e.*, who will run the pilot)?	What is the time-frame for implementing and assessing the specific action?	How will the effectiveness of this action be measured?	What does the analysis indicate?	When and how are the results shared with the faculty and others?	What was the final result? Institutionalize, revise, or discard the specific action? (Attach any documentation)
E.g., Students in [course] will receive ___ minutes additional instruction on X . . .	Professor Finn	The pilot will be run . . .	*E.g.*, The assessment task force will . . .	*E.g.*, Triangulated analysis indicates that the changes implemented as part of the pilot raised student performance to the desired threshold level. A Triangulated Analysis Form is attached as Appendix ___.	*E.g.*, 1. Provided faculty with Specific Action Plan via email on __/__/__ and . . .	*E.g.*, Institutionalized change via faculty vote on __/__/__. For further detail *see* Appendix ___.

* Adapted from http://www.apta.org/outcomesassessment/, with permission of the American Physical Therapy Association. Copyright © 2006 American Physical Therapy Association.

Final Thoughts

The authors hope that this Guide will serve you well as you undertake this new assessment journey. Realize that you are embarking on a new and little travelled path, but one that can lead to great rewards. Never forget that institutional assessment is ultimately all about serving our students. We owe them the best education we can provide.

Be patient with the process, and be dedicated. Do not get bogged down in the amount of work to do, just take that first step. And don't worry if you make a few wrong turns. We all will. Most importantly, keep moving, keep trying, do something.

Action List

Create a Triangulated Analysis for the performance criterion that you are assessing this cycle.

Activity 6: Evaluate data, including processes, to determine whether relevant criteria have been met, and if not why.

Step 1: Gather data collected.

Step 2: Score/tally the data collected.

- For <u>direct subjective tools</u>:
  - Finalize hot rubrics.
  - Develop rating scale and set benchmark for competency.
  - Norm scorers.
  - Score samples.
- For <u>direct objective tools</u>:
  - Develop rating scale and set benchmark for competency.
  - Tally data collected from samples.
- For <u>indirect quantitative tools</u>, tally data collected from samples.
- For <u>indirect qualitative tools</u>, tabulate data collected from samples and seek expert's assistance, if needed, to index and manage data.

Step 3: Analyze the data collected.

- For <u>direct tools and indirect quantitative tools</u>, apply the performance thresholds set during Implementation Stage.
- For <u>indirect qualitative tools</u>, consult with expert to interpret the results.
- Document your progress in Column G of the Triangulated Analysis Form, attach any rubrics and reports as appendices, and provide copies of these documents to the assessment coordinator.
- Indicate if there is a trigger for change or further analysis based upon findings.
- Compare results of three tools (triangulate your results), record what triangulated analysis indicates, and memorialize your findings in Column H of Triangulated Analysis Form.
- Review assessment processes, if necessary, and take any appropriate measures to ensure validity and reliability of data.

- Develop hypotheses as to what are the possible causes of the triangulated analysis findings, and fill out Column I of Triangulated Analysis Form.

Activity 7: Report findings to key stakeholders.

- For <u>faculty, administrators, and senior staff</u>, provide information listed in this Chapter.
- For <u>accrediting bodies</u>:
  - Contact accrediting bodies for required forms or samplesforms.
  - Contact members of university assessment committee to find out about reporting forms for regional accrediting bodies.
  - If no forms exist, provide information listed in this Chapter to accrediting bodies.
- <u>For students, potential students, and other stakeholders in the general public</u>, provide information listed in this Chapter. Consult with public relations department for appropriate/preferable dissemination methods.
- Fill out Column J of Triangulated Analysis Form.
- Attach any documents relating to communications as appendices.

Activity 8: Close the loop by developing and implementing any changes, if necessary.

Create a Specific Action Plan for Unfavorable Findings.

- Develop and implement an action plan (pilot project) aimed at improving student achievement of the outcome/criterion.
- Appoint change agents for the pilot project. (Fill out Column L of Specific Action Plan.)
- Set the time frame for the pilot project. (Fill out Column M of Specific Action Plan.)
- Determine how effectiveness of the pilot project will be measured. (Fill out Column N of Specific Action Plan.)
- Run the pilot project.
- Assess the efficacy of the actions taken under the Specific Action Plan. (Fill out Column O of Specific Action Plan.)
- Communicate findings with the faculty, administration, and other key stakeholders. (Fill out Column P of Specific Action Plan).
- Make recommendations following analysis of the pilot project and document final action taken by law school. (Fill out Column Q of Specific Action Plan.)

Appendix A

Glossary of Key Terms

Accreditation—The process through which an educational institution or program is certified as satisfying the official standards of its accrediting body. Accreditation begins with a self-study by the entity in question. The self-study is provided to the accrediting body, which uses it to prepare for an on-site visit by expert evaluators. Based on the self-study, the on-site visit, and any additional information gathered, the accrediting body determines whether certification is appropriate.

Add-on Assessment Activities—Assessment activities provided outside of the context of a course. They are the opposite of embedded assessment.

Alignment—*See* curriculum mapping.

Assessment Actors—Members of the law school community (administrators, faculty, and staff) charged with creating an institutional student learning outcomes assessment plan, implementing the plan, and/or evaluating the plan's results.

Assessment of Student Learning—A set of practices where student learning outcomes are created; data is gathered to measure the achievement of the outcomes; that data is analyzed; and that data is used to improve student learning.

Assessment Task Force—A group of assessment actors, typically composed of law faculty, which is assigned a learning outcome and charged with developing assessment measures for that outcome, evaluating the results, and leading the effort to make any needed changes.

Assessment Tools (*also known as assessment activities and assessment measures*)—The means by which one gathers evidence to demonstrate learning or the achievement of learning outcomes; they are indicators of performance.

Benchmark—A standard against which an individual student's performance is being compared.

Bloom's Taxonomy (*also known as Taxonomy of Education Objectives*)—A foundational theory of learning often relied on in higher education. It consists of a framework for categorizing educational goals created by Benjamin Bloom with collaborators Max Englehart, Edward Furst, Walter Hill, and David Krathwohl in 1956. The six categories recognized in ascending level of difficulty are knowledge, comprehension, application, analysis, synthesis, and evaluation. A revised version of the taxonomy was published in 2001. The categories in the revised taxonomy are remembering, understanding, applying, analyzing, evaluating, and creating.

Calibrate—To standardize a measuring device, such as a rubric, so that it can be used in an accurate and consistent way.

Census—An assessment of the entire population of a unit.

Classroom Assessment—*See* individual student assessment.

Cluster Random Sampling—Randomly selecting subgroups or sections and assessing everyone in that section.

Cold Rubric—A scoring guide that only includes a list of the dimensions of the assignment.

Competent—Properly qualified, capable of successfully completing a required task.

Control Group—A group of students who are not exposed to the change in question and serve as a benchmark.

Criterion-Referenced Benchmarks—Competency is measured based on whether a student satisfies certain prerequisites set by the assessor (*e.g.*, gets at least 35 out of 50 questions on a multiple-choice test right). Criterion-referenced assessment often uses rubrics. It is the opposite of norm-based assessment.

Curriculum Mapping (*also known as alignment*)—A grid of the courses in the curriculum that identifies which learning outcomes and performance criteria are addressed and assessed in each course.

Developmental Portfolio—A collection of student work product, which demonstrates the extent of a student's mastery of learning outcomes by showing the student's progress, including samples of the student's early work product and later work product throughout the student's academic career.

Dimensions—The relevant components of a task (*i.e.*, the specific knowledge, skills, and/or values involved) listed in a rubric that one must be able to observe in a student's performance for it to be considered successful.

Direct Assessment Measures—Any tool which uses student work product in some form to provide direct evidence of student learning. Examples include tests, essays, exercises, and other activities where students are asked to demonstrate their learning.

Embedded Assessment Activities—An activity that is a part of the student's course work or other testing procedure within a course. Students generally are graded on this work, and some or all of it is also used to assess learning outcomes.

Evaluator—The person or persons who analyze the data collected from an assessment activity and draw conclusions about the data.

External Standard—Criterion set by experts outside the law school.

Formative Assessment—Assessment conducted throughout the course of study through which students are provided feedback to improve their learning. Also defined in ABA Interpretation 314-1, as "measurements at different points during a particular course or at different points over the span of a student's education that provide meaningful feedback to improve student learning."

Goals/Objectives—Broad, abstract statements regarding general intentions of an institution that are not measurable. Goals typically focus on inputs rather than outcomes, indicating what the institution plans/hopes to teach rather than what students or graduates will learn. They are somewhere in between mission statements and learning outcomes in terms of their level of specificity. At some institutions, "objectives" are more specific goals of the institution. At other institutions, the terms "goals" and "objectives" are used interchangeably.

Hot Rubric—A scoring guide that includes the dimensions of the assigned task, a scale of the varying levels of achievement, and a description of what each level of achievement looks like. A hot rubric is used to evaluate a completed assignment.

Indexing—Reviewing transcripts or summaries of a focus group session and assigning a code/label to each piece of information that reflects the question to which it relates and the perspective expressed.

Indirect Assessment Measures—Assessment tools that utilize the opinions of the students or others about student learning to infer that learning has (or has not) taken place but do not allow for the direct examination of work product. Examples include reflective essays, surveys, and focus groups.

Individual Student Assessment (*also known as classroom assessment*)— Provides students with feedback for improvement and/or a measure of their achievement. Focuses on measuring the learning of individual students.

Inputs—Educational experiences or the resources that an institution devotes to producing its final product (*i.e.*, competent entry-level attorneys).

Institutional Assessment Committee—A group of assessment actors, typically composed primarily of law faculty, which is charged with overseeing the law school's institutional student learning outcomes assessment efforts. The primary task of this committee is typically the creation of an institutional student learning outcomes assessment plan for the school. The committee may or may not be charged with oversight of Implementation Stage and Evaluation Stage activities.

Institutional Assessment Coordinator (*also known as the Assistant Dean for Institutional Assessment, etc.*)—The primary administrator charged with coordinating the law school's institutional student learning outcomes assessment activities and ensuring that all accreditation standards relating to those activities are satisfied.

Institutional Effectiveness—An educational institution's performance as measured against its stated mission. The assessment of institutional effectiveness should be systematic, continuous, and well documented. The achievement of student learning outcomes provides one measure of institutional effectiveness. An institution's mission may also include non-instructional objectives that require additional measures.

Institutional Review Board (IRB)—In an educational setting, a group that reviews and approves research involving human subjects with the goal to ensure that all human subject research is conducted in accordance with all federal, institutional, and ethical guidelines.

Institutional Student Learning Outcomes Assessment—A set of practices, which focuses on the overall effectiveness of a school's program of education, where institutional learning outcomes are created; data is gathered to measure the achievement of the outcomes; that data is analyzed; and that data is used to improve student learning.

Internal/Local Standard—A standard based on criteria established by faculty for identifying a competent graduate.

Interpretation—Developing summary statements that reflect the common themes that emerged in a focus group session with regard to each question.

Learning and Teaching Center (*also known as Center for Excellence in Teaching, Center for Teaching and Learning, etc.*)—A facility and/or program devoted to providing resources and opportunities for faculty development in the area of teaching.

Learning Outcomes—The knowledge, skills, and values that an institution wants its graduates to have as a result of obtaining an education at its institution or upon completion of their studies.

Managing—The bringing together (collating) of all of the pieces of information assigned the same code/label by a facilitator after a focus group session.

Metacognition (*also known as student self-assessment*)—One's understanding of her own thinking or learning process.

Methodological Triangulation—Using multiple tools, ideally two direct tools and one indirect tool, to assess a desired criterion in an institutional plan to improve the reliability of the results.

Mini-Bar Examination (*also known as a baby bar exam*)—A simulated practice bar examination.

Mission Statement—Describes the essence of an institution and outlines the guiding principles, aspirations, and values of the institution, stated in broad, abstract terms.

Norming—An effort to calibrate the scoring of individual scorers.

Norm-Referenced Benchmark—Competency is measured by comparing the student or students' performance to the performance of other students. Grading on a curve is a form of norm-referenced assessment.

Objective Tools—Assessment activities that require neither specialized expertise to score correctly nor a subjective evaluation. Objective tools have a definite answer, such as multiple-choice and true/false questions.

Office of Institutional Research—An office that supports a university's strategic planning and decision-making processes through the collection, analysis, and dissemination of information relating to students, programs, policies, environment, facilities, etc.

Outcomes/Outputs Assessment—An ongoing, formalized, or systematic process to improve something, in which outcomes are created; data is gathered to measure the achievement of the outcomes; that data is analyzed; and then, the data is used to improve the achievement of the outcomes.

Outputs—Student work products, which document what students have learned.

Performance Criteria (*also known as assessment criteria, performance elements, or performance indicators*)—The more specific characteristics students must demonstrate to establish a particular outcome has been satisfied. The performance criteria are intended to address the ambiguities found in the learning outcomes. They force one to describe in concrete terms what each outcome requires.

Performance Thresholds—A minimum expectation level. Failure to achieve a threshold should trigger action of some kind on the part of an institution.

Proficiency—Mastery of the subject matter that goes beyond basic competency but does not require that a student demonstrate the expertise that would be expected of an experienced practitioner.

Program Review—A process used to examine the effectiveness of an academic/instructional program.

Programmatic Assessment—A set of practices, which focuses on the effectiveness of a particular program within the law school, such as a legal writing program, intellectual property track or concentration, etc., where program learning outcomes are created; evidence on attainment of the outcomes is gathered and analyzed; and the data is used to improve the program's offerings.

Prompt—The call of a question, which allows students to understand exactly what the author of the question wants them to do.

Qualitative Data—Data that is descriptive and does not use numerical scores. It is observable, but not measurable. Often, such results are reported verbally and are based upon interviews, focus groups, or responses to open-ended survey questions.

Quantitative Data—Data that can be measured (*i.e.*, assigned a number).

Regional Accreditors—Organizations recognized by the Council for Higher Education Accreditation to accredit/certify educational institutions within a particular geographic region that are authorized to grant post-secondary degrees, associate, bachelors, masters, and/or doctoral.

Reliability—The degree to which the tool yields the same results on repeated trials (*i.e.*, demonstrates consistent results). Reliability depends in large part on representative sampling and scoring consistency.

Rubric—A scoring guide used to describe the criteria under which a student's performance is to be evaluated.

Sampling—Assessing a representative group.

Scorer—The person or persons who actually score the data collected from subjective direct assessments using rubrics.

Scorer Reliability—Agreement or consistency in the scoring evaluations made by different scorers and by the same scorer at different points in time.

Scorer Triangulation—Using multiple scorers to assess performance on a tool to improve consistency in results.

Showcase Portfolio—A collection of student work product that demonstrates the extent of a student's mastery of learning outcomes by "showcasing" his best work product.

Simple Random Sampling—Sampling where everyone in the population has an equal chance to be selected for a sample.

Stratified Random Sampling—The dividing of a population into subgroups based on significant characteristics that are of interest to the institution, such as gender or race, and the selection of a representative sample from each subgroup.

Subjective Tools—Assessment activities that require specialized expertise to score correctly, such as essay exams, memoranda, and oral arguments.

Summative Assessment—"Assessment after the fact," assessment that occurs after a course of study. It provides no opportunity for individual students to improve their learning and typically provides little or no feedback to students. Also defined in ABA Interpretation 314-1 as "measurements at the culmination of a particular course or at the culmination of any part of a student's legal education that measure the degree of student learning."

Target—An aspirational goal of what an institution would like its students to achieve.

Test Blueprint—The mapping of the knowledge, skills, or values that an assessment tool is intended to measure.

University Assessment Committee—A group of assessment actors, typically faculty members or administrators representing each academic unit of the university, which is charged with overseeing the university's institutional student learning outcomes assessment efforts.

Validity—The degree to which a tool measures what it is supposed to measure and provides useful information, measuring what has actually been learned by the students.

Value-Added/Longitudinal Benchmark—Performance is measured by comparing students' performance on a test (or other instrument) after some period in law school to their performance on the same instrument when they began law school. The idea is to determine whether there has been value added by the students' progression through the curriculum.

Appendix B

Key Implementation and Evaluation Stage Forms

Assessment Blueprint Form

Outcome:
Criterion:
Assessment Cycle: 20__–20__
Assessment Task Force Members:

Column A	Column B	Column C	Column D	Column E	Column F
Tools/ Measures	Tool Type (Direct or Indirect; Objective or Subjective; Quantitative or Qualitative)	Where and when will data be collected (*i.e.,* in what class or other setting)?	What is the performance threshold?	Who will score/tabulate the data?	Who will evaluate the data?
Tool 1					
Tool 2					
Tool 3					

* Adapted from http://www.apta.org/outcomesassessment/, with permission of the American Physical Therapy Association. Copyright © 2006 American Physical Therapy Association.

Triangulated Analysis Form

	Column G	Column H	Column I	Column J	Column K
Outcome: **Criterion:** **Assessment Cycle: 20__–20__** **Assessment Task Force Members:**					
← Link with Assessment Blueprint	Record your findings and indicate if there is a trigger for change or further analysis.	Analysis of data collected for relevant criterion. What does your triangulated analysis indicate?	Hypothesis? What are the possible causes of the findings (favorable or unfavorable)? List as many as may apply.	Report findings to appropriate stakeholders.	→ Link with Specific Action Plan, if necessary
Tool 1					
Tool 2					
Tool 3					

* Adapted from http://www.apta.org/outcomesassessment/, with permission of the American Physical Therapy Association. Copyright © 2006 American Physical Therapy Association.

Specific Action Plan Form (Required Only for Unfavorable Findings)

Outcome:
Criterion:
Assessment Cycle: 20__–20__
Assessment Task Force Members:

Column K	Column L	Column M	Column N	Column O	Column P	Column Q
Specific action that constitutes the change (can be multiple actions).	Who are the change agents (*i.e.,* who will run the pilot)?	What is the time-frame for implementing and assessing the specific action?	How will the effectiveness of this action be measured?	What does the analysis indicate?	When and how are the results shared with the faculty and others?	What was the final result? Institutionalize, revise, or discard the specific action? (Attach any documentation)

* Adapted from http://www.apta.org/outcomesassessment/, with permission of the American Physical Therapy Association. Copyright © 2006 American Physical Therapy Association.

Appendix C

Example Law School Learning Outcomes

Special thanks to the following law schools for agreeing to share their learning outcomes. Their work should inspire us all.

Brigham Young University J. Reuben Clark Law School

For more information visit: http://www.law2.byu.edu/site/admissions/curriculum.

Expected Learning Outcomes—JD

1. Students will understand the fundamental principles of Civil Procedure, Contracts, Criminal Law, Property, Structures of the Constitution, Torts, Professional Responsibility, and a large number of elective courses.
2. Students will be able to engage in legal analysis, reasoning, and problem solving.
3. Students will be able to perform legal research.
4. Students will be able to communicate effectively orally and in writing regarding legal matters.
5. Students will be able to recognize and resolve ethical issues in light of ethical, moral, and religious principles.
6. Students will have the ability and desire to engage in lifelong learning and service.

Hamline University School of Law ("HUSL")

For more information visit: http://www.law.du.edu/documents/assessment-con ference/Sandeen-Getting-Buy-In-From-Your-Colleagues.pdf.

Learning Outcomes For Lawyer Achievement (LOLA)
As adopted by the law faculty on May 8, 2008.

GOAL #1 (KNOWLEDGE): Acquire the conceptual frameworks and substantive knowledge needed for competent professional service as a new attorney and as a basis for lifelong learning.

HUSL graduates should be able to …

1. <u>Demonstrate</u> competence in key foundational areas of U.S. law, including areas of substantive law tested on bar examinations.
2. <u>Demonstrate</u> competence in other student-elected areas of substantive law.
3. <u>Demonstrate</u> knowledge of the structure, components, and functioning of the U.S. legal system, including the markets for legal services.
4. <u>Demonstrate</u> an understanding of the operation of law in a global context.
5. <u>Demonstrate</u> an understanding of the ethical rules that govern the legal profession.

GOAL #2 (SKILLS): Learn, practice, and apply the skills and methods that are essential for effective lawyering.

HUSL graduates should be able to …

1. <u>Identify and apply</u> strategies to discover and achieve client objectives.
2. <u>Master</u> appropriate strategies and technologies to retrieve, use, and manage research materials and information effectively and efficiently.
3. <u>Comprehend and synthesize</u> the reasoning and rules contained in legal authorities and apply them to a variety of client situations.
4. <u>Communicate</u> effectively in writing and in speaking with diverse audiences in a variety of formal and informal settings.
5. <u>Demonstrate</u> the capacity to understand and appreciate the diverse backgrounds and perspectives of clients, colleagues, adversaries, and others while dealing sensitively and effectively with the issues presented.
6. <u>Advocate</u>, collaborate, and problem-solve effectively in formal and informal dispute resolution processes.

GOAL #3 (PROFESSIONALISM): Develop the personal attributes, attitudes, and practices befitting an honorable and respected profession.

HUSL graduates should be able to …

1. <u>Acquire</u> the knowledge and skills required to competently represent one's clients (see the lists above).

2. <u>Articulate</u> the roles lawyers play in promoting justice, improving the legal profession, and serving the community.
3. <u>Exercise</u> professional decorum consistent with a lawyer's professional responsibilities and leadership roles.
4. <u>Reflect</u> on one's own work and professional development.
5. <u>Engage</u> in effective time management.

Pepperdine University School of Law

For more information visit: http://law.pepperdine.edu/degrees-programs/juris -doctor/program-learning-outcomes/.

Program Learning Outcomes

The School of Law's Educational Goals for Its JD Program: Students who successfully complete the Law School's JD program will share the following characteristics:

- The ability to think like a lawyer
- A basic proficiency in professional lawyering skills
- An appreciation, understanding, and inculcation of the moral, ethical, and professional values and responsibilities of law-trained individuals

The effective integration of the apprenticeships of thinking, performing, and behaving (or thinking, doing, and being) will prepare students for productive careers as counselors, advocates, and judges; as business persons; as elected public servants, and as researchers, teachers, and philosophers of the law.

The cognitive apprenticeship (CA)

#	Outcomes
CA 1	Students will demonstrate knowledge and understanding of substantive law.
CA 2	Students will demonstrate proficiency in legal analysis and critical reasoning.

The professional lawyering skills apprenticeship (LS)

#	Outcomes
LS 1	Students will demonstrate proficiency in legal research and in written and oral communication.
LS 2	Students will demonstrate professional lawyering skills.

The moral, ethical, and professional identity apprenticeship (ME)

#	Outcomes
ME 1	Students will demonstrate knowledge and understanding of a lawyer's moral, ethical, and professional responsibilities.
ME 2	Students will demonstrate awareness of their responsibility to society, including providing pro bono services.

University of Dayton School of Law

For more information visit: https://udayton.edu/law/academics/learning-outcomes.php.

Learning Outcome 1: Graduates will demonstrate knowledge and understanding of the law and the American legal system.

Graduates will demonstrate achievement of this learning outcome by ...

> Criterion 1: Identifying, describing, and interpreting the fundamental terms, rules, and principles of law, including significant alternative formulations, such as minority rules.

> Criterion 2: Describing the American legal system's structures, processes, and procedures.

Learning Outcome 2: Graduates will exhibit issue-spotting skills.

Graduates will demonstrate achievement of this learning outcome by ...

> Criterion 1: Identifying each potentially applicable legal theory as it relates to the facts.

> Criterion 2: Identifying each legal rule relevant to each potentially applicable legal theory.

> Criterion 3: Identifying the legally significant facts relating to each applicable legal rule.

Learning Outcome 3: Graduates will demonstrate competency in analytical and problem-solving skills.

Graduates will demonstrate achievement of this learning outcome by ...

> Criterion 1: Critically reading the applicable authority, including identifying the key rules within each authority.

Criterion 2: Synthesizing the relevant rules of law into a logical framework for analysis.

Criterion 3: Where rules conflict, thoroughly analyzing which rule a court is likely to apply.

Criterion 4: Meticulously applying the identified rules to the facts, including evaluating potential counterarguments, to determine the likely outcome of the case.

Criterion 5: When appropriate, analogizing the facts to and distinguishing the facts from those of precedent cases in specific and helpful ways to determine the likely outcome of the case.

Criterion 6: Articulating practical considerations, such as cost and effects on other people.

Learning Outcome 4: Graduates will communicate effectively and efficiently to individuals and groups.

Graduates will demonstrate achievement of this learning outcome by ...

Criterion 1: Writing documents that are clear, concise, well-reasoned, organized, professional in tone, appropriate to the audience and the circumstances, and if appropriate, contain proper citation to authority.

Criterion 2: Speaking in a clear, concise, well-reasoned, organized, and professional manner that is appropriate to the audience and the circumstances.

Criterion 3: Actively listening to clients, colleagues, judges, and others.

Learning Outcome 5: Graduates will research effectively and efficiently.

Graduates will demonstrate achievement of this learning outcome by ...

Criterion 1: Devising and implementing a logical research plan, which reflects an understanding of the limitations created by time and financial constraints.

Criterion 2: Accurately assessing the weight of authority.

Criterion 3: Identifying and effectively employing the fundamental tools of legal research.

Learning Outcome 6: Graduates will demonstrate competency in legal practice skills.

Graduates will demonstrate achievement of this learning outcome by ...

Criterion 1: Capably managing a legal project (*e.g.*, case, memorandum, mediation) from its inception to its conclusion.

Criterion 2: Effectively planning and controlling their use of time.

Criterion 3: Identifying and effectively engaging in appropriate dispute resolution processes.

Learning Outcome 7: Graduates will recognize and resolve ethical and other professional dilemmas.

Graduates will demonstrate achievement of this learning outcome by ...

Criterion 1: Listing the sources of the law governing lawyers.

Criterion 2: Identifying and explaining the applicable law governing lawyers.

Criterion 3: Using the law governing lawyers to recognize ethical and other professional dilemmas.

Criterion 4: Applying the law governing lawyers to help resolve ethical and other professional dilemmas.

Criterion 5: Exercising professional judgment to help resolve ethical and other professional dilemmas.

Learning Outcome 8: Graduates will continue to develop professional skills and attributes.

Graduates will demonstrate achievement of this learning outcome by ...

Criterion 1: Exhibiting self-directed learning skills that will allow them to understand areas of the law with which they were previously unfamiliar.

Criterion 2: Participating in extracurricular opportunities to increase knowledge, hone skills, and inform values.

Learning Outcome 9: Graduates will exemplify the Marianist charism of service, community, and inclusivity.

Graduates will demonstrate achievement of this learning outcome by ...

Criterion 1: Exhibiting civility and treating others with respect.

Criterion 2: Displaying diversity skills, including sensitivity to social and cultural difference.

Criterion 3: Contributing to the profession's fulfillment of its responsibility to ensure that adequate legal services are provided to those who cannot afford to pay for them.

University of the Pacific McGeorge School of Law

For more information visit: http://www.mcgeorge.edu/Students/Academics/JD_Degree/Learning_Outcomes.htm.

Learning outcomes are the lawyering skills that students are expected to obtain through the completion of a legal education. Consistent with ABA Standards, upon completion of a J.D. degree, graduates of the Pacific McGeorge School of Law will demonstrate mastery of the following student learning outcomes at the level needed for admission to the bar and effective and ethical participation in the legal profession as an entry level attorney.

The curriculum at Pacific McGeorge School of Law has been designed to prepare students with the key skills and competencies needed to demonstrate these learning outcomes in the legal profession.

Each student will:

1. Demonstrate the ability to identify and understand key concepts in substantive law, legal theory, and procedure in domestic and international law contexts;
2. Apply knowledge and critical thinking skills to perform competent legal analysis, reasoning, and problem solving;
3. Demonstrate the ability to conduct domestic and international legal research;
4. Demonstrate communication skills, including effective listening and critical reading, writing in objective and persuasive styles, and oral advocacy and other oral communications;
5. Collaborate effectively with others in a variety of legal settings and contexts;
6. Apply knowledge of professional ethics to representation of clients, performance of duties as an officer of the courts, and to the resolution of ethical issues; and
7. Demonstrate professional judgment and professionalism through conduct consistent with the legal profession's values and standards.

Approved by Faculty on Feb. 18, 2011

Appendix D

Faculty Views on Law Student Learning Outcomes Sample Survey

Learning outcomes are the knowledge, skills, and attitudes/values that students should be able to demonstrate by the time they graduate. What do we value? In short, we need to answer three questions:

1) What does the model School of Law graduate know? (This question focuses on doctrinal principles.)
2) What can the model School of Law graduate do? (This question focuses on major skills, such as communication.)
3) What does the model School of Law graduate value? (This question focuses on the graduate's ethics and attitudes towards the profession.)

The Assessment Committee's first task is to compile a list of six to twelve fundamental learning outcomes, which reflect the University of Dayton School of Law's unique perspective. Your input on these outcomes is very much needed. This survey should take less than ten minutes to complete, but we hope that you will take the time to really think about your answers and to discuss them with your colleagues.

The ideal learning outcome is short, simple, and centered on the graduate, rather than the institution. In drafting learning outcomes, it is important to keep the following principles in mind.

Learning outcomes should be defined by terms that are:

- Measurable (though not necessarily quantifiable)
- Observable (We cannot measure what occurs in a graduate's mind (*e.g.*, the graduate understands concept X), but we can measure actions taken by a graduate (*e.g.*, the graduate defines, explains, and provides examples of concept X.))

- Performed by the graduate (Outcomes that are vague or do not refer to actions performed by the graduate cannot be easily assessed.)

Thank you for your participation.

1. The Assessment Committee has compiled a draft list of student learning outcomes for your review. FOR EACH POSSIBLE LEARNING OUTCOME, PLEASE INDICATE THE EXTENT TO WHICH YOU AGREE THAT IT IS AN ADVISABLE LEARNING OUTCOME.

	Strongly Agree	Agree	Neutral	Disagree	Strongly Disagree
Graduates will demonstrate knowledge and understanding of the law and the American legal system.	○	○	○	○	○
Graduates will exhibit issue-spotting skills.	○	○	○	○	○
Graduates will demonstrate competency in analytical and problem-solving skills.	○	○	○	○	○
Graduates will communicate effectively and efficiently to individuals and groups.	○	○	○	○	○
Graduates will research effectively and efficiently.	○	○	○	○	○
Graduates will demonstrate competency in legal practice skills.	○	○	○	○	○
Graduates will recognize and resolve ethical and other professional dilemmas.	○	○	○	○	○
Graduates will continue to develop professional skills and attributes.	○	○	○	○	○
Graduates will exemplify the Marianist charism of faith, service, community, and inclusivity.	○	○	○	○	○

2. Please list any suggestions you have for additional learning outcomes here.

3. Please set forth any additional questions, concerns, or suggestions you have for the Assessment Committee here.

Appendix E

Sample Curriculum Map

NOTE: This is a sample map and does not represent an actual map of an institution.

Learning Outcome 3—Graduates will demonstrate competency in analytical and problem-solving skills.

Criterion	Development Level Course Name I=Introduced[i] C=Competency P=Proficiency	Assessment Tools	Feedback W=Written O=Oral I=Individual G=Group
Criterion 4: Graduates will demonstrate achievement of this learning outcome by analogizing the facts to and distinguishing the facts from those of precedent cases in specific and helpful ways to determine the likely outcome of the case.	C-Torts I	Final[v]	I
	C-Torts II	Class Participation/Final	IGO
	C-Legal Research and Writing I (x3)[ii]	Multiple (Examples on File)	WIGO (x2)/I
	C-Evidence	Mid/Final/Writing Assign.	WIO
	C-Professional Responsibility	Multiple (Examples on File)	WIO
	C-Externship (x2)	Simulation/Writing Assign.	IGO
	C-Capstone (Civil Lit.)	Multiple (Examples on File)	WIGO
	C-Professional Responsibility	Quiz/Mid/Final	WIO
	C-Crim.	Quiz/Final/Writing Assign.	WI
	C-Civ. Pro.	Multiple (Examples on File)	WIGO
	C-Legal Research and Writing II (x3)	Multiple (Examples of File)	WIGO
	P-Real Prop. I[iii]	Final	WIO
	P-Clinic	Multiple (Examples on File)	WI
	P-Contracts I[iv]	Mid/Final	WI
	P-Contracts II	Final	WI
	P-Appellate Advocacy	Multiple (Examples on File)	WIO
	P-Transactional Drafting	Writing Assign./Class Participation	WIGO

Notes at end of section.

Learning Outcome 4—Graduates will communicate effectively and efficiently.

Criterion	Development Level Course Name *I=Introduced* *C=Competency* *P=Proficiency*	Assessment Tools	Feedback *W=Written* *O=Oral* *I=Individual* *G=Group*
Criterion 2: Graduates will speak in a clear, concise, well-reasoned, organized, and professional manner that is appropriate to the audience and the circumstances.	I-Real Prop. I I-Legal Research and Writing I (x2) C-ADR C-Legal Research and Writing II C-Transactional Drafting C-Externship (x2) C-Civ. Pro. C-Contracts I C-Contracts II P-Clinic P-Capstone (Civil Lit.) P-Appellate Advocacy[vi]	Class Participation Multiple (Examples on File) Simulation Multiple (Examples on File) Negotiation/Class Partic. Multiple (Examples on File) Class Participation Class Participation Class Participation Multiple (Examples on File) Multiple (Examples on File) Multiple (Examples on File)	O IGO IG IGO O IO I IO IO IO I IGO

Notes at end of section.

Learning Outcome 9—Graduates will exemplify the Marianist charism of faith, service, community, and inclusivity.

Criterion	Development Level Course Name *I=Introduced*[vii] *C=Competency* *P=Proficiency*	Assessment Tools	Feedback *W=Written* *O=Oral* *I=Individual* *G=Group*
Criterion 1: Graduates will contribute to the profession's fulfillment of its responsibility to ensure that adequate legal services are provided to those who cannot afford to pay for them.	I-Externship I-Capstone (Civil Lit.) I-Professional Responsibility I-Contracts I I-Contracts II	Simulation/Writing Assign. Writing Assign. Multiple (Examples on file) Multiple (Examples on file) Multiple (Examples on file)	W WI WIG WI WI

Notes at end of section.

Notes

i. Although in this column there is no course listing "I," its absence does not indicate a gap in coverage of the criterion in question. A rating of "C" indicates both that the skill, knowledge, etc. is introduced and that students are expected to demonstrate competency by the end of the course.

ii. "(x3)" indicates that there were 3 professors who taught Legal Research and Writing I and all 3 provided responses. Any time the symbol "(x#)" appears in the chart, that indicates that more than one response was submitted for that course. In a perfect world, there would be consistent developmental expectations for the same course (even if taught by different professors). However, there will be instances where a professor's response is out of line with those of her counterparts. There may be an honest disagreement among the professors as to what level of development is appropriate, and/or there may be some misunderstanding as to the meaning of the various developmental levels.

iii. "P" or "Proficient" is the highest level of development. Recognizing that even talented graduates still have things to learn, the ABA requires competency, as opposed to proficiency, in the achievement of learning outcomes. One would expect a natural progression in the level of development sought over the course of a student's time at the law school. For example, a first-year course might serve to introduce students to oral advocacy, and upper-level courses might seek to create competency and possibly even proficiency in oral advocacy skills. This footnote highlights a situation in which the professor in a first-year, first-semester course indicated that students are expected to become proficient in a skill. It creates a "red flag" that should be addressed by the assessment actors undertaking the survey. They can do so by discussing this rating with the professor, including her understanding of the developmental levels and her methods of assessment, to make a determination if students are actually proficient in this skill after one semester.

iv. The curriculum map will also allow the assessment actors undertaking the survey to identify concerning marking trends by certain professors. In this example, this professor teaches Contracts I and II, first-year courses, and lists the expected developmental level for every performance criteria as "proficient." It is important to be sensitive to the fact that outcomes assessment is new to all, and it will take some time and effort to get everyone on the same page in terms of the various developmental levels.

v. The assessment actors should use the "Assessment Tools" column to review what is being used to measure achievement of the skill, value, etc. This information is helpful for two reasons. First, it can help them determine if the developmental level identified by the instructor appears accurate. For example, if only the Socratic Method is being used and the skill is not being measured on an exam, paper, etc. can you really be certain that students are developing competency? On the other hand, if multiple tools are being used, this is a better indicator that the instructor's rating is accurate. Second, this information can be used by an Assessment Task Force to determine what embedded tools might be used in the Assessment Blueprint. Knowing what measures are already in place can save the Task force an incredible amount of time.

vi. "Appellate Advocacy" refers to an upper level writing course. Here, one would expect to see the developmental level listed as a "C"/"P" as part of the natural progression. In contrast, one would expect to see the developmental level listed as an "I"/"C" for Legal Research and Writing I and "C" for Legal Research and Writing II.

vii. This column demonstrates a "hole" identified by curricular mapping.

The criterion at issue is merely "Introduced" in a handful of required courses. Students are never asked to demonstrate any level of development. Therefore, there will need to be a discussion as to whether the law school wants to (or has to) keep this criterion. If it keeps it, then there will need to be a discussion as to how it can be incorporated further into the curriculum or extra-curricular activities.

Appendix F

Curriculum Mapping Survey Sample Form

Introduction to Curriculum Mapping

In addition to the development and refinement of the learning outcomes, the law school will also be using curriculum mapping as another important tool to assess our program of legal education. First, curriculum mapping will be used to determine whether, and the extent to which, our curriculum ensures that students achieve the desired learning outcomes. Second, curriculum mapping will also be used to test the appropriateness of our (proposed or current) learning outcomes. For example, to the extent that a learning outcome or performance criterion is not addressed anywhere within the curriculum, based upon the evidence gathered from the curriculum mapping survey, we will then determine whether it should remain as a learning outcome, and if so, what needs to occur within the curriculum or extra-curricular offerings to ensure its coverage. All of this will be done with faculty input. To that end, the Institutional Assessment Committee has prepared a survey to be completed by all professors who teach required courses in the law school curriculum.

The survey directly relates to our institutional learning outcomes and their related performance criteria. For each performance criterion, please determine whether you address the identified performance criterion in your course. If you do, please:

1. Specify the level of depth in which the criterion is developed in your course by using one of the three categories described below.
2. Provide a description of how you assess that students reach the desired level of development regarding each criterion (example of common assessment tools are given below).
3. Specify whether feedback is provided to the students.

We will collect and compile this data in a curriculum map. To do so, we need your responses no later than [_____]. Thank you in advance for your assistance with this important project.

The Three Categories: Introduced (I), Competency (C), and Proficiency (P)

These are the three categories we are using to determine the level of depth in which each criterion is being developed in our required curriculum.

The definition of each follows:

I = Students are **introduced** to this knowledge, skill, or value, but are not tested or otherwise assessed as to what they have learned. (This knowledge, skill, or value may be developed in another course in more depth.)

C = Students are instructed and assessed on this knowledge, skill, or value and are expected to demonstrate basic **competency** by the end of the course.

P = Students have advanced instruction in and/or additional practice with and are assessed on this knowledge, skill, or value and are expected to demonstrate **proficiency** by the end of the course. ("Proficiency" means that a student demonstrates a mastery of the subject matter that goes beyond basic competency. However, it does not require that a student demonstrate the expertise that would be expected of an experienced practitioner.)

You should fill in the letter that best describes the level of depth at which you address the performance criterion. Please choose only one letter per criterion. **If you do not address a given performance criterion in your course, you should leave it blank.**

Please note that we do not expect that all or even most performance criteria will be addressed in every course. It may be that certain criteria are addressed in only one or two courses. Additionally, we expect that it will not be uncommon, particularly in first-year courses to see that many topics are simply introduced. Further, very few topics will reach the proficiency level except for those covered in capstones and the like. This survey is being circulated to assess our overall program of legal education on an institutional level.

Examples of Assessment Tools

There are numerous ways to assess student learning. Some common examples or tools that you may employ are: final exam, mid-term exam, quiz, writing assignment, seminar paper, in-class simulation, presentation, class participation, or any other method you use to determine whether students are learning what you are teaching.

Feedback

There are a number of ways in which to evaluate or assess student performance and provide feedback. In the third column, please indicate whether you provide written feedback (W), oral feedback (O), group feedback (G), or individual feedback (I) or any combination of the above. Also, feel free to indicate any other methods by which you provide feedback.

Survey

Part One: Check the statement below that bests describes your past experience with this course.

____ I have never taught this course before.

____ I last taught this course in 20__/20__.

____ I last taught this course in 20__/20__.

____ I last taught this course in 20__/20__.

____ I last taught this course **before** 20__/20__.

Learning Outcome 1—Graduates will demonstrate knowledge and understanding of the law and the American legal system.

Learning Outcome 2—Graduates will . . .

Criterion	Development Level I=Introduced C=Competency P=Proficiency	Assessment Tools	Feedback W=Written O=Oral I=Individual G=Group
Criterion 1: Graduates will identify, describe, and interpret the fundamental terms, rules, and principles of law, including significant alternative formulations, such as minority rules.			
Criterion 2: . . .			

Criterion	Development Level *I=Introduced* *C=Competency* *P=Proficiency*	Assessment Tools	Feedback *W=Written* *O=Oral* *I=Individual* *G=Group*
Criterion 1: . . .			
Criterion 2: . . .			

Index